C-795   CAREER EXAMINATION SERIES

This is your
PASSBOOK for...

Social Case Worker

Test Preparation Study Guide
Questions & Answers

NATIONAL LEARNING CORPORATION®

COPYRIGHT NOTICE

This book is SOLELY intended for, is sold ONLY to, and its use is RESTRICTED to individual, bona fide applicants or candidates who qualify by virtue of having seriously filed applications for appropriate license, certificate, professional and/or promotional advancement, higher school matriculation, scholarship, or other legitimate requirements of education and/or governmental authorities.

This book is NOT intended for use, class instruction, tutoring, training, duplication, copying, reprinting, excerption, or adaptation, etc., by:

1) Other publishers
2) Proprietors and/or Instructors of "Coaching" and/or Preparatory Courses
3) Personnel and/or Training Divisions of commercial, industrial, and governmental organizations
4) Schools, colleges, or universities and/or their departments and staffs, including teachers and other personnel
5) Testing Agencies or Bureaus
6) Study groups which seek by the purchase of a single volume to copy and/or duplicate and/or adapt this material for use by the group as a whole without having purchased individual volumes for each of the members of the group
7) Et al.

Such persons would be in violation of appropriate Federal and State statutes.

PROVISION OF LICENSING AGREEMENTS – Recognized educational, commercial, industrial, and governmental institutions and organizations, and others legitimately engaged in educational pursuits, including training, testing, and measurement activities, may address request for a licensing agreement to the copyright owners, who will determine whether, and under what conditions, including fees and charges, the materials in this book may be used them. In other words, a licensing facility exists for the legitimate use of the material in this book on other than an individual basis. However, it is asseverated and affirmed here that the material in this book CANNOT be used without the receipt of the express permission of such a licensing agreement from the Publishers. Inquiries re licensing should be addressed to the company, attention rights and permissions department.

All rights reserved, including the right of reproduction in whole or in part, in any form or by any means, electronic or mechanical, including photocopying, recording, or by any information storage and retrieval system, without permission in writing from the Publisher.

Copyright © 2024 by
National Learning Corporation

212 Michael Drive, Syosset, NY 11791
(516) 921-8888 • www.passbooks.com
E-mail: info@passbooks.com

PUBLISHED IN THE UNITED STATES OF AMERICA

PASSBOOK® SERIES

THE *PASSBOOK® SERIES* has been created to prepare applicants and candidates for the ultimate academic battlefield – the examination room.

At some time in our lives, each and every one of us may be required to take an examination – for validation, matriculation, admission, qualification, registration, certification, or licensure.

Based on the assumption that every applicant or candidate has met the basic formal educational standards, has taken the required number of courses, and read the necessary texts, the *PASSBOOK® SERIES* furnishes the one special preparation which may assure passing with confidence, instead of failing with insecurity. Examination questions – together with answers – are furnished as the basic vehicle for study so that the mysteries of the examination and its compounding difficulties may be eliminated or diminished by a sure method.

This book is meant to help you pass your examination provided that you qualify and are serious in your objective.

The entire field is reviewed through the huge store of content information which is succinctly presented through a provocative and challenging approach – the question-and-answer method.

A climate of success is established by furnishing the correct answers at the end of each test.

You soon learn to recognize types of questions, forms of questions, and patterns of questioning. You may even begin to anticipate expected outcomes.

You perceive that many questions are repeated or adapted so that you can gain acute insights, which may enable you to score many sure points.

You learn how to confront new questions, or types of questions, and to attack them confidently and work out the correct answers.

You note objectives and emphases, and recognize pitfalls and dangers, so that you may make positive educational adjustments.

Moreover, you are kept fully informed in relation to new concepts, methods, practices, and directions in the field.

You discover that you are actually taking the examination all the time: you are preparing for the examination by "taking" an examination, not by reading extraneous and/or supererogatory textbooks.

In short, this PASSBOOK®, used directedly, should be an important factor in helping you to pass your test.

SOCIAL CASE WORKER

DUTIES AND RESPONSIBILITIES
Under supervision, provides casework services in one of several general or specialized areas of activity, such as family and child welfare work, medical, social work, psychiatric social work, or youth guidance services; performs related work.

EXAMPLES OF TYPICAL TASKS
Provides casework services in the specialized area of family and child welfare. Interviews parents, relatives, agency officers and/or members of the community regarding the physical, social, emotional, etc., problems of dependent and neglected children to determine the desirability of their placement in private child-care agencies or in Department of Welfare secured and approved foster homes; engages in adoption services; arranges maternity shelter care for unmarried mothers in planning for the suitable care of the child; provides medical social work services to persons receiving medical care and treatment in a hospital or clinic, or to recipients of public assistance from the City Department of Welfare; utilizes social casework methods in dealing with the ill and the physically handicapped with proper stress on the meaning of disability and its treatment in relation to the individual, the family and the community and with the aim of assisting the patient in making an adjustment to the community based on his physical capacities and limitations; applies psychiatric social casework concepts and techniques in the observation, care and treatment of emotionally disturbed, maladjusted, mentally ill or mentally defective persons in a hospital, clinic or institution; interprets psychiatric findings and recommendations to the patients and their families, plans for discharge and after care, and aids in the adjustment of the social and personal problems incident to the illness; provides youth guidance social casework services. Interviews children and their parents to discuss behavior problems and to determine what services may be indicated; prepares children and their families to accept the service and makes referral to an appropriate agency or resource for treatment; provides direct service for a selected small caseload; maintains a cooperative working relationship with other agencies and the community; participates in conferences, training programs, special studies, etc.; prepares and maintains case records, reports, summaries, etc., confers and consults with professional and technical personnel in utilizing a multidiscipline approach; applies social work knowledge and specialized skills to help individuals to meet their social, economic and relationship needs.

HOW TO TAKE A TEST

I. YOU MUST PASS AN EXAMINATION

A. WHAT EVERY CANDIDATE SHOULD KNOW

Examination applicants often ask us for help in preparing for the written test. What can I study in advance? What kinds of questions will be asked? How will the test be given? How will the papers be graded?

As an applicant for a civil service examination, you may be wondering about some of these things. Our purpose here is to suggest effective methods of advance study and to describe civil service examinations.

Your chances for success on this examination can be increased if you know how to prepare. Those "pre-examination jitters" can be reduced if you know what to expect. You can even experience an adventure in good citizenship if you know why civil service exams are given.

B. WHY ARE CIVIL SERVICE EXAMINATIONS GIVEN?

Civil service examinations are important to you in two ways. As a citizen, you want public jobs filled by employees who know how to do their work. As a job seeker, you want a fair chance to compete for that job on an equal footing with other candidates. The best-known means of accomplishing this two-fold goal is the competitive examination.

Exams are widely publicized throughout the nation. They may be administered for jobs in federal, state, city, municipal, town or village governments or agencies.

Any citizen may apply, with some limitations, such as the age or residence of applicants. Your experience and education may be reviewed to see whether you meet the requirements for the particular examination. When these requirements exist, they are reasonable and applied consistently to all applicants. Thus, a competitive examination may cause you some uneasiness now, but it is your privilege and safeguard.

C. HOW ARE CIVIL SERVICE EXAMS DEVELOPED?

Examinations are carefully written by trained technicians who are specialists in the field known as "psychological measurement," in consultation with recognized authorities in the field of work that the test will cover. These experts recommend the subject matter areas or skills to be tested; only those knowledges or skills important to your success on the job are included. The most reliable books and source materials available are used as references. Together, the experts and technicians judge the difficulty level of the questions.

Test technicians know how to phrase questions so that the problem is clearly stated. Their ethics do not permit "trick" or "catch" questions. Questions may have been tried out on sample groups, or subjected to statistical analysis, to determine their usefulness.

Written tests are often used in combination with performance tests, ratings of training and experience, and oral interviews. All of these measures combine to form the best-known means of finding the right person for the right job.

II. HOW TO PASS THE WRITTEN TEST

A. NATURE OF THE EXAMINATION

To prepare intelligently for civil service examinations, you should know how they differ from school examinations you have taken. In school you were assigned certain definite pages to read or subjects to cover. The examination questions were quite detailed and usually emphasized memory. Civil service exams, on the other hand, try to discover your present ability to perform the duties of a position, plus your potentiality to learn these duties. In other words, a civil service exam attempts to predict how successful you will be. Questions cover such a broad area that they cannot be as minute and detailed as school exam questions.

In the public service similar kinds of work, or positions, are grouped together in one "class." This process is known as *position-classification*. All the positions in a class are paid according to the salary range for that class. One class title covers all of these positions, and they are all tested by the same examination.

B. FOUR BASIC STEPS

1) Study the announcement

How, then, can you know what subjects to study? Our best answer is: "Learn as much as possible about the class of positions for which you've applied." The exam will test the knowledge, skills and abilities needed to do the work.

Your most valuable source of information about the position you want is the official exam announcement. This announcement lists the training and experience qualifications. Check these standards and apply only if you come reasonably close to meeting them.

The brief description of the position in the examination announcement offers some clues to the subjects which will be tested. Think about the job itself. Review the duties in your mind. Can you perform them, or are there some in which you are rusty? Fill in the blank spots in your preparation.

Many jurisdictions preview the written test in the exam announcement by including a section called "Knowledge and Abilities Required," "Scope of the Examination," or some similar heading. Here you will find out specifically what fields will be tested.

2) Review your own background

Once you learn in general what the position is all about, and what you need to know to do the work, ask yourself which subjects you already know fairly well and which need improvement. You may wonder whether to concentrate on improving your strong areas or on building some background in your fields of weakness. When the announcement has specified "some knowledge" or "considerable knowledge," or has used adjectives like "beginning principles of..." or "advanced ... methods," you can get a clue as to the number and difficulty of questions to be asked in any given field. More questions, and hence broader coverage, would be included for those subjects which are more important in the work. Now weigh your strengths and weaknesses against the job requirements and prepare accordingly.

3) Determine the level of the position

Another way to tell how intensively you should prepare is to understand the level of the job for which you are applying. Is it the entering level? In other words, is this the position in which beginners in a field of work are hired? Or is it an intermediate or advanced level? Sometimes this is indicated by such words as "Junior" or "Senior" in the class title. Other jurisdictions use Roman numerals to designate the level – Clerk I, Clerk II, for example. The word "Supervisor" sometimes appears in the title. If the level is not indicated by the title, check the description of duties. Will you be working under very close supervision, or will you have responsibility for independent decisions in this work?

4) Choose appropriate study materials

Now that you know the subjects to be examined and the relative amount of each subject to be covered, you can choose suitable study materials. For beginning level jobs, or even advanced ones, if you have a pronounced weakness in some aspect of your training, read a modern, standard textbook in that field. Be sure it is up to date and has general coverage. Such books are normally available at your library, and the librarian will be glad to help you locate one. For entry-level positions, questions of appropriate difficulty are chosen -- neither highly advanced questions, nor those too simple. Such questions require careful thought but not advanced training.

If the position for which you are applying is technical or advanced, you will read more advanced, specialized material. If you are already familiar with the basic principles of your field, elementary textbooks would waste your time. Concentrate on advanced textbooks and technical periodicals. Think through the concepts and review difficult problems in your field.

These are all general sources. You can get more ideas on your own initiative, following these leads. For example, training manuals and publications of the government agency which employs workers in your field can be useful, particularly for technical and professional positions. A letter or visit to the government department involved may result in more specific study suggestions, and certainly will provide you with a more definite idea of the exact nature of the position you are seeking.

III. KINDS OF TESTS

Tests are used for purposes other than measuring knowledge and ability to perform specified duties. For some positions, it is equally important to test ability to make adjustments to new situations or to profit from training. In others, basic mental abilities not dependent on information are essential. Questions which test these things may not appear as pertinent to the duties of the position as those which test for knowledge and information. Yet they are often highly important parts of a fair examination. For very general questions, it is almost impossible to help you direct your study efforts. What we can do is to point out some of the more common of these general abilities needed in public service positions and describe some typical questions.

1) General information

Broad, general information has been found useful for predicting job success in some kinds of work. This is tested in a variety of ways, from vocabulary lists to questions about current events. Basic background in some field of work, such as sociology or economics, may be sampled in a group of questions. Often these are principles which have become familiar to most persons through exposure rather than through formal training. It is difficult to advise you how to study for these questions; being alert to the world around you is our best suggestion.

2) Verbal ability

An example of an ability needed in many positions is verbal or language ability. Verbal ability is, in brief, the ability to use and understand words. Vocabulary and grammar tests are typical measures of this ability. Reading comprehension or paragraph interpretation questions are common in many kinds of civil service tests. You are given a paragraph of written material and asked to find its central meaning.

3) Numerical ability

Number skills can be tested by the familiar arithmetic problem, by checking paired lists of numbers to see which are alike and which are different, or by interpreting charts and graphs. In the latter test, a graph may be printed in the test booklet which you are asked to use as the basis for answering questions.

4) Observation

A popular test for law-enforcement positions is the observation test. A picture is shown to you for several minutes, then taken away. Questions about the picture test your ability to observe both details and larger elements.

5) Following directions

In many positions in the public service, the employee must be able to carry out written instructions dependably and accurately. You may be given a chart with several columns, each column listing a variety of information. The questions require you to carry out directions involving the information given in the chart.

6) Skills and aptitudes

Performance tests effectively measure some manual skills and aptitudes. When the skill is one in which you are trained, such as typing or shorthand, you can practice. These tests are often very much like those given in business school or high school courses. For many of the other skills and aptitudes, however, no short-time preparation can be made. Skills and abilities natural to you or that you have developed throughout your lifetime are being tested.

Many of the general questions just described provide all the data needed to answer the questions and ask you to use your reasoning ability to find the answers. Your best preparation for these tests, as well as for tests of facts and ideas, is to be at your physical and mental best. You, no doubt, have your own methods of getting into an exam-taking mood and keeping "in shape." The next section lists some ideas on this subject.

IV. KINDS OF QUESTIONS

Only rarely is the "essay" question, which you answer in narrative form, used in civil service tests. Civil service tests are usually of the short-answer type. Full instructions for answering these questions will be given to you at the examination. But in case this is your first experience with short-answer questions and separate answer sheets, here is what you need to know:

1) Multiple-choice Questions

Most popular of the short-answer questions is the "multiple choice" or "best answer" question. It can be used, for example, to test for factual knowledge, ability to solve problems or judgment in meeting situations found at work.

A multiple-choice question is normally one of three types—
- It can begin with an incomplete statement followed by several possible endings. You are to find the one ending which *best* completes the statement, although some of the others may not be entirely wrong.
- It can also be a complete statement in the form of a question which is answered by choosing one of the statements listed.

- It can be in the form of a problem – again you select the best answer.

Here is an example of a multiple-choice question with a discussion which should give you some clues as to the method for choosing the right answer:

When an employee has a complaint about his assignment, the action which will *best* help him overcome his difficulty is to
    A. discuss his difficulty with his coworkers
    B. take the problem to the head of the organization
    C. take the problem to the person who gave him the assignment
    D. say nothing to anyone about his complaint

In answering this question, you should study each of the choices to find which is best. Consider choice "A" – Certainly an employee may discuss his complaint with fellow employees, but no change or improvement can result, and the complaint remains unresolved. Choice "B" is a poor choice since the head of the organization probably does not know what assignment you have been given, and taking your problem to him is known as "going over the head" of the supervisor. The supervisor, or person who made the assignment, is the person who can clarify it or correct any injustice. Choice "C" is, therefore, correct. To say nothing, as in choice "D," is unwise. Supervisors have and interest in knowing the problems employees are facing, and the employee is seeking a solution to his problem.

2) True/False Questions

The "true/false" or "right/wrong" form of question is sometimes used. Here a complete statement is given. Your job is to decide whether the statement is right or wrong.

SAMPLE: A roaming cell-phone call to a nearby city costs less than a non-roaming call to a distant city.

This statement is wrong, or false, since roaming calls are more expensive.
This is not a complete list of all possible question forms, although most of the others are variations of these common types. You will always get complete directions for answering questions. Be sure you understand *how* to mark your answers – ask questions until you do.

V. RECORDING YOUR ANSWERS

Computer terminals are used more and more today for many different kinds of exams.
For an examination with very few applicants, you may be told to record your answers in the test booklet itself. Separate answer sheets are much more common. If this separate answer sheet is to be scored by machine – and this is often the case – it is highly important that you mark your answers correctly in order to get credit.
An electronic scoring machine is often used in civil service offices because of the speed with which papers can be scored. Machine-scored answer sheets must be marked with a pencil, which will be given to you. This pencil has a high graphite content which responds to the electronic scoring machine. As a matter of fact, stray dots may register as answers, so do not let your pencil rest on the answer sheet while you are pondering the correct answer. Also, if your pencil lead breaks or is otherwise defective, ask for another.

Since the answer sheet will be dropped in a slot in the scoring machine, be careful not to bend the corners or get the paper crumpled.

The answer sheet normally has five vertical columns of numbers, with 30 numbers to a column. These numbers correspond to the question numbers in your test booklet. After each number, going across the page are four or five pairs of dotted lines. These short dotted lines have small letters or numbers above them. The first two pairs may also have a "T" or "F" above the letters. This indicates that the first two pairs only are to be used if the questions are of the true-false type. If the questions are multiple choice, disregard the "T" and "F" and pay attention only to the small letters or numbers.

Answer your questions in the manner of the sample that follows:

32. The largest city in the United States is
    A. Washington, D.C.
    B. New York City
    C. Chicago
    D. Detroit
    E. San Francisco

1) Choose the answer you think is best. (New York City is the largest, so "B" is correct.)
2) Find the row of dotted lines numbered the same as the question you are answering. (Find row number 32)
3) Find the pair of dotted lines corresponding to the answer. (Find the pair of lines under the mark "B.")
4) Make a solid black mark between the dotted lines.

VI. BEFORE THE TEST

Common sense will help you find procedures to follow to get ready for an examination. Too many of us, however, overlook these sensible measures. Indeed, nervousness and fatigue have been found to be the most serious reasons why applicants fail to do their best on civil service tests. Here is a list of reminders:

- Begin your preparation early – Don't wait until the last minute to go scurrying around for books and materials or to find out what the position is all about.
- Prepare continuously – An hour a night for a week is better than an all-night cram session. This has been definitely established. What is more, a night a week for a month will return better dividends than crowding your study into a shorter period of time.
- Locate the place of the exam – You have been sent a notice telling you when and where to report for the examination. If the location is in a different town or otherwise unfamiliar to you, it would be well to inquire the best route and learn something about the building.
- Relax the night before the test – Allow your mind to rest. Do not study at all that night. Plan some mild recreation or diversion; then go to bed early and get a good night's sleep.
- Get up early enough to make a leisurely trip to the place for the test – This way unforeseen events, traffic snarls, unfamiliar buildings, etc. will not upset you.
- Dress comfortably – A written test is not a fashion show. You will be known by number and not by name, so wear something comfortable.

- Leave excess paraphernalia at home – Shopping bags and odd bundles will get in your way. You need bring only the items mentioned in the official notice you received; usually everything you need is provided. Do not bring reference books to the exam. They will only confuse those last minutes and be taken away from you when in the test room.
- Arrive somewhat ahead of time – If because of transportation schedules you must get there very early, bring a newspaper or magazine to take your mind off yourself while waiting.
- Locate the examination room – When you have found the proper room, you will be directed to the seat or part of the room where you will sit. Sometimes you are given a sheet of instructions to read while you are waiting. Do not fill out any forms until you are told to do so; just read them and be prepared.
- Relax and prepare to listen to the instructions
- If you have any physical problem that may keep you from doing your best, be sure to tell the test administrator. If you are sick or in poor health, you really cannot do your best on the exam. You can come back and take the test some other time.

VII. AT THE TEST

The day of the test is here and you have the test booklet in your hand. The temptation to get going is very strong. Caution! There is more to success than knowing the right answers. You must know how to identify your papers and understand variations in the type of short-answer question used in this particular examination. Follow these suggestions for maximum results from your efforts:

1) Cooperate with the monitor

The test administrator has a duty to create a situation in which you can be as much at ease as possible. He will give instructions, tell you when to begin, check to see that you are marking your answer sheet correctly, and so on. He is not there to guard you, although he will see that your competitors do not take unfair advantage. He wants to help you do your best.

2) Listen to all instructions

Don't jump the gun! Wait until you understand all directions. In most civil service tests you get more time than you need to answer the questions. So don't be in a hurry. Read each word of instructions until you clearly understand the meaning. Study the examples, listen to all announcements and follow directions. Ask questions if you do not understand what to do.

3) Identify your papers

Civil service exams are usually identified by number only. You will be assigned a number; you must not put your name on your test papers. Be sure to copy your number correctly. Since more than one exam may be given, copy your exact examination title.

4) Plan your time

Unless you are told that a test is a "speed" or "rate of work" test, speed itself is usually not important. Time enough to answer all the questions will be provided, but this does not mean that you have all day. An overall time limit has been set. Divide the total time (in minutes) by the number of questions to determine the approximate time you have for each question.

5) Do not linger over difficult questions

If you come across a difficult question, mark it with a paper clip (useful to have along) and come back to it when you have been through the booklet. One caution if you do this – be sure to skip a number on your answer sheet as well. Check often to be sure that you have not lost your place and that you are marking in the row numbered the same as the question you are answering.

6) Read the questions

Be sure you know what the question asks! Many capable people are unsuccessful because they failed to *read* the questions correctly.

7) Answer all questions

Unless you have been instructed that a penalty will be deducted for incorrect answers, it is better to guess than to omit a question.

8) Speed tests

It is often better NOT to guess on speed tests. It has been found that on timed tests people are tempted to spend the last few seconds before time is called in marking answers at random – without even reading them – in the hope of picking up a few extra points. To discourage this practice, the instructions may warn you that your score will be "corrected" for guessing. That is, a penalty will be applied. The incorrect answers will be deducted from the correct ones, or some other penalty formula will be used.

9) Review your answers

If you finish before time is called, go back to the questions you guessed or omitted to give them further thought. Review other answers if you have time.

10) Return your test materials

If you are ready to leave before others have finished or time is called, take ALL your materials to the monitor and leave quietly. Never take any test material with you. The monitor can discover whose papers are not complete, and taking a test booklet may be grounds for disqualification.

VIII. EXAMINATION TECHNIQUES

1) Read the general instructions carefully. These are usually printed on the first page of the exam booklet. As a rule, these instructions refer to the timing of the examination; the fact that you should not start work until the signal and must stop work at a signal, etc. If there are any *special* instructions, such as a choice of questions to be answered, make sure that you note this instruction carefully.

2) When you are ready to start work on the examination, that is as soon as the signal has been given, read the instructions to each question booklet, underline any key words or phrases, such as *least, best, outline, describe* and the like. In this way you will tend to answer as requested rather than discover on reviewing your paper that you *listed without describing*, that you selected the *worst* choice rather than the *best* choice, etc.

3) If the examination is of the objective or multiple-choice type – that is, each question will also give a series of possible answers: A, B, C or D, and you are called upon to select the best answer and write the letter next to that answer on your answer paper – it is advisable to start answering each question in turn. There may be anywhere from 50 to 100 such questions in the three or four hours allotted and you can see how much time would be taken if you read through all the questions before beginning to answer any. Furthermore, if you come across a question or group of questions which you know would be difficult to answer, it would undoubtedly affect your handling of all the other questions.

4) If the examination is of the essay type and contains but a few questions, it is a moot point as to whether you should read all the questions before starting to answer any one. Of course, if you are given a choice – say five out of seven and the like – then it is essential to read all the questions so you can eliminate the two that are most difficult. If, however, you are asked to answer all the questions, there may be danger in trying to answer the easiest one first because you may find that you will spend too much time on it. The best technique is to answer the first question, then proceed to the second, etc.

5) Time your answers. Before the exam begins, write down the time it started, then add the time allowed for the examination and write down the time it must be completed, then divide the time available somewhat as follows:
    - If 3-1/2 hours are allowed, that would be 210 minutes. If you have 80 objective-type questions, that would be an average of 2-1/2 minutes per question. Allow yourself no more than 2 minutes per question, or a total of 160 minutes, which will permit about 50 minutes to review.
    - If for the time allotment of 210 minutes there are 7 essay questions to answer, that would average about 30 minutes a question. Give yourself only 25 minutes per question so that you have about 35 minutes to review.

6) The most important instruction is to *read each question* and make sure you know what is wanted. The second most important instruction is to *time yourself properly* so that you answer every question. The third most important instruction is to *answer every question*. Guess if you have to but include something for each question. Remember that you will receive no credit for a blank and will probably receive some credit if you write something in answer to an essay question. If you guess a letter – say "B" for a multiple-choice question – you may have guessed right. If you leave a blank as an answer to a multiple-choice question, the examiners may respect your feelings but it will not add a point to your score. Some exams may penalize you for wrong answers, so in such cases *only*, you may not want to guess unless you have some basis for your answer.

7) Suggestions
    a. Objective-type questions
        1. Examine the question booklet for proper sequence of pages and questions
        2. Read all instructions carefully
        3. Skip any question which seems too difficult; return to it after all other questions have been answered
        4. Apportion your time properly; do not spend too much time on any single question or group of questions

5. Note and underline key words – *all, most, fewest, least, best, worst, same, opposite,* etc.
6. Pay particular attention to negatives
7. Note unusual option, e.g., unduly long, short, complex, different or similar in content to the body of the question
8. Observe the use of "hedging" words – *probably, may, most likely,* etc.
9. Make sure that your answer is put next to the same number as the question
10. Do not second-guess unless you have good reason to believe the second answer is definitely more correct
11. Cross out original answer if you decide another answer is more accurate; do not erase until you are ready to hand your paper in
12. Answer all questions; guess unless instructed otherwise
13. Leave time for review

  b. Essay questions
1. Read each question carefully
2. Determine exactly what is wanted. Underline key words or phrases.
3. Decide on outline or paragraph answer
4. Include many different points and elements unless asked to develop any one or two points or elements
5. Show impartiality by giving pros and cons unless directed to select one side only
6. Make and write down any assumptions you find necessary to answer the questions
7. Watch your English, grammar, punctuation and choice of words
8. Time your answers; don't crowd material

8) Answering the essay question

Most essay questions can be answered by framing the specific response around several key words or ideas. Here are a few such key words or ideas:

M's: manpower, materials, methods, money, management
P's: purpose, program, policy, plan, procedure, practice, problems, pitfalls, personnel, public relations

  a. Six basic steps in handling problems:
1. Preliminary plan and background development
2. Collect information, data and facts
3. Analyze and interpret information, data and facts
4. Analyze and develop solutions as well as make recommendations
5. Prepare report and sell recommendations
6. Install recommendations and follow up effectiveness

  b. Pitfalls to avoid
1. *Taking things for granted* – A statement of the situation does not necessarily imply that each of the elements is necessarily true; for example, a complaint may be invalid and biased so that all that can be taken for granted is that a complaint has been registered

2. *Considering only one side of a situation* – Wherever possible, indicate several alternatives and then point out the reasons you selected the best one
3. *Failing to indicate follow up* – Whenever your answer indicates action on your part, make certain that you will take proper follow-up action to see how successful your recommendations, procedures or actions turn out to be
4. *Taking too long in answering any single question* – Remember to time your answers properly

IX. AFTER THE TEST

Scoring procedures differ in detail among civil service jurisdictions although the general principles are the same. Whether the papers are hand-scored or graded by machine we have described, they are nearly always graded by number. That is, the person who marks the paper knows only the number – never the name – of the applicant. Not until all the papers have been graded will they be matched with names. If other tests, such as training and experience or oral interview ratings have been given, scores will be combined. Different parts of the examination usually have different weights. For example, the written test might count 60 percent of the final grade, and a rating of training and experience 40 percent. In many jurisdictions, veterans will have a certain number of points added to their grades.

After the final grade has been determined, the names are placed in grade order and an eligible list is established. There are various methods for resolving ties between those who get the same final grade – probably the most common is to place first the name of the person whose application was received first. Job offers are made from the eligible list in the order the names appear on it. You will be notified of your grade and your rank as soon as all these computations have been made. This will be done as rapidly as possible.

People who are found to meet the requirements in the announcement are called "eligibles." Their names are put on a list of eligible candidates. An eligible's chances of getting a job depend on how high he stands on this list and how fast agencies are filling jobs from the list.

When a job is to be filled from a list of eligibles, the agency asks for the names of people on the list of eligibles for that job. When the civil service commission receives this request, it sends to the agency the names of the three people highest on this list. Or, if the job to be filled has specialized requirements, the office sends the agency the names of the top three persons who meet these requirements from the general list.

The appointing officer makes a choice from among the three people whose names were sent to him. If the selected person accepts the appointment, the names of the others are put back on the list to be considered for future openings.

That is the rule in hiring from all kinds of eligible lists, whether they are for typist, carpenter, chemist, or something else. For every vacancy, the appointing officer has his choice of any one of the top three eligibles on the list. This explains why the person whose name is on top of the list sometimes does not get an appointment when some of the persons lower on the list do. If the appointing officer chooses the second or third eligible, the No. 1 eligible does not get a job at once, but stays on the list until he is appointed or the list is terminated.

X. HOW TO PASS THE INTERVIEW TEST

The examination for which you applied requires an oral interview test. You have already taken the written test and you are now being called for the interview test – the final part of the formal examination.

You may think that it is not possible to prepare for an interview test and that there are no procedures to follow during an interview. Our purpose is to point out some things you can do in advance that will help you and some good rules to follow and pitfalls to avoid while you are being interviewed.

What is an interview supposed to test?

The written examination is designed to test the technical knowledge and competence of the candidate; the oral is designed to evaluate intangible qualities, not readily measured otherwise, and to establish a list showing the relative fitness of each candidate – as measured against his competitors – for the position sought. Scoring is not on the basis of "right" and "wrong," but on a sliding scale of values ranging from "not passable" to "outstanding." As a matter of fact, it is possible to achieve a relatively low score without a single "incorrect" answer because of evident weakness in the qualities being measured.

Occasionally, an examination may consist entirely of an oral test – either an individual or a group oral. In such cases, information is sought concerning the technical knowledges and abilities of the candidate, since there has been no written examination for this purpose. More commonly, however, an oral test is used to supplement a written examination.

Who conducts interviews?

The composition of oral boards varies among different jurisdictions. In nearly all, a representative of the personnel department serves as chairman. One of the members of the board may be a representative of the department in which the candidate would work. In some cases, "outside experts" are used, and, frequently, a businessman or some other representative of the general public is asked to serve. Labor and management or other special groups may be represented. The aim is to secure the services of experts in the appropriate field.

However the board is composed, it is a good idea (and not at all improper or unethical) to ascertain in advance of the interview who the members are and what groups they represent. When you are introduced to them, you will have some idea of their backgrounds and interests, and at least you will not stutter and stammer over their names.

What should be done before the interview?

While knowledge about the board members is useful and takes some of the surprise element out of the interview, there is other preparation which is more substantive. It *is* possible to prepare for an oral interview – in several ways:

1) Keep a copy of your application and review it carefully before the interview

This may be the only document before the oral board, and the starting point of the interview. Know what education and experience you have listed there, and the sequence and dates of all of it. Sometimes the board will ask you to review the highlights of your experience for them; you should not have to hem and haw doing it.

2) Study the class specification and the examination announcement

Usually, the oral board has one or both of these to guide them. The qualities, characteristics or knowledges required by the position sought are stated in these documents. They offer valuable clues as to the nature of the oral interview. For example, if the job involves supervisory responsibilities, the announcement will usually indicate that knowledge of modern supervisory methods and the qualifications of the candidate as a supervisor will be tested. If so, you can expect such questions, frequently in the form of a hypothetical situation which you are expected to solve. NEVER go into an oral without knowledge of the duties and responsibilities of the job you seek.

3) Think through each qualification required

Try to visualize the kind of questions you would ask if you were a board member. How well could you answer them? Try especially to appraise your own knowledge and background in each area, *measured against the job sought*, and identify any areas in which you are weak. Be critical and realistic – do not flatter yourself.

4) Do some general reading in areas in which you feel you may be weak

For example, if the job involves supervision and your past experience has NOT, some general reading in supervisory methods and practices, particularly in the field of human relations, might be useful. Do NOT study agency procedures or detailed manuals. The oral board will be testing your understanding and capacity, not your memory.

5) Get a good night's sleep and watch your general health and mental attitude

You will want a clear head at the interview. Take care of a cold or any other minor ailment, and of course, no hangovers.

What should be done on the day of the interview?

Now comes the day of the interview itself. Give yourself plenty of time to get there. Plan to arrive somewhat ahead of the scheduled time, particularly if your appointment is in the fore part of the day. If a previous candidate fails to appear, the board might be ready for you a bit early. By early afternoon an oral board is almost invariably behind schedule if there are many candidates, and you may have to wait. Take along a book or magazine to read, or your application to review, but leave any extraneous material in the waiting room when you go in for your interview. In any event, relax and compose yourself.

The matter of dress is important. The board is forming impressions about you – from your experience, your manners, your attitude, and your appearance. Give your personal appearance careful attention. Dress your best, but not your flashiest. Choose conservative, appropriate clothing, and be sure it is immaculate. This is a business interview, and your appearance should indicate that you regard it as such. Besides, being well groomed and properly dressed will help boost your confidence.

Sooner or later, someone will call your name and escort you into the interview room. *This is it.* From here on you are on your own. It is too late for any more preparation. But remember, you asked for this opportunity to prove your fitness, and you are here because your request was granted.

What happens when you go in?

The usual sequence of events will be as follows: The clerk (who is often the board stenographer) will introduce you to the chairman of the oral board, who will introduce you to the other members of the board. Acknowledge the introductions before you sit down. Do not be surprised if you find a microphone facing you or a stenotypist sitting by. Oral interviews are usually recorded in the event of an appeal or other review.

Usually the chairman of the board will open the interview by reviewing the highlights of your education and work experience from your application – primarily for the benefit of the other members of the board, as well as to get the material into the record. Do not interrupt or comment unless there is an error or significant misinterpretation; if that is the case, do not hesitate. But do not quibble about insignificant matters. Also, he will usually ask you some question about your education, experience or your present job – partly to get you to start talking and to establish the interviewing "rapport." He may start the actual questioning, or turn it over to one of the other members. Frequently, each member undertakes the questioning on a particular area, one in which he is perhaps most competent, so you can expect each member to participate in the examination. Because time is limited, you may also expect some rather abrupt switches in the direction the questioning takes, so do not be upset by it. Normally, a board member will not pursue a single line of questioning unless he discovers a particular strength or weakness.

After each member has participated, the chairman will usually ask whether any member has any further questions, then will ask you if you have anything you wish to add. Unless you are expecting this question, it may floor you. Worse, it may start you off on an extended, extemporaneous speech. The board is not usually seeking more information. The question is principally to offer you a last opportunity to present further qualifications or to indicate that you have nothing to add. So, if you feel that a significant qualification or characteristic has been overlooked, it is proper to point it out in a sentence or so. Do not compliment the board on the thoroughness of their examination – they have been sketchy, and you know it. If you wish, merely say, "No thank you, I have nothing further to add." This is a point where you can "talk yourself out" of a good impression or fail to present an important bit of information. Remember, *you close the interview yourself.*

The chairman will then say, "That is all, Mr. _____, thank you." Do not be startled; the interview is over, and quicker than you think. Thank him, gather your belongings and take your leave. Save your sigh of relief for the other side of the door.

How to put your best foot forward

Throughout this entire process, you may feel that the board individually and collectively is trying to pierce your defenses, seek out your hidden weaknesses and embarrass and confuse you. Actually, this is not true. They are obliged to make an appraisal of your qualifications for the job you are seeking, and they want to see you in your best light. Remember, they must interview all candidates and a non-cooperative candidate may become a failure in spite of their best efforts to bring out his qualifications. Here are 15 suggestions that will help you:

1) Be natural – Keep your attitude confident, not cocky

If you are not confident that you can do the job, do not expect the board to be. Do not apologize for your weaknesses, try to bring out your strong points. The board is interested in a positive, not negative, presentation. Cockiness will antagonize any board member and make him wonder if you are covering up a weakness by a false show of strength.

2) Get comfortable, but don't lounge or sprawl

Sit erectly but not stiffly. A careless posture may lead the board to conclude that you are careless in other things, or at least that you are not impressed by the importance of the occasion. Either conclusion is natural, even if incorrect. Do not fuss with your clothing, a pencil or an ashtray. Your hands may occasionally be useful to emphasize a point; do not let them become a point of distraction.

3) Do not wisecrack or make small talk

This is a serious situation, and your attitude should show that you consider it as such. Further, the time of the board is limited – they do not want to waste it, and neither should you.

4) Do not exaggerate your experience or abilities

In the first place, from information in the application or other interviews and sources, the board may know more about you than you think. Secondly, you probably will not get away with it. An experienced board is rather adept at spotting such a situation, so do not take the chance.

5) If you know a board member, do not make a point of it, yet do not hide it

Certainly you are not fooling him, and probably not the other members of the board. Do not try to take advantage of your acquaintanceship – it will probably do you little good.

6) Do not dominate the interview

Let the board do that. They will give you the clues – do not assume that you have to do all the talking. Realize that the board has a number of questions to ask you, and do not try to take up all the interview time by showing off your extensive knowledge of the answer to the first one.

7) Be attentive

You only have 20 minutes or so, and you should keep your attention at its sharpest throughout. When a member is addressing a problem or question to you, give him your undivided attention. Address your reply principally to him, but do not exclude the other board members.

8) Do not interrupt

A board member may be stating a problem for you to analyze. He will ask you a question when the time comes. Let him state the problem, and wait for the question.

9) Make sure you understand the question

Do not try to answer until you are sure what the question is. If it is not clear, restate it in your own words or ask the board member to clarify it for you. However, do not haggle about minor elements.

10) Reply promptly but not hastily

A common entry on oral board rating sheets is "candidate responded readily," or "candidate hesitated in replies." Respond as promptly and quickly as you can, but do not jump to a hasty, ill-considered answer.

11) Do not be peremptory in your answers

A brief answer is proper – but do not fire your answer back. That is a losing game from your point of view. The board member can probably ask questions much faster than you can answer them.

12) Do not try to create the answer you think the board member wants

He is interested in what kind of mind you have and how it works – not in playing games. Furthermore, he can usually spot this practice and will actually grade you down on it.

13) Do not switch sides in your reply merely to agree with a board member

Frequently, a member will take a contrary position merely to draw you out and to see if you are willing and able to defend your point of view. Do not start a debate, yet do not surrender a good position. If a position is worth taking, it is worth defending.

14) Do not be afraid to admit an error in judgment if you are shown to be wrong

The board knows that you are forced to reply without any opportunity for careful consideration. Your answer may be demonstrably wrong. If so, admit it and get on with the interview.

15) Do not dwell at length on your present job

The opening question may relate to your present assignment. Answer the question but do not go into an extended discussion. You are being examined for a *new* job, not your present one. As a matter of fact, try to phrase ALL your answers in terms of the job for which you are being examined.

Basis of Rating

Probably you will forget most of these "do's" and "don'ts" when you walk into the oral interview room. Even remembering them all will not ensure you a passing grade. Perhaps you did not have the qualifications in the first place. But remembering them will help you to put your best foot forward, without treading on the toes of the board members.

Rumor and popular opinion to the contrary notwithstanding, an oral board wants you to make the best appearance possible. They know you are under pressure – but they also want to see how you respond to it as a guide to what your reaction would be under the pressures of the job you seek. They will be influenced by the degree of poise you display, the personal traits you show and the manner in which you respond.

ABOUT THIS BOOK

This book contains tests divided into Examination Sections. Go through each test, answering every question in the margin. We have also attached a sample answer sheet at the back of the book that can be removed and used. At the end of each test look at the answer key and check your answers. On the ones you got wrong, look at the right answer choice and learn. Do not fill in the answers first. Do not memorize the questions and answers, but understand the answer and principles involved. On your test, the questions will likely be different from the samples. Questions are changed and new ones added. If you understand these past questions you should have success with any changes that arise. Tests may consist of several types of questions. We have additional books on each subject should more study be advisable or necessary for you. Finally, the more you study, the better prepared you will be. This book is intended to be the last thing you study before you walk into the examination room. Prior study of relevant texts is also recommended. NLC publishes some of these in our Fundamental Series. Knowledge and good sense are important factors in passing your exam. Good luck also helps. So now study this Passbook, absorb the material contained within and take that knowledge into the examination. Then do your best to pass that exam.

EXAMINATION SECTION

EXAMINATION SECTION
TEST 1

DIRECTIONS: Each question or incomplete statement is followed by several suggested answers or completions. Select the one that BEST answers the question or completes the statement. *PRINT THE LETTER OF THE CORRECT ANSWER IN THE SPACE AT THE RIGHT.*

1. When a worker is planning a future interview with a client, of the following, the MOST important consideration is the
   A. recommendations he will make to the client
   B. place where the client will be interviewed
   C. purpose for which the client will be interviewed
   D. personality of the client

   1.____

2. For a worker to make a practice of reviewing the client's case record, if available, prior to the interview is usually
   A. *inadvisable*, because knowledge of the client's past record will tend to influence the worker's judgment
   B. *advisable*, because knowledge of the client's background will help the worker to identify discrepancies in the client's responses
   C. *inadvisable*, because such review is time-consuming and of questionable value
   D. *advisable*, because knowledge of the client's background will help the worker to understand the client's situation

   2.____

3. Assume that a worker makes a practice of constantly re-assuring clients with serious and complex problems by making such statements as: *I'm sure you'll soon be well; I know you'll get a job soon*; or *Everything will be all right.*
   Of the following, the MOST likely result of such practice is to
   A. encourage the client and make him feel that the worker understands what the client is going through
   B. make the client doubtful about the worker's understanding of his difficulties and the worker's ability to help
   C. confuse the client and cause him to hesitate to take any action on his own initiative
   D. help the client to be more realistic about his situation and the probability that it will improve

   3.____

4. In order to get the maximum amount of information from a client during an interview, of the following, it is MOST important for the worker to communicate to the client the feeling that the worker is
   A. interested in the client
   B. a figure of authority
   C. efficient in his work habits
   D. sympathetic to the client's lifestyle

   4.____

5. Of the following, the worker who takes extremely detailed notes during an interview with a client is MOST likely to
   A. encourage the client to talk freely
   B. distract and antagonize the client
   C. help the client feel at ease
   D. understand the client's feelings

6. You find that many of the clients you interview are verbally abusive and unusually hostile to you.
   Of the following, the MOST appropriate action for you to take FIRST is to
   A. review your interviewing techniques and consider whether you may be provoking these clients
   B. act in a more authoritative manner when interviewing troublesome clients
   C. tell these clients that you will not process their applications unless their troublesome behavior ceases
   D. disregard the clients' troublesome behavior during the interviews

7. During an interview, you did not completely understand several of your client's responses. In each instance, you rephrased the client's statement and asked the client if that was what he meant.
   For you to use such a technique during interviews would be considered
   A. *inappropriate*; you may have distorted the client's meaning by rephrasing his statements
   B. *inappropriate*; you should have asked the same question until you received a comprehensible response
   C. *appropriate*; the client will have a chance to correct you if you have misinterpreted his responses
   D. *appropriate*; a worker should rephrase clients' responses for the records

8. A worker is interviewing a client who has just had a severe emotional shock because of an assault on her by a mugger.
   Of the following, the approach which would generally be MOST helpful to the client is for the worker to
   A. comfort the client and encourage her to talk about the assault
   B. sympathize with the client but refuse to talk about the assault
   C. tell the client to control her emotions and think positively about the future
   D. proceed with the interview in an impersonal and unemotional manner

9. A worker finds that her questions are misinterpreted by many of the clients she interviews.
   Of the following, the MOST likely reason for this problem is that the
   A. client is not listening attentively
   B. client wants to avoid the subject being discussed
   C. worker has failed to express her meaning clearly
   D. worker has failed to put the client at ease

10. For a worker to look directly at the client and observe him during the interview is, generally,
    A. *inadvisable*; this will make the client nervous and uncomfortable
    B. *advisable*; the client will be more likely to refrain from lying
    C. *inadvisable*; the worker will not be able to take notes for the case record
    D. *advisable*; this will encourage conversation and accelerate the progress of the interview

11. You are interviewing a client who is applying for social services for the first time. In order to encourage this client to freely give you the information needed for you to establish his eligibility, of the following, the BEST way to start the interview is by
    A. asking questions the client can easily answer
    B. conveying the impression that his responses to your questions will be checked
    C. asking two or three similar but important questions
    D. assuring the client that your sole responsibility is *getting the facts*

12. Workers are encouraged to record significant information obtained from clients and services provided for clients.
    Of the following, the MOST important reason for this practice is that these case records will
    A. help to reduce the need for regular supervisory conferences
    B. indicate to workers which clients are taking up the most time
    C. provide information which will help the agency to improve its services to clients
    D. make it easier to verify the complaints of clients

13. As a worker in the employment eligibility section, you find that interviews can be completed in a shorter period of time if you ask questions which limit the client to a certain answer.
    For you to use such a technique would be considered
    A. *inappropriate*, because this type of question usually requires advance preparation
    B. *inappropriate*, because this type of question may inhibit the client from saying what he really means
    C. *appropriate*, because you know the areas into which the questions should be directed
    D. *appropriate*, because this type of question usually helps clients to express themselves clearly

14. Assume that a worker at a juvenile detention center is planning foster care placement for a child.
    For the worker to have the child participate in the planning is generally considered to be
    A. time-consuming and of little practical value in preparing the child for placement
    B. valuable in helping the child adjust to future placement

C. useful, because the child will be more likely to cooperate with others in the center
D. anxiety-provoking because the child will feel that he has been abandoned

15. You have been assigned to interview the mother of a five-year-old son in her home to get information useful in locating the child's absent father. During the interview, you notice many serious bruises on the child's arms and legs, which the mother explains are due to the child's clumsiness.
Of the following, your BEST course of action is to
    A. accept the mother's explanation and concentrate on getting information which will help you to locate the father
    B. advise the mother to have the child examined for a medical condition that may be causing his clumsiness
    C. make a surprise visit to the mother later, to see whether someone is beating the child
    D. complete your interview with the mother and report the case to your supervisor for investigation of possible child abuse

15.____

16. During an interview, the former landlord of an absent father offers to help you to locate the father if you will give the landlord confidential information you have on the financial situation of the father.
Of the following, you should
    A. immediately end the interview with the landlord
    B. urge the landlord to help you but explain that you are not permitted to give him confidential information
    C. freely give the landlord the confidential information he requests about the father
    D. give the landlord the information only if he promises to keep it confidential

16.____

17. You feel that your client, a released mental patient, is not adjusting well to living on his own in an apartment. To gather more information, you interview privately his next-door neighbor, who claims that the client is creating a disturbance and speaks of the client in an angry and insulting manner.
Of the following, the BEST action for you to take in this situation is to
    A. listen patiently to the neighbor to try to get the facts about your client's behavior
    B. inform the neighbor that he has no right to speak insultingly about a mentally ill person
    C. make an appointment to interview the neighbor some other time when he isn't so upset
    D. tell the neighbor that you were not aware of the client's behavior and that you will have the client moved

17.____

18. As a worker assigned to an income maintenance center, you are interviewing a client to determine his eligibility for a work program. Suddenly, the client begins to shout that he is in no condition to work and that you are persecuting him for no reason.

18.____

Of the following, your BEST response to this client is to
- A. advise the client to stop shouting or you will call for the security guard
- B. wait until the client calms down, then order him to come back for another interview
- C. insist that you are not persecuting the client and that he must complete the interview
- D. wait until the client calms down, say that you understand how he feels, and try to continue the interview

19. You are counseling a mother whose 17-year-old son has recently been returned home from a mental institution. Although she is willing to care for her son at home, she is frightened by his strange and sometimes violent behavior and does not know the best arrangement to make for his care.
Of the following, your MOST appropriate response to this mother's problem is to
    - A. describe the supportive services and alternatives to home care which are available
    - B. help her to accept her son's strange and violent behavior
    - C. tell her that she will not be permitted to care for her son at home if she is frightened by his behavior
    - D. convince her that she is not responsible for her son's mental condition

20. Assume that, as an intake worker, you are interviewing an elderly man who comes to the center several times a month to discuss topics with you which are not related to social service. You realize that the man is lonely and enjoys these conversations.
Of the following, it would be MOST appropriate to
    - A. politely discourage the man from coming in to pass the time with you
    - B. avoid speaking to this man the next time he comes into the center
    - C. explore with the client his feelings about joining a Senior Citizens' Center
    - D. continue to hold these conversations with the man

21. A client you are interviewing in the housing elibility section tends to ramble on after each response that he gives, so that man clients are kept waiting.
In this situation, of the following, it would be MOST advisable to
    - A. try to direct the interview, in order to obtain the necessary information
    - B. reduce the number of questions asked so that you can shorten the interview
    - C. arrange a second interview for the client so that you can give him more time
    - D. tell the client that he is wasting everybody's time

22. A non-minority worker in an employment eligibility unit is about to interview a minority client on public assistance for job placement when the client says:
What does your kind know about my problems? You've never had to survive out on these streets.
Of the following, the worker's MOST appropriate response to this situation is to

A. postpone the interview until a minority worker is available to interview the client
B. tell the client that he must cooperate with the worker if he wants to continue receiving public assistance
C. explain to the client the function of the worker in this unit and the services he provides
D. assure the client that you do not have to be a member of a minority group to understand the effects of poverty

23. As a worker in a family services unit, you have been assigned to follow-up a case folder recently forwarded from the protective-diagnostic unit.
After making appropriate clerical notations in your records such as name of client and date of receipt, which of the following would be the MOST appropriate step to take next?
A. Confer with your supervisor
B. Read and review all reports included in the case folder
C. Arrange to visit with the client at his home
D. Confer with representatives of any other agencies which have been in contact with the client

23._____

24. As a worker in the employment section, you are interviewing a young client who seriously underestimates the amount of education and training he will require for a certain occupation.
For you to tell the client that you think he is mistaken would, generally, be considered
A. *inadvisable*, because workers should not express their opinions to clients
B. *inadvisable*, because clients have the right to self-determination
C. *advisable*, because clients should generally be alerted to their misconceptions
D. *advisable*, because workers should convince clients to adopt a proper lifestyle

25._____

25. As an intake worker, you are counseling a mother and her unmarried, thirteen-year-old daughter, who is six months pregnant, concerning the advisability of placing the daughter's baby for adoption. The mother insists on adoption, but the daughter remains silent and appears undecided.
Of the following, you should encourage the daughter to
A. make the final decision on adoption herself
B. keep her baby despite her mother's insistence on adoption
C. accept her mother's insistence on adoption
D. make the decision on adoption together with her mother

25._____

KEY (CORRECT ANSWERS)

1. C
2. D
3. B
4. A
5. B

6. A
7. C
8. A
9. C
10. D

11. A
12. C
13. B
14. B
15. D

16. B
17. A
18. D
19. A
20. C

21. A
22. C
23. B
24. C
25. D

TEST 2

DIRECTIONS: Each question or incomplete statement is followed by several suggested answers or completions. Select the one that BEST answers the question or completes the statement. *PRINT THE LETTER OF THE CORRECT ANSWER IN THE SPACE AT THE RIGHT.*

1. You are interviewing a legally responsible absent father who refuses to make child support payments because he claims the mother physically abuses the child.
   Of the following, the BEST way for you to handle his situation is to tell the father that you
   A. will report his complaint about the mother, but he is still responsible for making child support payments
   B. suspect that he is complaining about the mother in order to avoid his own responsibility for making child support payments
   C. are concerned with his responsibility to make child support payments, not with the mother's abuse of the child
   D. cannot determine his responsibility for making child support payments until his complaint about the mother is investigated

   1.____

2. On a visit to a home where child abuse is alleged, you find the mother preparing lunch for her two children. She tells you that she knows that a neighbor is spreading lies about her treatment of the children.
   Which one of the following is the BEST action for you to take?
   A. Thank the mother for her assistance, leave the home, and indicate in your report that the allegation of child abuse is false
   B. Tell the mother that, since you have been sent to visit her, there must be some truth to the allegations
   C. Explain the purpose of your visit and observe whatever interaction takes place between the children and the mother
   D. Conclude the interview, since you have observed the mother preparing a good lunch for the children

   2.____

3. You are interviewing an elderly woman who lives alone to determine her eligibility for homemaker service at public expense. Though obviously frail and in need of this service, the woman is not completely cooperative, and, during the interview, is often silent for a considerable period of time.
   Of the following, the BEST way for you to deal with these periods of silence is to
   A. realize that she may be embarrassed to have to apply for homemaker service at public expense, and emphasize her right to this service
   B. postpone the interview and make an appointment with her for a later date, when she may be better able to cooperate
   C. explain to the woman that you have many clients to interview and need her cooperation to complete the interview quickly
   D. recognize that she is probably hiding something and begin to ask questions to draw her out

   3.____

4. During a conference with an adolescent boy at a juvenile detention center, you find out for the first time that he would prefer to be placed in foster care rather than return to his natural parents.
To uncover the reasons why the boy dislikes his own home, of the following, it would be MOST advisable for you to
   A. ask the boy a number of short, simple questions about his feelings
   B. encourage the boy to talk freely and express his feelings as best he can
   C. interview the parents and find out why the boy doesn't want to live at home
   D. administer a battery of psychological tests in order to make an assessment of the boy's problems

5. Of the following, the BEST way to determine which activities should be provided for members of a Senior Citizens' Center is to
   A. ask the neighborhood community board to submit their recommendations
   B. meet with the professional staff of the center to get their opinions
   C. encourage the members of the center to express their personal preferences
   D. study the schedules prepared by other Senior Citizens' Centers for guidance

6. You are interviewing a mother who is applying for Aid to Families with Dependent Children because the husband has deserted the family. The mother becomes annoyed at having to answer your questions and tells you to leave her apartment.
Which one of the following actions would be MOST appropriate to take FIRST in this situation?
   A. Return to the office and close the case for lack of cooperation
   B. Tell the mother that you will get the information from her neighbors if she does not cooperate
   C. Tell the mother that you must stay until you get answers to your questions
   D. Explain to the mother the reasons for the interview and the consequences of her failure to cooperate

7. A worker assigned to visit homebound clients to determine their eligibility for Medicaid must understand each client's situation as completely as possible.
Of the following source which may provide insight into the client's situation, the one that is generally MOST revealing is:
   A. Close relatives of the client, who have known him for many years
   B. Next-door neighbors, who have observed the daily living habits of the client
   C. The client himself, who can provide his own description of his situation
   D. The records of other social agencies that may have served the client

8. A worker counseling juvenile clients finds that, although he can tolerate most of their behavior, he becomes infuriated when they lie to him.
Of the following, the worker can BEST deal with his anger at his clients' lying by

A. recognizing his feelings of anger and learning to control expression of these feelings to his clients
B. warning his clients that he cannot be responsible for his anger when a client lies to him
C. using willpower to suppress his feelings of anger when a client lies to him
D. realizing that lying is a common trait of juveniles and not directed against him personally

9. During an interview at the employment eligibility section, one of your clients, a former drug addict, has expressed an interest in attending a community counseling center and resuming his education.
In this case, the MOST appropriate action that you should take FIRST is to
   A. determine whether this ambition is realistic for a former drug addict
   B. send the client's application to a community counseling center which provides services to former addicts
   C. ask the client whether he is really motivated or is just seeking your approval
   D. encourage and assist the client to take this step, since his interest is a positive sign

9.____

10. Because of habitual neglect by his mother, a five-year-old boy has been placed in a foster home.
For the worker to encourage the mother to visit the boy in the foster home is, generally,
   A. *desirable*, because the boy will be helped by continuing his ties with his mother
   B. *undesirable*, because the boy will be upset by his mother's visits and will have a harder time adjusting to the foster home
   C. *desirable*, because the mother will learn from the foster parents how she should treat the boy
   D. *undesirable*, because the mother should be punished for her neglect of the boy by complete separation from him

10.____

11. You are interviewing a client who, during previous appointments, has not responded to your requests for information required to determine his continued eligibility for services. On this occasion, the client again offers an excuse which you feel is not acceptable.
For you to advise the client of the probable loss of services because of his lack of cooperation is
   A. *inappropriate*, because the threat to withhold services will harm the relationship between worker and client
   B. *inappropriate*, because workers should not reveal to clients that they do not believe their statements
   C. *appropriate*, because social services are a reward given to cooperative clients
   D. *appropriate*, because the worker should inform clients of the consequences of their lack of cooperation

11.____

4 (#2)

12. Assume that you are counseling an adolescent boy in a juvenile detention center who has been a ringleader in smuggling pot into the center. During your regular interview with this boy, of the following, it would be *advisable* to
    A. tell him you know that he has been involved in smuggling pot and that you are trying to understand the reasons for his misbehavior
    B. ignore his pot smuggling in order to reassure him that you understand and accept him, even though you do not agree with his standards of behavior
    C. warn him that you have reported his pot smuggling and that he will be punished for his misbehavior
    D. show him that you disagree of his pot smuggling, but assure him that you will not report him for his misbehavior

12.____

13. Your unit has received several complaints about a homeless elderly woman living outdoors in various locations in the area. To help determine the need for protective services for this woman, you interview several persons in the neighborhood who are familiar with her, but all are uncooperative or reluctant to give information.
    Of the following, your BEST approach to these persons is to explain to them that
    A. you will take legal steps against them if they do not cooperate with you
    B. their cooperation may enable you to help this homeless woman
    C. you need their cooperation to remove this homeless woman from their neighborhood
    D. they will be responsible for any harm that comes to this homeless woman

13.____

14. A foster mother complains to the worker that a ten-year-old boy placed with her is overaggressive and unmanageable. The worker, knowing that the boy has been placed unsuccessfully several times before, constantly reassures the foster mother that the boy is improving steadily.
    For the worker to do this, generally,
    A. *good practice*, because the foster mother may accept the professional opinion of the worker and keep the boy
    B. *poor practice*, because the foster mother may be discouraged from discussing the boy's problems with the worker
    C. *good practice*, because the foster mother may feel guilty if she gives up the boy when he is improving
    D. *poor practice*, because the boy should not remain with a foster mother who complains about his behavior

14.____

15. Assume that, as a worker in the liaison and adjustment unit, you are interviewing a client regarding an adjustment in budget. The client begins to scream at you that she holds you responsible for the decrease in her allowance.
    Of the following, which is the BEST way for you to handle this situation?
    A. Attempt to discuss the matter calmly with the client and explain her right to a hearing
    B. Urge the client to appeal and assure her of your support

15.____

C. Tell the client that her disorderly behavior will be held against her
D. Tell the client that the reduction is due to red tape and is not your fault

16. As a worker assigned to a juvenile detention center, you are having a counseling interview with a recently admitted boy who is having serious problems in adjusting to confinement in the center. During the interview, the boy frequently interrupts to ask you personal questions.
Of the following, the BEST way for you to deal with these questions is to
    A. tell him in a friendly way that your job is to discuss his problems, not yours
    B. try to understand how the questions relate to the boy's own problems and reply with discretion
    C. take no notice of the questions and continue with the interview
    D. try to win the boy's confidence by answering his questions in detail

17. A worker is interviewing an elderly woman who hesitates to provide necessary information about her finances to determine whether she is eligible for supplementary assistance. She fears that this information will be reported to others and that her neighbors will find out that she is destitute and applying for welfare.
Of the following, the worker's MOST appropriate response is to
    A. tell her that, if she hesitates to give this information, the agency will get it from other sources
    B. assure her that this information is kept strictly confidential, and will not be given to unauthorized persons
    C. convince her that her application will be turned down unless she provides this information as soon as possible
    D. ask for the name and address of her nearest relative and obtain the information from that person

18. You are counseling a couple whose children have been placed in a foster home because of the couple's quarrelling and child neglect. When you interview the wife by herself, she tells you that she knows the husband often cheats on her with other women, but she is too afraid of the husband's temper to tell him how much this hurts her.
For you to immediately reveal to the husband the wife's unhappiness concerning his cheating is, generally,
    A. *good practice*, because it will help the husband to understand why his wife quarrels with him
    B. *poor practice*, because information received from the wife should not be given to the husband without her permission
    C. *good practice*, because the husband will direct his anger at you rather than at his wife
    D. *poor practice*, because the wife may have told you a false story about her husband in order to win your sympathy

19. A worker in an employment eligibility section is beginning a job placement interview with a tall, strongly-built young man. As the man sits down, the worker comments: *I know a big fellow like you wouldn't be interested in any clerical job.*
For the worker to make such a comment is, generally,
   A. *appropriate*, because it creates an air of familiarity which may put the man at ease
   B. *inappropriate*, because the man may be sensitive about his physical size
   C. *appropriate*, because the worker is using his judgment to help speed up the interview
   D. *inappropriate*, because the man may feel he is being pressured into agreeing with the worker

19.____

20. Workers at a juvenile detention center are responsible for establishing constructive relationships with the youths confined to the center in order to help them adjust to detention.
Of the following, the BEST way for a worker to deal with a youth who acts over-aggressive and hostile is to
   A. take appropriate disciplinary measures
   B. attempt to distract the youth by encouraging him to engage in physical sports
   C. try to discover the real reasons for the youth's hostile behavior
   D. urge the youth to express his anger against the institution instead of *taking it out* on you

20.____

21. A worker in a men's shelter is counseling a middle-aged client for alcoholism. During counseling, the client confesses that, many years ago, he had often enjoyed sexually abusing his ten-year-old daughter. The worker tells the client that he personally finds the client's behavior *morally disgusting.*
For the worker to tell the client this is, generally,
   A. *acceptable counseling practice*, because it may encourage the client to feel guilty about his behavior
   B. *unacceptable counseling practice*, because the client may try to shock the worker by confessing other similar behavior
   C. *acceptable counseling practice*, because *letting off steam* in this manner may relieve tension between the worker and the client
   D. *unacceptable counseling practice*, because the client may hesitate to discuss his behavior frankly with the worker in the future

21.____

22. During your discussion with a foster mother who has had a nine-year-old boy in placement for about one month, you are told that the child is disruptive in school and has been unruly and hostile toward the foster family. The boy had been quiet and docile before placement.
In this situation, it would be MOST appropriate to suggest to the foster mother that
   A. this behavior is normal for a nine-year-old boy
   B. children placed in foster homes usually go through a period of testing their foster parents

22.____

C. the child must have picked up these patterns from the foster family
D. this behavior is probably a sign that she is too strict with the boy

23. During an interview in the housing eligibility section, your client, who wants to move to a larger apartment, asks you to decide on a suitable neighborhood for her.
    For you, the worker, to make such a decision for the client would generally be considered
    A. *appropriate*, because you can save time and expense by sharing your knowledge of neighborhoods with the client
    B. *inappropriate*, because workers should not help clients with this type of decision
    C. *appropriate*, because this will help the client to develop confidence in her ability to make decisions
    D. *inappropriate*, because the client should be encouraged to accept the responsibility of making this decision

23.____

24. Your client, an elderly man left unable to care for himself after a stroke, has been referred for home-attendant services, but insists that he does not need these services. You believe that the man considers this to be an insult to his pride and that he will not allow himself to admit that he needs help.
    Of the following, the MOST appropriate action for you to take is to
    A. withdraw the referral for home-attendant services and allow the client to try to take care of himself
    B. process the request for home-attendant services on the assumption that the client will soon realize that he cannot care for himself
    C. discuss with the client your interpretation of his problem and attempt to persuade him to accept home-attendant services
    D. tell the client that he will have no further opportunity to apply for home-attendant services if he does not accept them at this time

24.____

25. A worker making a field visit to investigate a complaint of child abuse finds that the parents of the child are a racially mixed couple. The child appears poorly dressed and unruly.
    Of the following, the MOST appropriate approach for the worker to take in this situation is to
    A. take the child aside and ask him privately if either of his parents ever mistreats him
    B. determine if prejudice against the couple has led them to use the child as a scapegoat
    C. question the non-minority parent closely for signs of resentment of the child's mixed parentage
    D. observe the relationship between parents and child for indications of abuse by the parents

25.____

KEY (CORRECT ANSWERS)

1. A
2. C
3. A
4. B
5. C

6. D
7. C
8. A
9. D
10. A

11. D
12. A
13. B
14. B
15. A

16. B
17. B
18. B
19. D
20. C

21. D
22. B
23. D
24. C
25. D

EXAMINATION SECTION
TEST 1

DIRECTIONS: Each question or incomplete statement is followed by several suggested answers or completions. Select the one that BEST answers the question or completes the statement. *PRINT THE LETTER OF THE CORRECT ANSWER IN THE SPACE AT THE RIGHT.*

1. The PRIMARY function of the Department of Social Services is to
   A. refer needy persons to legally responsible relatives for support
   B. enable needy persons to become self-supporting
   C. refer ineligible persons to private agencies
   D. grant aid to needy eligible persons
   E. administer public assistance programs in which the federal and state governments do not participate

    1._____

2. A public assistance program objective should be designed to
   A. provide for eligible persons in accordance with their individual requirements and with consideration of the circumstances in which they live
   B. provide for eligible persons at a standard of living equal to that enjoyed while they were self-supporting
   C. make sure that assistance payments from public funds are not too liberal
   D. guard against providing a better living for persons receiving aid than is enjoyed by the most frugal independent families
   E. eliminate the need for private welfare agencies

    2._____

3. It is often stated that it would be better to abolish the need for relief rather than to extend the existing public assistance programs.
   This statement suggests that
   A. existing legislation makes it too easy for people to apply for and receive assistance
   B. public assistance should be limited to institutional care for rehabilitative purposes
   C. the support of needy persons should be the responsibility of their own families and relatives rather than that of the government
   D. the existing criteria used to determine *need* for public assistance are too liberal and should be modified to include a *work* test
   E. attempts should be made to eradicate those forces in our social organization which cause poverty

    3._____

4. The one of the following types of public assistance which is frequently described as a *special privilege* is
   A. veteran assistance
   B. emergency assistance
   C. aid to dependent children
   D. old-age assistance
   E. vocational rehabilitation of the handicapped

    4._____

17

5. The principle of *settlement* holds that each community is responsible for the care of its own members and that communities should not bear the costs of care for needy non-residents.
   This was an intrinsic principle of the
   A. English Poor Laws
   B. Home Rule Amendment
   C. Single Tax Proposal
   D. National Bankruptcy Regulations
   E. Proportional Representation Act

5.____

6. The FIRST form of state social security legislation developed in the United States was
   A. health insurance
   B. unemployment compensation
   C. workmen's compensation
   D. old-age insurance
   E. old-age assistance

6.____

7. The plan for establishing a federal department with Cabinet status to be known as the Department of Health, Education, and Welfare, was
   A. vetoed by the President after having been passed by Congress
   B. disapproved by the Senate after having been passed by the House of Representatives
   C. rejected by both the Senate and the House of Representatives
   D. enacted into legislation during a past session of Congress
   E. determined to be unconstitutional

7.____

8. Census Bureau reports show certain definite social trends in our population. One of these trends which was a major contributing factor in the establishment of the federal old-age insurance system was the
   A. increased rate of immigration to the United States
   B. rate at which the number of Americans living to 65 years of age and beyond is increasing
   C. increasing amounts spent for categorical relief in the country as a whole
   D. decreasing number of legally responsible relatives who have been unable to assist the aged since the Depression of 1929
   E. number of states which have failed to meet their obligations in the care of the aged

8.____

9. The Federal Housing Administration is the agency which
   A. insures mortgages made by lending institutions for new construction or remodeling of old construction
   B. provides federal aid for state and local governments for slum clearance and housing for very low income families
   C. subsidizes the building industry through direct grants
   D. provides for the construction of low-cost housing projects owned and operated by the federal government
   E. combines city planning with government subsidies for large-scale housing

9.____

10. Reports show that more men than women are physically handicapped MAINLY because
    A. women are instinctively more cautious than men
    B. men are more likely to have congenital deformities
    C. women tend to see surgical remedies because of greater concern over personal appearance
    D. men have lower ability to recover from injury
    E. men are more likely to be exposed to hazardous conditions

11. Of the following, the explanation married women give MOST frequently for seeking employment outside the home is that they wish to
    A. escape the drudgeries of home life
    B. develop secondary employment skills
    C. maintain an emotionally satisfying career
    D. provide the main support for the family
    E. supplement the family income

12. Of the following home conditions, the one MOST likely to cause emotional disturbances in children is
    A. increased birthrate following the war
    B. disrupted family relationships
    C. lower family income than that of neighbors
    D. higher family income than that of neighbors
    E. overcrowded living conditions

13. Casual unemployment, as distinguished from other types of unemployment, is traceable MOST readily to
    A. a decrease in the demand for labor as a result of scientific progress
    B. more or less haphazard changes in the demand for labor in certain industries
    C. periodic changes in the demand for labor in certain industries
    D. disturbances and disruptions in industry resulting from international trade barriers
    E. increased mobility of the population

14. Labor legislation, although primarily intended for the benefit of the employee, may aid the employer by
    A. increasing his control over the immediate labor market
    B. prohibiting government interference with operating policies
    C. protecting him, through equalization of labor costs, from being undercut by other employers
    D. transferring to the general taxpayer the principal costs of industrial hazards of accident and unemployment
    E. increasing the pensions of civil service employees

15. When employment and unemployment figures both decline, the MOST probable conclusion is that
    A. the population has reached a condition of equilibrium
    B. seasonal employment has ended

C. the labor force has decreased
D. payments for unemployment insurance have been increased
E. industrial progress has reduced working hours

16. In evaluating the adequacy of an individual's income, a social service worker should place primary emphasis on
    A. its value in relation to the average income
    B. the source of the income
    C. its relation to the earning capacity of the individual
    D. its purchasing power
    E. the purposes for which it is spent

17. An individual with an I.Q. of 100 may be said to have demonstrated _____ intelligence.
    A. superior
    B. absolute
    C. substandard
    D. approximately average
    E. high average

18. While state legislatures differ in many respects, all of them are MOST NEARLY alike in
    A. provisions for retirement of members
    B. rate of pay
    C. length of legislative sessions
    D. method of selection of their members
    E. length of term of office

19. If a state passed a law in a field under Congressional jurisdiction and if Congress subsequently passed contrary legislation, the state provision would be
    A. regarded as never having existed
    B. valid until the next session of the state legislature which would be obliged to repeal it
    C. superseded by the federal statute
    D. ratified by Congress
    E. still operative in the state involved

20. Power to pardon offenses committed against the people of the United States is vested in the
    A. Supreme Court of the United States
    B. United States District Courts
    C. Federal Bureau of Investigation
    D. United States Parole Board
    E. President of the United States

21. As distinguished from formal social control of an individual's behavior, an example of informal social control is that exerted by
    A. public opinion
    B. religious doctrine
    C. educational institutions
    D. statutes
    E. public health measures

22. The PRINCIPAL function of the jury in a jury trial is to decide questions of
    A. equity
    B. fact
    C. injunction
    D. contract
    D. law

23. Of the following rights of an individual, the one which usually depends on citizenship as distinguished from those given anyone living under the laws of the United States is the right to
    A. receive public assistance
    B. hold an elective office
    C. petition the government for redress of grievances
    D. receive equal protection of the laws
    E. be accorded a trial by jury

24. The name of Thomas Malthus is MOST closely associated with a work on
    A. population
    B. political justice
    C. capitalism
    D. social contract
    E. wealth of nations

25. A chronic functional disease characterized by fits or attacks in which there is a loss of consciousness with a succession of convulsions is called
    A. epilepsy
    B. dipsomania
    C. catalepsy
    D. Hodgkin's disease
    E. paresis

KEY (CORRECT ANSWERS)

1. D
2. A
3. E
4. A
5. A

6. C
7. D
8. B
9. A
10. E

11. E
12. B
13. B
14. C
15. C

16. D
17. D
18. D
19. C
20. E

21. A
22. B
23. B
24. A
25. A

TEST 2

DIRECTIONS: Each question or incomplete statement is followed by several suggested answers or completions. Select the one that BEST answers the question or completes the statement. *PRINT THE LETTER OF THE CORRECT ANSWER IN THE SPACE AT THE RIGHT.*

Questions 1-10.

DIRECTIONS: Questions 1 through 10, inclusive, are based on the following table, which gives a partial summary of certain groups of cases in the social services center of a public assistance agency.

SOCIAL SERVICES CENTER CASELOAD SUMMARY, JUNE-SEPTEMBER

	June	July	August	September
Total Cases Under Care at End of Month	13,790	11,445	13,191	12,209
Home relief	4,739	2,512	6,055	5,118
Old-age assistance	5,337	b	5,440	2,265
Aid to dependent children	3,487	1,621	1,520	4,594
Aid to the Blind	227	251	176	232
Net Change During Month	-344	c	1,746	-982
Applications Made During Month	1,542	789	3,153	1,791
Total Cases Accepted during Month	534	534	2,879	982
Home relief	278	213	342	338
Old-age assistance	43	161	1,409	f
Aid to dependent children	195	153	1,115	307
Aid to the blind	18	7	13	14
Total Cases Closed During Month	878	d	1,133	1,964
To private employment	326	1,197	460	870
To unemployment insurance	96	421	126	205
Reclassified	176	326	178	399
All other reasons	280	935	e	490
Total Cases Carried Over to Next Month	a	11,445	13,191	12,209

1. The number which should be placed in the blank indicated by *a* is
   - A. 12,912
   - B. 13,446
   - C. 13,790
   - D. 14,134
   - E. None of the above

2. The number which should be placed in the blank indicated by *b* is
   - A. 6,385
   - B. 7,601
   - C. 8,933
   - D. 7,061
   - E. None of the above

3. The number which should be placed in the blank indicated by *c* is
   - A. -2,345
   - B. -344
   - C. 344
   - D. 3,413
   - E. None of the above

2 (#2)

4. The number which should be placed in the blank indicated by *d* is   4.____
   A. 2,789   B. 2,345   C. 7,601
   D. 3,879   E. None of the above

5. Of the total number of cases closed during the month of August, the percentage   5.____
   closed for reasons other than reclassification or receipt of unemployment
   insurance is APPROXIMATELY
   A. 13.8%   B. 73.17%   C. 26.83%   D. 40.60%   E. 24.63%

6. In comparing June and July, the figures indicate that with respect to the total   6.____
   cases under care at the end of each month,
   A. the percentage of total cases accepted during the month was lower in
      June
   B. the percentage of total cases accepted during the month was higher in
      June
   C. the percentage of total cases accepted during both months was the same
   D. there were more cases under care at the end of July
   E. there is insufficient data for comparison of the total cases under care at
      the end of each month

7. The total number of cases accepted during the entire period in the category in   7.____
   which most cases were accepted was
   A. 1,409   B. 1,936   C. 1,770   D. 4,929   E. 20,103

8. In comparing July and September, the figures indicate that   8.____
   A. more cases were closed in September because of private employment
   B. the total number of cases accepted during the month consisted of a
      greater proportion of home relief cases in September
   C. in one of these months, there were more total cases under care at the
      end of the month than at the beginning of the month
   D. aid to dependent children cases at the beginning of September numbered
      almost three times as many as at the beginning of July
   E. none of the above is correct

9. The total number of applications made during the four-month period was   9.____
   A. more than four times the number of cases closed because of private
      employment during the same period
   B. less than the combined totals of aid to dependent children cases under
      care in June and July
   C. 4,376 more than the total number of cases accepted during August
   D. 23 times as large as the number of cases reclassified in July
   E. 5,916 less than the total number of cases carried over to September

10. The ratio of old-age assistance cases accepted in August to the total number   10.____
    of such cases under care at the end of that month is expressed with the
    GREATEST degree of accuracy by the figures
    A. 1:4   B. 1:25   C. 4:1   D. 7:128   E. 10:39

11. The term *mores* refers to
    A. English meadows
    B. bribery
    C. Moorish worship
    D. telegraphic code
    E. social customs

12. *Disparity* refers MOST directly to
    A. difference
    B. argument
    C. low wages
    D. separation
    E. injustice

13. The technical term used to express the ratio between mental and chronological age is called the
    A. mentality rating
    B. culture level index
    C. psychometric standard
    D. achievement index
    E. intelligence quotient

14. In social services work, the disorganizing factors in a personal or familial situation which prevent or hinder rehabilitation are called
    A. median deviations
    B. transference situations
    C. rank correlations
    D. liabilities
    E. collective representations

15. The period in the life of man when mental abilities begin to deteriorate is known as
    A. puberty
    B. adolescence
    C. gerontology
    D. senility
    E. antiquity

Questions 16-25.

DIRECTIONS: Questions 16 through 25, inclusive, contain two blank spaces each. You are to select the words which will fill the blanks so that the sentence will be true and sensible. For the *first* blank in each question, select a word or phrase preceded by letter A, B, C, D, or E. For the *second* blank in the question, select a word or phrase preceded by letter V, W, X, Y, or Z. Use the two letters you have selected as your answer and print both these letters in the correspondingly numbered space at the right.

16. _____ is to public assistance as citizenship is to _____.
    A. need
    B. school attendance
    C. worthiness
    D. child
    E. welfare center
    V. passport
    W. alien
    X. immigration
    Y. excise tax
    Z. indictment

17. _____ is to home relief as public institutional care is to _____.
    A. compensation
    B. supplementation
    C. direct relief
    D. survivor's insurance
    E. fiscal period
    V. removal of custody
    W. adoption
    X. indoor relief
    Y. day care
    Z. voucher assistance

18. _____ is to face sheet as income is to _____.   18.____
    A. client   B. cash relief
    C. relief standard   D. case record
    E. emergency assistance
    V. wages   W. home
    X. debts   Y. taxes
    Z. bonus

19. _____ is to demography as man is to _____.   19.____
    A. politics   B. racial relations   C. stigmata
    D. social statistics   E. democracy
    V. population   W. geography   X. woman
    Y. marriage   Z. anthropology

20. _____ is to tuberculosis as Terman is to _____.   20.____
    A. Wasserman   B. Mantoux   C. Schick
    D. Ascheim-Zondek   E. Snellen
    V. litmus test   W. means test   X. lie detector test
    Y. intelligence test   Z. CAVD test

21. _____ is to dementia as feeblemindedness is to _____.   21.____
    A. anger   B. luxation   C. insanity
    D. diagnosis   E. psychiatry
    V. myopia   W. amentia   X. tibia
    Y. criminal   Z. childhood

22. Frustration is to _____ as _____ is to relaxation.   22.____
    A. satisfaction   B. goal   C. need
    D. desire   E. motive
    V. tension   W. behavior   X. adjustment
    Y. readjustment   Z. reaction

23. _____ is to embezzlement as parole is to _____.   23.____
    A. intent   B. larceny   C. desertion
    D. guilt   E. conviction
    V. bail   W. plea   X. probation
    Y. innocence   Z. reformatory

24. Abandonment is to _____ as coercion is to _____.   24.____
    A. abduction   B. discovery   C. guardian
    D. adultery   E. desertion
    V. desertion   W. impotence   X. crime
    Y. coition   Z. constraint

25. _____ is to homicide as felony is to _____.   25.____
    A. courthouse   B. mayhem   C. negligence
    D. witness   E. manslaughter
    V. judge   W. crime   X. autopsy
    Y. civil suit   Z. prosecutor

KEY (CORRECT ANSWERS)

1. C
2. D
3. A
4. E
5. B

6. A
7. B
8. E
9. E
10. E

11. E
12. A
13. E
14. D
15. D

16. AV
17. CX
18. DV
19. DZ
20. BY

21. CW
22. AV
23. BX
24. EZ
25. EW

TEST 3

DIRECTIONS: Each question or incomplete statement is followed by several suggested answers or completions. Select the one that BEST answers the question or completes the statement. *PRINT THE LETTER OF THE CORRECT ANSWER IN THE SPACE AT THE RIGHT.*

Questions 1-3.

DIRECTIONS: Questions 1 through 3, inclusive, are to be answered on the basis of the following passage.

Aid to dependent children shall be given to a parent or other relative as herein specified for the benefit of a child or children under sixteen years of age or of a minor or minors between sixteen and eighteen years of age if in the judgment of the administrative agency: (1) the granting of an allowance will be in the interest of such child or minor, and (2) the parent or other relative is a fit person to bring up such child or minor so that his physical, mental, and moral well-being will be safeguarded, and (3) aid is necessary to enable such parent or other relative to do so, and (4) such child or minor is a resident of the state on the date of application for aid, and (5) such minor between sixteen and eighteen years of age is regularly attending school in accordance with the regulations of the department. An allowance may be granted for the aid of such child or minor who has been deprived or parental support or care by reason of the death, continued absence from the home, or physical or mental incapacity of a parent, and who is living with his father, mother, grandfather, grandmother, brother, sister, stepfather, stepmother, stepbrother, stepsister, uncle or aunt. In making such allowances, consideration shall be given to the ability of the relative making application and of any other relatives to support and care for or to contribute to the support and care of such child or minor. In making all such allowances, it shall be made certain that the religious faith of the child or minor shall be preserved and protected.

1. The preceding passage is concerned PRIMARILY with
   A. the financial ability of persons applying for public assistance
   B. compliance on the part of applicants with the *settlement* provisions of the law
   C. the fitness of parents or other relatives to bring up physically, mentally, or morally delinquent children between the ages of sixteen and eighteen
   D. eligibility for aid to dependent children
   E. the religious faith of children or minors coming within the provisions of this law

1.____

2. On the basis of the preceding passage, the MOST accurate of the following statements is:
   A. Mary Doe, mother of John, age 18, is entitled to aid for her son if he is attending school regularly
   B. Evelyn Stowe, mother of Eleanor, age 13, is not entitled to aid for Eleanor if she uses her home for immoral purposes
   C. Ann Roe, cousin of Helen, age 14, is entitled to aid for Helen if the latter is living with her
   D. Peter Moe, uncle of Henry, age 15, is not entitled to aid for Henry if the latter is living with him

2.____

E. Harriet Hoe, mother of Paul, age 7, is not entitled to aid for him if she has been divorced from her husband

3. The above passage is PROBABLY an excerpt of the
   A. Administrative Code
   B. Social Welfare Law
   C. Federal Security Act
   D. City Charter
   E. Colonial Laws of the state

   3.____

4. Recent amendment of the Social Security Act has produced major changes in the administration of public assistance.
   The one of the following which is NOT included among these changes is the
   A. availability of federal funds in matching payments for home relief to veterans who are employable but unemployed
   B. establishment of federal grants-in-aid for a category of assistance to be known as aid to the permanently and totally disabled
   C. extension of the four categories of assistance to Puerto Rico and the Virgin Islands
   D. sharing by the federal government of costs of assistance to needy aged and blind persons in public medical institutions
   E. availability of federal funds within present federal maxima in matching indirect payments for medical care in old-age assistance, aid to the blind, and aid to dependent children

   4.____

5. The length of residence required to make a person eligible for the various forms of public assistance available in the United States
   A. is the same in all states but is different among public assistance programs in a given state
   B. is the same in all states and among different public assistance programs in a given state
   C. is the same in all states for different categories
   D. varies among states and among different public assistance programs in a given state
   E. varies only in the local agencies of a given state

   5.____

6. The Social Welfare Law requires that whenever an applicant for aid to dependent children resides in a place where there is a central index or a social service exchange, the public welfare official shall register the case with such index or exchange.
   This requirement is for the purpose of
   A. preventing duplication and coordinating the work of public and private agencies
   B. establishing prior claims on the amounts of assistance furnished when repayments are made
   C. having the social service exchange determine which agency should handle the case
   D. providing statistical data regarding the number of persons receiving grants for aid to dependent children
   E. making sure that opportunities for private employment are available to persons receiving assistance

   6.____

7. A person who knowingly brings a needy person from another state into the state for the purpose of making him a public charge, is guilty of
   A. violation of the Displaced Persons Act
   B. violation of the Mann Act
   C. a felony
   D. a misdemeanor
   E. no offense

7.____

8. Among the following needy persons, the one NOT eligible to receive veteran assistance is the
   A. husband of a veteran, if living with the veteran
   B. minor grandchild of a veteran, if living with the veteran
   C. incapacitated child of a deceased veteran
   D. stepmother of stepfather of a veteran, if living with the veteran
   E. non-veteran brother or sister of a veteran, if living with the veteran

8.____

9. The term *state residence*, as defined in the Social Welfare Law, means continuous residence within the state for a period of AT LEAST
   A. one year   B. two years   C. six months
   D. one month   E. one day

9.____

10. In order to be eligible for old-age assistance in this state, applicants must have resided continuously in the state prior to the date of application for
    A. three months   B. six months   C. one year
    D. five years   E. no specific period

10.____

11. Under the Social Security Act, public assistance payments do NOT provide for
    A. old-age assistance
    B. care of children in foster homes
    C. aid to the blind
    D. aid to dependent children
    E. aid to the permanently and totally disabled

11.____

12. The Social Welfare Law provides that certain relatives of a recipient of public assistance or care, or of a person liable to become in need thereof, be responsible for the support of such person if they are of sufficient ability.
    The one of the following who is NOT a legally responsible relative is a(n)
    A. mother
    B. child
    C. grandparent
    D. uncle
    E. step-parent, for a minor stepchild

12.____

13. Of the following, the distinguishing characteristics of a *dependent child* as defined in the Social Welfare Law, refer to a child who is
    A. in the custody of, or wholly or partly maintained by an authorized organization of charitable, eleemosynary, correctional, or reformatory character

13.____

B. in such condition of want or suffering or who under improper guardianship as to injure or endanger the morals of himself or others
C. between 16 and 18 years of age and solely dependent upon his parents for support and maintenance
D. under 16 years of age and deserted or abandoned by parents or other persons lawfully charged with his care
E. incorrigible or ungovernable and beyond the control of his parents or guardian

14. Recent adoption laws tend to place increased emphasis upon
    A. informal signing of adoption papers
    B. lowered residence requirements for adoption
    C. establishment of the child's inheritance rights
    D. social investigation of the home before adoption
    E. increased boarding rates paid to adoptive parents

15. Any person or organization soliciting donations in public places is required to have a license issued by the
    A. Police Department   B. Department of Sanitation
    C. Division of Labor Relations D. Department of Social Services
    E. Department of Licenses

16. A person who, though himself, in good health, harbors disease germs which may be passed on to others, is called a(n)
    A. instigator   B. carrier   C. incubator
    D. inoculator   E. malingerer

17. Diseases most commonly caused by certain working environments or conditions are known as _____ diseases.
    A. infectious   B. contagious   C. occupational
    D. hereditary   E. compensatory

18. The process of destroying micro-organisms which cause disease or infection is called
    A. contamination   B. immunization C. inoculation
    D. sterilization   E. infestation

19. Proper utilization of the term *carious* would involve reference to
    A. teeth
    B. curiosity
    C. shipment of food packages to needy persons in Europe
    D. hazardous or precarious situations
    E. lack of reasonable precautions

20. The chemical agent which has been used extensively to prevent the spread of typhus infection is
    A. cortisone   B. D.D.T.   C. penicillin
    D. ephedrine   E. sulfanilamide

21. The medical term for *hardening of the arteries* is 21.____
    A. carcinoma B. arthritis C. thrombosis
    D. arteriosclerosis E. phlebitis

22. A set of symptoms which occur together is called a 22.____
    A. sympathin B. syncope C. syndrome
    D. synecdoche E. syllogism

23. If the characteristics of a person were being studied by competent observers, it would be expected that their observations would differ MOST markedly with respect to their evaluation of the person's 23.____
    A. intelligence B. nutritional characteristics
    C. temperamental characteristics D. weight
    E. height

24. If there are evidences of dietary deficiency in families where cereals make up a major portion of the diet, the MOST likely reason for this deficiency is that 24.____
    A. cereals cause absorption of excessive quantities of water
    B. persons who concentrate their diet on cereals do not chew their food properly
    C. carbohydrates are deleterious
    D. other essential food elements are omitted
    E. children eat cereals too rapidly

25. Although malnutrition is generally associated with poverty, dietary studies of population groups in the United States reveal that 25.____
    A. malnutrition is most often due to a deficiency of nutrients found chiefly in high-cost foods
    B. there has been overemphasis of the causal relationship between poverty and malnutrition
    C. malnutrition is found among people with sufficient money to be well fed
    D. a majority of the population in all income groups is undernourished
    E. malnutrition is not a factor in the incidence of rickets

KEY (CORRECT ANSWERS)

1. D
2. B
3. B
4. A
5. D

6. A
7. D
8. E
9. A
10. E

11. B
12. D
13. A
14. D
15. D

16. B
17. C
18. D
19. A
20. B

21. D
22. C
23. C
24. D
25. C

TEST 4

DIRECTIONS: Each question or incomplete statement is followed by several suggested answers or completions. Select the one that BEST answers the question or completes the statement. *PRINT THE LETTER OF THE CORRECT ANSWER IN THE SPACE AT THE RIGHT.*

1. A medically trained person who treats mental diseases is called a(n)
   A. psychologist
   B. sociologist
   C. psychiatrist
   D. physiologist
   E. opthamologist

   1.____

2. Of the following social agencies, the which must rely MOST on short-contact interviewing is the
   A. child-guidance clinic
   B. Travelers' Aid Society
   C. Social Service Exchange
   D. Hospital for Crippled Children
   E. juvenile court

   2.____

3. The organization which has as one of its primary functions the mitigation of suffering caused by famine, fire, floods, and other national calamities is the
   A. National Safety Council
   B. Salvation Army
   C. Public Administration Services
   D. American National Red Cross
   E. American Legion

   3.____

4. The MAIN difference between public welfare and private social agencies is that in public agencies
   A. case records are open to the public
   B. the granting of assistance cannot be sufficiently flexible to meet the varying needs of individual recipients
   C. only financial assistance may be provided
   D. all policies and procedures must be based upon statutory authorizations
   E. economical and efficient administration are stressed because their funds are obtained through public taxation

   4.____

5. Proper handling of a case in which the applicant requires temporary congregate care would involve a referral initially to
   A. a private agency
   B. a religious institution
   C. the state welfare agency
   D. the federal government
   E. one of the municipal shelters

   5.____

6. A recipient of relief who is in need of the services on an attorney but is unable to pay the customary fees, should generally be referred to the
   A. Small Claims Court
   B. Domestic Relations Court
   C. County Lawyers Association
   D. City Law Department
   E. Legal Aid Society

   6.____

7. A person who is not satisfied with the action taken by the Department of Social Services on his application for old-age assistance may appeal to the State Department of Social Welfare for an impartial review and a *fair hearing.*

   7.____

The final decision in such a hearing is made by the
A. State Board of Social Welfare
B. State Commissioner of Social Welfare
C. Commissioner of Social Services
D. Attorney-General of the State
E. Federal Security Agency

8. An injured worker should file his claim for workmen's compensation with the
A. State Labor Relations Board
B. Division of Placement and Unemployment Insurance
C. State Industrial Commission
D. Workmen's Compensation Board
E. State Insurance Board

8.____

9. In order to supplement the care and guidance furnished to young people by the family and other social institutions, the legislature created a temporary agency known as the State Youth Commission.
Among the powers and duties of this Commission are those listed below, with the EXCEPTION of
A. supervising the administration of state institutions for juvenile delinquents
B. authorizing payment of state aid to municipalities in accordance with the provisions of the Youth Commission Act
C. making studies and recommendations regarding the guidance and treatment of juvenile delinquents
D. devising plans for the creation and operation of youth bureaus and recreation projects
E. making necessary studies and analyses of the problems of youth guidance and the prevention of juvenile delinquency

9.____

10. One of the institutions operated by the State Department of Social Welfare is the
A. State School for the Blind, Batavia
B. State Training School for Boys, Warwick
C. State Reconstruction Home, West Haverstraw
D. State School for Mental Defectives, Newark
E. Woodbourne Institute for Defective Delinquents, Woodbourne

10.____

11. The one of the following which is NOT included among the responsibilities of the Bureau of Public Assistance of the Social Security Administration is
A. reviewing and approving state plans for public assistance and the operation of these plans, in order to determine their continuing conformity to the Social Security Act
B. administering provisions for grants by the federal government to states for old-age assistance, aid to the blind, aid to dependent children, and aid to the permanently and totally disabled
C. carrying out the Social Security Administration's functions in connection with the federal-state unemployment insurance system

11.____

D. reviewing state estimates for public assistance and certifying the amount of federal grants to states
E. collecting, analyzing, and publishing data on the operation of all forms of public assistance in the states, including general assistance

12. Because of the number of able-bodied employable persons on relief, the Department of Social Services once adopted the policy of
    A. removing all employables from the relief rolls
    B. subjecting such persons to special review in order to determine whether they are concealing facts about employment
    C. assigning such persons to various city departments for appropriate employment commensurate with the amount of relief grants
    D. forcing all men on the employable list to apply to other governmental agencies as provisional civil service workers
    E. requesting selective service boards to give preference to such employable persons of appropriate age for induction into the armed forces

13. The type of insurance found MOST frequently among families such as those assisted by the Department of Social Services is
    A. accident   B. straight life   C. endowment
    D. industrial   E. personal liability

14. Of the following items in the standard budget of the Department of Social Services, the one for which actual expenditures would be MOST constant throughout the year is
    A. fuel   B. housing
    C. medical care   D. clothing
    E. household replacements

15. The MOST frequent cause of *broken homes* is attributed to the
    A. temperamental incompatibilities of parents and in-laws
    B. extension of the system of children's courts
    C. psychopathic irresponsibility of the parents
    D. institutionalization of one of the spouses
    E. death of one or both spouses

16. In rearing children, the problems of the widower are usually greater than those of the widow, largely because of the
    A. tendency of widowers to impose excessively rigid moral standards
    B. increased economic hardship
    C. added difficulty of maintaining a desirable home
    D. possibility that a stepmother will be added to the household
    E. prevalent masculine prejudice against pursuits which are inherently feminine

17. Foster-home placement of children is often advocated in preference to institutionalization PRIMARILY because
    A. the law does not provide for local supervision of children's institutions
    B. institutions furnish a more expensive type of care
    C. the number of institutions is insufficient compared to the number of children needing car
    D. children are not well treated in institutions
    E. foster homes provide a more normal environment for children

18. Of the following, the category MOST likely to yield the greatest reduction in cost to the taxpayer under improved employment conditions is
    A. home relief, including aid to the homeless
    B. aid to the blind
    C. aid to dependent children
    D. old-age assistance
    E. aid to the permanently and totally disabled

19. One of the MOST common characteristics of the chronic alcoholic is
    A. low intelligence level
    B. wanderlust
    C. psychosis
    D. independence
    E. egocentricity

20. Of the following factors leading toward the cure of the alcoholic, the MOST important is thought to be
    A. removal of all alcohol from the immediate environment
    B. development of a sense of personal adequacy
    C. social disapproval of drinking
    D. segregation from former companions
    E. intensive supervision by parole officers

21. An interview is BEST conducted in private primarily because
    A. the person interviewed will tend to be less self-conscious
    B. the interviewer will be able to maintain his continuity of thought better
    C. it will insure that the interview is *off the record*
    D. people tend to *show off* before an audience
    E. constant interruption by visitors and telephone calls will irritate the interviewer

22. An interviewer will be better able to understand the person interviewed and his problems if he recognizes that much of the person's behavior is due to motives
    A. which are deliberate
    B. of which he is unaware
    C. which are inexplicable
    D. which are kept under control
    E. which are calculated to deceive

23. When an applicant for public assistance is repeatedly told that *everything will be all right*, the effect that can usually be expected is that he will
    A. develop overt negativistic reactions toward the agency
    B. become too closely identified with the interviewer

C. doubt the interviewer's ability to understand and help with his problems
D. have greater confidence in the interviewer
E. make no appreciable change in his attitude toward the interviewer

24. While interviewing a client, it is preferable that the social service worker
    A. take no notes in order to avoid disturbing the client
    B. focus primary attention on the client while the client is talking
    C. take no notes in order to impress upon the client the worker's ability to remember all the pertinent facts of his case
    D. record all details in order to show the client that what he says is important
    E. record all details in order to impress upon the client the official character of his statements

24.____

25. During an interview, a curious applicant asks several questions about the social service worker's private life.
    As the interviewer, you should
    A. refuse to answer such questions
    B. answer his questions fully
    C. explain that your primary concern is with his problems and that discussion of your personal affairs will not be helpful in meeting his needs
    D. explain that it is the responsibility of the interviewer to ask questions and not to answer them
    E. answer only enough of his questions to the extent necessary to establish a friendly relationship with him

25.____

KEY (CORRECT ANSWERS)

1. C
2. B
3. D
4. D
5. E

6. E
7. B
8. D
9. A
10. B

11. C
12. C
13. D
14. B
15. E

16. C
17. E
18. A
19. E
20. B

21. A
22. B
23. C
24. C
25. C

TEST 5

DIRECTIONS: Each question or incomplete statement is followed by several suggested answers or completions. Select the one that BEST answers the question or completes the statement. *PRINT THE LETTER OF THE CORRECT ANSWER IN THE SPACE AT THE RIGHT.*

1. An interviewer can BEST establish a good relationship with the person being interviewed by
    A. assuming casual interest in the statements made by the person being interviewed
    B. asking questions which enable the person to show pride in his knowledge
    C. taking the point of view of the person interviewed
    D. controlling the interview to a major extent
    E. showing a genuine interest in the person

1._____

2. An interviewer's attention must be directed toward himself as well as toward the person interviewed.
   This statement means that the interviewer should
    A. keep in mind the extent to which his own prejudices may influence his judgment
    B. rationalize the statements made by the person interviewed
    C. gain the respect and confidence of the person interviewed
    D. avoid being too impersonal
    E. avoid using indirect methods in eliciting information from the person interviewed

2._____

3. More complete expression will be obtained from a person being interviewed if the interviewer can create the impression that
    A. the data secured will become part of a permanent record
    B. official information must be accurate in every detail
    C. it is the duty of the person interviewed to give accurate data
    D. the interviewer checks additional sources to get complete data
    E. the person interviewed is participating in a discussion of his own problems

3._____

4. The practice of asking leading questions should be avoided in an interview because the
    A. interviewer risks revealing his attitudes to the person being interviewed
    B. interviewer may be led to ignore the objective attitudes of the person interviewed
    C. answers may be unwarrantedly influenced
    D. person interviewed will resent the attempt to lead him and will be less cooperative
    E. replies to such questions are always verbose

4._____

5. A good technique for the interviewer to use in an effort to secure reliable data and to reduce the possibility of misunderstanding is to
   A. use casual undirected conversation, enabling the person being interviewed to talk about himself, and thus secure the desired information
   B. adopt the procedure of using direct questions regularly
   C. extract the desired information from the person being interviewed by putting him on the defensive
   D. explain to the person being interviewed the information desired and the reason for needing it
   E. explain that he is an experienced interviewer and can detect false statements

6. As a social service worker interviewing an applicant for public assistance, your attitude toward his veracity should be that the information he has furnished you is
   A. *untruthful* until you have had an opportunity to check the information
   B. *truthful* only insofar as verifiable facts are concerned
   C. *untruthful* because clients tend to interpret everything in their own favor
   D. *truthful* until you have information to the contrary
   E. *untruthful* because most applicants are unreliable

7. When a public assistance agency assigns its most experienced interviewers to conduct initial interviews with applicants, the MOST important reason for its action is that
   A. experienced workers are always older, and therefore command the respect of applicants
   B. the applicant may be given a complete understanding of the procedures to be followed and the time involved in obtaining assistance payments
   C. applicants with fraudulent intentions will be detected, and prevented from obtaining further services from the agency
   D. the agency may immediately obtain an accurate and complete plan to be followed in giving assistance to the applicant
   E. the applicant may be given an understanding of the purpose of the assistance program and of the bases for granting assistance, in addition to the routine information

8. As a social service worker conducting the first interview with an applicant for public assistance, you should
   A. ask questions requiring *yes* or *no* answers in order to simplify the interview
   B. rephrase several of the key questions as a check on his previous statements
   C. let him tell his own story while keeping him to the relevant facts
   D. avoid showing any sympathy for the applicant while he is revealing his personal needs and problems
   E. ask only direct questions so as to demonstrate your impersonal approach

9. An aged person who is unable to produce immediate proof of age has made an application for old-age assistance. He states that it will take about a week to obtain the necessary proof and that he does not have enough money to provide meals for himself until then.
   If it appears that he is in immediate need, he should be told that
   A. the law requires proof of age before any assistance can be granted
   B. temporary assistance will be provided pending the completion of the investigation
   C. a personal loan will be provided from a revolving fund
   D. he should arrange for a small loan from private sources
   E. he will have to produce an affidavit witnessed by two relatives who will vouch for the accuracy of his statements before any assistance can be provided

10. If the social service worker learns during the interview that the client has applied for public assistance without the knowledge of her husband, even though he is a member of the same household, the worker should
    A. appear not to notice this oversight, but watch for other evidences of marital discord
    B. make no mention of this to the applicant, but before taking final action send a note to the husband asking him to come in
    C. discuss this situation with the client and help her recognize the value of her husband's participation in the application
    D. point out to the applicant the implications of her behavior and ask for an explanation of her motives
    E. tell the applicant that the husband's needs will be excluded from the budget until he appears for a personal interview

11. Responsibility for fully informing the public about the availability of public assistance can MOST successfully be discharged by
    A. local public assistance agencies   B. social service exchanges
    C. community chest organizations   D. councils of social agencies
    E. service clubs

12. Of the sources through which a welfare agency can seek information about the family background and economic needs of a particular client, the MOST important consists of
    A. records and documents covering the client
    B. interviews with the client's relatives
    C. the client's own story
    D. direct contacts with former employers
    E. information offered by the client's neighbors

13. The one of the following sources of evidence which would MOST likely to give information needed to verify residence is
    A. family affidavits   B. medical and hospital bills
    C. an original birth certificate   D. rental receipts
    E. an insurance policy

14. In public assistance agencies, vital statistics are a resource used by the workers MAINLY to
    A. help establish eligibility through verification of births, deaths, and marriages
    B. help establish eligibility through verification of divorce proceedings
    C. secure proof of unemployment and eligibility for unemployment compensation
    D. secure indices of the cost of living in the larger cities
    E. discourage applications from ineligible persons

15. Case record should be considered confidential in order to
    A. make it impossible for agencies to know each other's methods
    B. permit worker to make objective rather than subjective comments
    C. prevent recipients from comparing amounts of assistance given to different families
    D. keep pertinent information from other social workers
    E. protect clients and their families

16. Because the social service worker generally is not trained as a psychiatrist, he should, when encountering psychiatric problems in the performance of his departmental duties,
    A. ignore such problems because they are beyond the scope of his responsibilities
    B. inform the affected persons that he recognizes their problems personally but will take no official cognizance of them
    C. ask to be relieved of the cases in which these problems are met and recommend that they be assigned to a psychiatrist
    D. recognize such problems where they exist and make referrals to the proper sources for treatment
    E. ask his supervisor to assign a psychiatric case worker to accompany him on all subsequent visits to the client

17. The family budget is a device used by the Department of Social Services to
    A. determine changes in the cost-of-living index
    B. estimate the needs of families and the amount of assistance necessary to meet this needs
    C. evaluate its financial condition
    D. estimate probable expenditures during a given period
    E. determine whether an applicant is eligible for categorical assistance or for general relief

18. The amount included for food for each client in Department of Social Services budgets should
    A. be based on quantitative caloric estimates of energy requirements rather than on variety in the kinds of foods
    B. be high enough to provide minimum subsistence, but low enough to discourage ineligible applicants
    C. exclude special dietary needs which are relatively expensive

D. cover food idiosyncrasies of various members of the household
E. meet the generally accepted standards for proper nutrition

19. The program for aid to dependent children is PRIMARILY directed toward
    A. the placement and supervision of children in selected foster homes
    B. provision of assistance whereby children can remain in their own homes or in the homes of relatives
    C. rehabilitation of neglected and delinquent children
    D. provision of specialized services to children in areas of special need
    E. provision of assistance to widows of good moral character for the care of their children

19.____

20. Since need is a condition of eligibility in the old-age assistance program, an assistance payment to an aged recipient should be based upon a consideration of
    A. the length of time he received general relief prior to his application for old-age assistance
    B. his attitude toward the agency
    C. his total needs and resources
    D. the probable duration of his dependency
    E. the average monthly cost of institutional care

20.____

21. From a social point of view, the reason for the growth of the practice of giving public assistance in the form of cash payments is the
    A. resultant reduction in complaints coming to the agency
    B. increased necessity for developing nationwide comparative statistics
    C. facilitation of recovery for relief improperly granted
    D. public's increasing belief in the essential justice of this type of assistance

21.____

22. In closing the case of a client, the social service worker should attempt to give the client a(n)
    A. feeling of being rejected by the agency as a worthy person
    B. idea of the progress of similar cases being handled by the agency
    C. understanding that his case could be reopened for full relief, if necessary, but not for emergency assistance
    D. explanation of the conditions upon which he might make re-application
    E. explanation of the limitations of the agency in meeting his needs

22.____

23. There is widespread agreement among nearly all planning groups concerned with public assistance that
    A. need for public assistance should be the primary, if not the only, condition of eligibility; and that all arbitrary conditions of eligibility such as citizenship, ownership of home, and moral character should be eliminated from all public assistance programs
    B. public assistance grants should be paid by voucher rather than in cash because most recipients do not use cash allowances for the purposes for which they are intended
    C. the names of persons receiving public assistance should be publicized in order to prevent fraud

23.____

D. public assistance should be discontinued immediately whenever the unemployed father of a family receiving assistance refuses a job offer
E. public assistance should not be provided for any persons who own property or who have any financial resources

24. Of fundamental importance to the work of social worker in the Department of Social Services is
    A. the knowledge of when to use the power of the Department to subdue an angry client
    B. an ability to classify clients according to common characteristics as described in case records
    C. the ability to explain eligibility in terms of legal requirements with clarity and simplicity
    D. the realization that persons who apply for public assistance have become independent because of lack of industriousness and are therefore unable to manage their own affairs
    E. a general knowledge of the executive, administrative, and supervisory functions of the Department

25. Although a social worker in the Department of Social Services has several responsibilities, his PRIMARY one is to
    A. nullify any restrictive rules and regulations issued by the State Department of Social Welfare
    B. carry out his own interpretation of the function of the Department of Social Services
    C. carry out the objectives of Department of Social Services programs as set forth in the Social Welfare Law
    D. avoid community criticism of the manner in which the programs of the Department of Social Services are conducted
    E. give relief to all applicants who claim they are eligible

KEY (CORRECT ANSWERS)

1.	E		11.	A
2.	A		12.	C
3.	E		13.	D
4.	C		14.	A
5.	D		15.	E
6.	D		16.	D
7.	E		17.	B
8.	C		18.	E
9.	B		19.	B
10.	C		20.	C

21. D
22. D
23. A
24. C
25. C

EXAMINATION SECTION

TEST 1

DIRECTIONS: Each question or incomplete statement is followed by several suggested answers or completions. Select the one that BEST answers the question or completes the statement. *PRINT THE LETTER OF THE CORRECT ANSWER IN THE SPACE AT THE RIGHT.*

1. The one of the following which is the PRINCIPAL medium of casework service is
    A. skilled diagnosis and realistic treatment planning
    B. personal communication or relationship established between the client and the worker
    C. agency organization in relation to program objectives
    D. the combined knowledge, skill, and attitude of the worker

    1._____

2. Treatment aimed at helping the client maintain his adaptive pattern is directed toward
    A. alleviating undue pressures in the client's everyday life and strengthening his emotional reactions to psychological pressure
    B. modifying the client's unrealistic life pattern by confronting him with explanations for his behavior
    C. assuming a passive role in order to avoid disturbing the client's adjustment
    D. working with those aspects of the client's problems which are related to environmental factors

    2._____

3. On account of the multi-faceted and dynamic nature of clients' problems, of the following, it is NECESSARY for the social worker to
    A. analyze the total problem before proceeding with treatment
    B. develop a comprehensive treatment plan which approaches the main aspects of the total problem
    C. separate the personality and behavioral aspects of the problem from the social setting
    D. select some part of the problem as the unit for work

    3._____

4. The one of the following which is the MOST important consideration in evaluating the ego strength of an angry, deprived, mistreated, frustrated, evasive client is the client's ability to
    A. verbalize his problems to someone
    B. redirect his anger towards an object
    C. form a relationship with an accepting worker
    D. hold a job

    4._____

5. When a client is torn between choices that immobilize him or make his problem less manageable, the social worker should base his practice with the client on the following, with the EXCEPTION of
   A. identification of the client's problem
   B. persuading the client to act according to his instructions
   C. determination with the client of preferred approaches in dealing with the problem
   D. enabling the client to take constructive action to deal with the problem

6. Assume that a social worker reports that a mother with whom she is working claims that the school is discriminating against her children because she is a welfare recipient. Her children have a history of truancy and poor school achievement. The worker feels that the mother's assessment of the situation has some validity.
   Of the following, the BEST course of action for the worker to take is to
   A. support the mother's defense of her children and report the alleged discrimination by the school to the Board of Education
   B. inquire further into the reasons for the children's truancy and poor achievement with the children, the mother, and school officials
   C. explore with the mother her feelings about receiving public assistance, and encourage her to find a job so she won't need assistance
   D. disengage herself from her close involvement in this case since she has stopped being objective

7. A social worker has as a client a 17-year-old boy who is part of a group whose norm of behavior is cutting classes, frequent absenteeism, sexual promiscuity, and petty thievery. He wants to finish school and to grow up, but the present peer-group pressure militates against this, and he is damaging his values by following the group's norms.
   The social worker would be MOST helpful to this boy if, of the following, he takes the role of a
   A. mediator, to help support the boy against the demands of the group, and also to give him direct help in defending himself psychologically
   B. resource person, to refer the boy to a youth agency that would be able to work with the boy in his peer group
   C. interpreter, to help the boy realize the inappropriateness of his behavior in the peer group
   D. peer model, to help the boy identify with a young, successful person

8. A fifteen-year-old boy has been referred to a social worker with a history of arrests for repeated acts of minor delinquency, suspension from school for truancy, and a hostile attitude towards treatment. He is financially supported by his parents, but they seem to have stopped giving him emotional support and say that he is uncontrollable.
The boy's interests would be served BEST if, of the following, the social worker's role were that of
   A. psychosocial counselor using traditional insight development
   B. educator in teaching the boy the skills he would need to succeed
   C. catalyst in family therapy, to help the boy and his parents handle their feelings and the reality problems constructively
   D. crisis intervenor, taking an assertive role to give direction and specific help

8._____

9. The one of the following which is a COMMON error made by new social workers who are beginning to find out about the influence of unconscious desires and emotions on human behavior is to
   A. probe the client unnecessarily
   B. become over-assured that they can solve the client's problem
   C. slow up the pace of the interview
   D. look for the proper treatment method based on the client's neuroses

9._____

10. Although we can judge statements about objective verifiable matters to be true or false, we are not similarly justified in passing judgment on subjective attitudes.
Of the following, this statement BEST explains the rationale behind the social work principle of
   A. empathy   B. abreaction
   C. non-judgmentality D. confidentiality

10._____

11. The one of the following which BEST describes the meaning of ambivalence in social work is: The
   A. social worker refrains from imposing his moral judgments on the client
   B. supervisor assists the worker in understanding the psychological causes for the client's behavior
   C. client is seeking someone who will understand the subjective reasons for his behavior
   D. client has conflicting interests, desires, and emotions

11._____

12. The CORRECT definition of the term *acceptance* as used in social work is as follows:
   A. A decision made at intake to accept the client as a case for the agency to handle
   B. The concept of a positive and active understanding by the worker of the feelings a client expresses through his behavior
   C. The concept that the worker does not pass judgment on the client's behavior
   D. Communication to the client that the worker does not condone and accept his antisocial behavior

12._____

13. Psychiatrists are usually concerned with the total functioning and integration of the human personality.
    Of the following, social workers USUALLY concentrate on
    A. the same thing but for shorter periods of time
    B. the same thing but without prescribing medication
    C. helping the client to deal with the presenting problem
    D. making the proper referrals to assist the client in dealing with his problem

14. The one of the following which is a DESCRIPTIVE term for a client who is resistive, breaks appointments, withholds information, beclouds issues, related to others in a primitive, often distorted fashion, and acts out his wishes and conflicts in his contact with the worker is
    A. psychotic
    B. manic depressive
    C. paranoid schizophrenic
    D. character disorder

15. The one of the following which is a MAJOR reason why it is so difficult for social workers to exert influence on social policy is:
    A. Social workers are trained to implement existing policies, not to change those that are unworkable
    B. Those who make policy are influenced by numerous forces, persons, values, and aspirations, not all of which relate directly to the policy decisions to be made
    C. As a result of the heavy concentration on casework in the graduate schools, most social workers put more emphasis on working with individuals, rather than on social policy
    D. Psychological and psychiatric concepts are disputed by experts in the field, so that it is difficult to diagnose motives

16. The one of the following which is the BEST explanation of the rationale of *crisis intervention* as a treatment method is:
    A. A little help, rationally directed and purposefully focused at an extremely critical time in the client's life, can be more effective than more extensive help given during a less critical period
    B. Because clients are more likely to react precipitously at times of crisis, social workers must give particular emphasis at such times to providing direct and aggressive advice and assistance
    C. The social worker should make full use of the client's vulnerable emotional state at a time of crisis in order to bring him face to face with his defense mechanisms and with the realities of life
    D. The client's urgent need for emotional support at times of crisis should be used by the social worker at such times to gain the client's confidence and trust

17. In establishing contact with a new, unfamiliar group, of the following, the group worker's usual FIRST action should be to
    A. discuss the sponsoring agency and its function
    B. give special attention to the less aggressive members
    C. reinforce the authority of the natural group leader
    D. approach the group at their own level of language and interests

18. If a group worker should become aware that some members of his group feel resentful toward him, of the following, it would GENERALLY be advisable for the worker to
    A. make a special effort to please the resentful members
    B. offer to resign from leadership of the group
    C. attempt to convey to the resentful members his own attitude of acceptance of them
    D. enlist the support of other group members to convince the resentful ones of his good intentions

18._____

19. Assume that, during the sixth weekly session of activity group therapy with a group of adolescent boys, they engage in horseplay, use obscene language, and become quite uncontrollable.
Of the following, it can SAFELY be concluded that the
    A. boys are testing the worker to learn his limits of tolerance
    B. worker's status as the group leader is being seriously challenged
    C. composition of the group should be changed
    D. worker should end the session and dismiss the boys

19._____

20. Of the following, the role of the group worker at meetings of a group which has its own officers is to
    A. withdraw from the activities of the group
    B. make decisions for the group if required
    C. clarify issues and teach skills when necessary
    D. handle hostile or aggressive members

20._____

21. Schizophrenia in children USUALLY becomes manifest
    A. during the latency period
    B. during adolescence only
    C. when the mother has a history of schizophrenia
    D. during early childhood or adolescence

21._____

22. Sickle cell anemia is a blood disease MOST commonly found in children whose parents are
    A. Caucasian   B. interracial
    B. black or Latin American   D. oriental

22._____

23. A decline in hearing and vision takes place in healthy persons during the period BEGINNING at age
    A. 30   B. 40   C. 50   D. 60

23._____

24. The MOST common complaint made by psychiatric patients is concerned with
    A. depression   B. panic   C. insomnia   D. fatigue

24._____

25. The one of the following which is *most likely* to cause the reappearance in old age of a previously compensated neurosis is
    A. decrease in social status, loss of persons and possessions or presence of injuries and illnesses
    B. decrease in sensory and cognitive capacities resulting in poor reality testing
    C. cerebro-arteriosclerosis or other cerebrovascular disturbance
    D. decrease in financial resources, resulting in heightened anxiety

25._____

KEY (CORRECT ANSWERS)

1. B
2. A
3. D
4. C
5. B

6. B
7. A
8. C
9. A
10. C

11. D
12. B
13. C
14. D
15. B

16. A
17. D
18. C
19. A
20. C

21. D
22. C
23. B
24. A
25. A

TEST 2

DIRECTIONS: Each question or incomplete statement is followed by several suggested answers or completions. Select the one that BEST answers the question or completes the statement. *PRINT THE LETTER OF THE CORRECT ANSWER IN THE SPACE AT THE RIGHT.*

1. Of the following, group approaches are COMMONLY used for 1._____
    A. encounter, discussion, training, and administration
    B. education, counseling, therapy, and recreation
    C. counseling, recreation, catharsis, and crisis intervention
    D. counseling, leadership, administration, and training

2. The purposes of group counseling are the following, with the EXCEPTION of 2._____
    A. avoidance of treating pathology as such
    B. helping clients attain a better level of functioning
    C. modifying social and familial problems
    D. resolving intra-psychic conflicts

3. The separation of public assistance recipients into categories had its origins in the 3._____
    A. Elizabethan poor law
    B. numerous amendments to the Social Security Act
    C. legislation of the Massachusetts Bay Colony
    D. Social Security Act of 1935

4. The one of the following which is the FIRST form of social insurance to be widely developed in the United States is 4._____
    A. workmen's compensation or industrial accident insurance
    B. unemployment insurance programs
    C. temporary disability insurance
    D. old age insurance for industrial workers

5. The doctrine of less eligibility, which has been considered over the years as a policy for public assistance programs, means most nearly that 5._____
    A. grants should always be below subsistence level in order to give recipients an incentive to seek employment
    B. eligibility for public assistance should be established on the basis of a limited number of basic budgetary needs
    C. income derived from public assistance benefits should not exceed the amount earned by the lowest paid independent worker in the community
    D. categories of need should be established in each community and ranked in order of priority in order to determine eligibility for assistance

6. Social insurance programs such as OASDHI and unemployment insurance have been CRITICIZED widely because, of the following,
   a. there is an inherent conflict between the intent to prevent poverty on the one hand, and wage-relatedness of the programs on the other
   b. there is no relationship between the amount or the benefits and differences in cost of living in various localities within a state
   c. the programs do not include review of personal and family problems
   d. a large percentage of the grants go to persons who are otherwise financially able to support themselves

7. The one of the following which would be the basis of a family allowance plan SIMILAR to programs in effect in Canada and France is:
   a. Family size, for all needy families with minor children whose current annual income is below specified levels
   b. The total number of persons in the household, including all adults except those receiving social security benefits
   c. The number of minor children, available to all families and requiring no means test
   d. Income level, available to all families with minor children

8. A MAJOR criticism of social and health programs as they exist today has been the tendency towards a *problem focus* rather than a *social goals* approach.
   Of the following, this approach has resulted in
   a. a lack of an integrated, systematic development of programs that deal adequately with social and health problems
   b. excessive expenditures for the social and health problems that have received the most attention, at the expense of other equally serious problems
   c. a federal and nationwide approach rather than the more desirable *geographic approach*, which would bring delivery of services closer to the people
   d. the development of legislation which shows little evidence of recognition of the contributions that could be made by social planners

9. A striking feature of American culture is its tendency to identify standards of personal excellence with competitive occupational achievement.
   The one of the following which is the CONSEQUENCE of this feature for those unable to make one's own living through work is to
   a. increase incentive to find a productive job
   b. lower the individual's feeling of self-worth and generate a feeling of powerlessness
   c. give the individual a need to control the environment
   d. encourage increased educational attainment

10. Of the following, the objectives and curriculum content of graduate schools of social work today GENERALLY indicate an *increased* emphasis on

    a. prevention and institutional change in addition to treatment
    b. knowledge of individual personality factors and treatment methods
    c. the separate methods and goals of classroom study and field work
    d. the use of the one-to-one instructor-student relationship for both classroom study and field work

10._____

11. At present, there is a general consensus among social welfare educators and administrators that not every job requires a professional social worker with a master's degree in social work.
    The one of the following which is the MOST important reason for this viewpoint is that personnel with lower educational qualifications can

    a. be used as a valuable temporary expedient for jobs that would otherwise remain unfilled
    b. perform certain social work tasks as well or even better than workers with master's degrees
    c. gain experience that will spur them on to attend a graduate school of social work in order to obtain the degree
    d. be used to reduce substantially personnel costs in public and private social work agencies

11._____

12. In an era of rapid change, of the following, the REAL test of the social work profession is to

    a. meet constructively the demands of that change
    b. hold to its traditional practices
    c. abandon its methods for new approaches
    d. wait to see what happens to other professions

12._____

13. The psychologist who is USUALLY associated with a theory of self-psychology which has as its basic concept the assertion that a man has a tendency to actualize himself, i.e., to maintain and improve himself, is

    A. Karl Jung   B. Sigmund Freud
    C. B.F. Skinner   D. Carl Rogers

13._____

14. Of the types of mental breakdown listed below, the disorder that ordinarily occurs at the MOST advanced age is

    A. cerebral arteriosclerosis
    B. neurasthenia
    C. dementia praecox
    D. paresis

14._____

15. Principles of crisis intervention in social casework have been derived LARGELY from the theoretical formulations of

    a. Harry Stack Sullivan and Clara Thompson
    b. August P. Hollingshead and Frederick C. Redlich
    c. Otto Rank and Jessie Taft
    d. Erich Lindemann and Gerald Caplan

15._____

16. Of the following, the MOST important reason that those responsible for the care of a child in placement should *never* depreciate the child's natural parents or the home from which he came is that the
    a. child's self-esteem depends on how he feels about his natural parents and his previous experiences
    b. natural parents may have been incapable of being adequate parents
    c. child may feel the substitute parents are jealous of his natural parents
    d. child will be forced into the position of defending his natural parents and will resent the substitute parents

17. Although day care was originally established mainly as a social service for working mothers, it has been found that, of the following,
    a. working mothers of physically and mentally handicapped children do not benefit from day care facilities
    b. most working mothers would prefer to leave their children with friends or relatives rather than at a day care center
    c. it would be economically feasible and beneficial for communities to establish day care centers which would be available to all mothers in the community
    d. day care can also be an educational experience for a child and be helpful in the development of peer relationships

18. Research studies of language development in young children have shown that, of the following,
    a. the multiple mothering of children in a large family retards language development
    b. language retardation in otherwise normal children is usually related to inadequate language stimulation
    c. language retardation is always associated with slow motor development
    d. children are usually slow in learning to talk when more than one language is spoken in the home

19. The *battered child syndrome* is reported to be one of the most difficult problems facing health officials. When a worker knows of a case of a child being severely physically abused, of the following, he SHOULD
    a. get psychiatric consultation to understand the parents' motives
    b. advise the child to stay away from the parents
    c. help the parents to see what they're doing is wrong
    d. report the case to child protective authorities

20. The one of the following which is a *psychological principle* which can BEST be described as a situation in which an individual experiences some ambivalence and indecisiveness in choosing one or more desired objects or goals is
    A. task-orientation   B. conflict
    C. apathy   D. projection

21. The *treatment method* which allows or encourages the client to express his charged feelings around a pressing emotional need is known as
    A. exploring
    B. synthesizing
    C. catharsis
    D. ventilating

21._____

22. The *emotional release* that results from recall of a previously forgotten painful experience is known as
    A. introjection
    B. abreaction
    C. sublimation
    D. free association

22._____

23. The *action* whereby an individual directs his aggression against an innocent bystander rather than expressing it against the source of his difficulties, is called
    A. displacement
    B. projection
    C. introjection
    D. abreaction

23._____

24. An *attempt* to attribute emotionally caused behavior to reasonable factors MORE acceptable to the individual is known as
    A. projection
    B. rationalization
    C. introjection
    D. free association

24._____

25. The UNCONSCIOUS *application* of elements of the experiences in a former relationship to a new relationship is known as
    A. projection
    B. abreaction
    C. transference
    D. sublimation

25._____

KEY (CORRECT ANSWERS)

1.	B	11.	B
2.	D	12.	A
3.	A	13.	D
4.	A	14.	A
5.	C	15.	D
6.	A	16.	A
7.	C	17.	D
8.	A	18.	B
9.	B	19.	D
10.	A	20.	B

21. D
22. B
23. A
24. B
25. C

58

EXAMINATION SECTION
TEST 1

DIRECTIONS: Each question or incomplete statement is followed by several suggested answers or completions. Select the one that BEST answers the question or completes the statement. *PRINT THE LETTER OF THE CORRECT ANSWER IN THE SPACE AT THE RIGHT.*

Questions 1-4.

DIRECTIONS: Questions 1 through 4 are to be answered SOLELY on the basis of the information in the paragraphs below.

Some authorities have questioned whether the term "culture of poverty" should be used since "culture" means a design for living which is passed down from generation to generation. The culture of poverty is, however, a very useful concept if it is used with care, with recognition that poverty is a subculture, and with avoidance of the "cookie-cutter" approach. With regard to the individual, the cookie-cutter view assumes that all individuals in a culture turn out exactly alike, as if they were so many cookies. It overlooks the fact that, at least in our urban society, every individual is a member of more than one subculture; and which subculture most strongly influences his response in a given situation depends on the interaction of a great many factors, including his individual makeup and history, the specifics of the various subcultures to which he belongs, and the specifics of the given situation. It is always important to avoid the cookie-cutter view of culture, with regard to the individual and to the culture or subculture involved.

With regard to the culture as a whole, the cookie-cutter concept again assumes homogeneity and consistency. It forgets that within any one culture or subculture there are conflicts and contradictions, and that at any given moment an individual may have to choose, consciously, between conflicting values or patterns. Also, most individuals, in varying degrees, have a dual set of values - those by which they live and those they cherish as best. This point has been made and documented repeatedly about the culture of poverty.

1. The *cookie-cutter* approach assumes that

    A. members of the same *culture* are all alike
    B. *culture* stays the same from generation to generation
    C. the term *culture* should not be applied to groups who are poor
    D. there are value conflicts within most cultures

2. According to the passage, every person in our cities

    A. is involved in the conflicts of urban culture
    B. recognizes that poverty is a subculture
    C. lives by those values to which he is exposed
    D. belongs to more than one subculture

3. The above passage emphasizes that a culture is likely to contain within it

    A. one dominant set of values
    B. a number of contradictions

C. one subculture to which everyone belongs
D. members who are exactly alike

4. According to the above passage, individuals are sometimes forced to choose between

   A. cultures
   B. subcultures
   C. different sets of values
   D. a new culture and an old culture

Questions 5-8.

DIRECTIONS: Questions 5 through 8 are to be answered SOLELY on the basis of the following passage.

There are approximately 33 million poor people in the United States; 14.3 million of them are children, 5.3 million are old people, and the remainder are in other categories. Altogether, 6.5 million families live in poverty because the heads of the households cannot works they are either too old or too sick or too severely handicapped, or they are widowed or deserted mothers of young children. There are the working poor, the low-paid workers, the workers in seasonal industries, and soldiers with no additional income who are heads of families. There are the underemployed: those who would like full-time jobs but cannot find them, those employees who would like year-round work but lack the opportunity, and those who are employed below their level of training. There are the non-working poor: the older men and women With small retirement incomes and those with no income, the disabled, the physically and mentally handicapped, and the chronically sick.

5. According to the above passage, APPROXIMATELY what percent of the poor people in the United States are children?

   A. 33   B. 16   C. 20   D. 44

6. According to the above passage, people who work in seasonal industries are LIKELY to be classified as

   A. working poor   B. underemployed
   C. non-working poor   D. low-paid workers

7. According to the above passage, the category of non-working poor includes people who

   A. receive unemployment insurance
   B. cannot find full-time work
   C. are disabled or mentally handicapped
   D. are soldiers with wives and children

8. According to the above passage, among the underemployed are those who

   A. can find only part-time work
   B. are looking for their first jobs
   C. are inadequately trained
   D. depend on insufficient retirement incomes

Questions 9-18.

DIRECTIONS: Questions 9 through 18 are to be answered SOLELY on the basis of the information given in the following charts.

CHILD CARE SERVICES 1997-2001

CHILDREN IN FOSTER HOMES AND VOLUNTARY INSTITUTIONS, BY TYPE OF CARE, IN NEW YORK CITY AND UPSTATE* NEW YORK

| Year End | FOSTER FAMILY HOMES | | | Total in Foster Family Homes | Total in Voluntary Institutions | Total in Other | Total Number of Children |
	Boarding Homes	Adoptive or Free Homes	Wage, Work or Self-Supportine				
New York City							
1997	12,389	1,773	33	14,195	7,187	1,128	22,510
1998	13,271	1,953	42	15,266	7,227	1,237	23,730
1999	14,012	2,134	32	16,178	7,087	1,372	24,637
2000	14,558	2,137	29	16,724	6,717	1,437	24,778
2001	14,759	2,241	37	17,037	6,777	1,455	25,264
Upstate							
1997	14,801	2,902	90	17,793	3,012	241	21,046
1998	15,227	2,943	175	18,345	3,067	291	21,703
1999	16,042	3,261	64	19,367	2,940	273	22,580
2000	16,166	3,445	60	19,671	2,986	362	23,121
2001	16,357	3,606	55	20,018	3.024	485	23,527

Upstate is defined as all of New York State, excluding New York City.

NUMBER OF CHILDREN, BY AGE, UNDER FOSTER FAMILY CARE IN NEW YORK CITY IN 2001

| Borough | Children's Ages | | | | | Total All Ages |
	One Year or Younger	Two Years	Three Years	Four Years	Over Four Years	
Manhattan	1,054	1,170	1,060	1,325	445	5,070
Bronx	842	1,196	1,156	1,220	484	4,882
Brooklyn	707	935	470	970	361	?
Queens	460	555	305	793	305	2,418
Richmond	270	505	160	173	112	1.224
Total All Boroughs	3,337	4,361	3,151	4,481	?	17,037

9. According to the table, Child Care Services, 1997-2001, the number of children in New York City boarding homes was AT LEAST twice the number of children in New York City voluntary institutions in _____ of the five years.

    A. *only* one   B. *only* two   C. *only* three   D. all

9._____

10. If the number of children cared for in voluntary institutions in New York State increases from 2001 to 2002 by exactly the same number as from 2000 to 2001, then the 2002 year-end total of children in voluntary institutions in New York State will be

    A. 3,062   B. 6,837   C. 7,494   D. 9,899

11. If the total number of children under child care services in New York City in 1997 was 25% more than in 1996, then the 1996 New York City total was MOST NEARLY

    A. 11,356   B. 11,647   C. 16,883   D. 18,008

12. From 1997 through 2001, the New York State five-year average of children in Child Care Services classified as *other* is MOST NEARLY

    A. 330   B. 728   C. 1,326   D. 1,656

13. Of all the children under foster family care in the Bronx in 2001, the percentage who were one year of age or younger is MOST NEARLY

    A. 16%   B. 17%   C. 18%   D. 19%

14. Suppose that in New York State the *wage, work, or self-supporting* type of foster family care is given only to children between the ages of 14 and 18, and that, of the children in *adoptive or free home* foster care in each of the five years listed, only one percent each year are between the ages of 14 and 18.
    The TOTAL number of 14 to 18-year-olds under foster family care in Upstate New York exceeded 95 in _____ of the five years.

    A. each   B. four   C. three   D. two

15. The average number of two-year-olds under foster family care in New York City's boroughs in 2001 is MOST NEARLY

    A. 872   B. 874   C. 875   D. 882

16. The difference between the total number of children of all ages under foster family care in Brooklyn in 2001 and the total number under foster care in Richmond that year is

    A. 1,224   B. 2,219   C. 3,443   D. 4,667

17. Suppose that by the end of 2002 the number of children one year or younger under foster family care in Queens will be twice the 2001 total, while the number of two-year-olds will be four-fifths the 2001 total.
    The 2002 total of children two years or younger under foster family care in Queens will be

    A. 2,418   B. 1,624   C. 1,364   D. 1,015

18. The TOTAL number oi children over four years of age under foster care in New York City in 2001 was

    A. 1,607   B. 1,697   C. 1,707   D. 1,797

19. At the start of a year, a family was receiving a public assistance grant of $191 twice a month, on the 1st and 15th of each month. On March 1, their rent allowance was decreased from $75 to $71 a month since they had moved to a smaller apartment. On August 1, their semimonthly food allowance, which had been $40.20, was raised by 10%. In that year, the TOTAL amount of money disbursed to this family was

    A. $2,272.10
    B. $3,290.70
    C. $4,544.20
    D. $4,584.20

19.____

20. It is discovered that a client has received double public assistance for 2 months by having been enrolled at two service centers of the Department of Social Services. The client should have received $84.00 twice a month instead of the double amount. He now agrees to repay the money by equal deductions from his public assistance check over a period of 12 months.
    What will the amount of his NEXT check be?

    A. $56   B. $70   C. $77   D. $80

20.____

21. Suppose a study is being made of the composition of 3,550 families receiving public assistance. Of the first 1,050 families reviewed, 18% had four or more children.
    If, in the remaining number of families, the percentage with four or more children is half as high as the percentage in the group already reviewed, then the percentage of families with four or more children in the entire group of families is MOST NEARLY

    A. 12   B. 14   C. 16   D. 27

21.____

22. Suppose that food prices have risen 13%, and an increase of the same amount has been granted in the food allotment given to people receiving public assistance.
    If a family has been receiving $405 a month, 35% of which is allotted for food, then the TOTAL amount of public assistance this family receives per month will be changed to

    A. $402.71   B. $420.03   C. $423.43   D. $449.71

22.____

23. Assume that the food allowance is to be raised 5% in August but will be retroactive for four months to April. The retroactive allowance is to be divided into equal sections and added to the public assistance checks for August, September, October, November, and December.
    A family which has been receiving $420 monthly, 40% of which was allotted for food, will receive what size check in August?

    A. $426.72   B. $428.40   C. $430.50   D. $435.12

23.____

24. A blind client, who receives $105 public assistance twice a month, inherits 14 shares of stock worth $90 each. The client is required to sell the stock and spend his inheritance before receiving more public assistance.
    Using his public assistance allowance as a guide, how many months are his new assets expected to last?

    A. 6   B. 7   C. 8   D. 12

24.____

25. The Department of Social Services has 16 service centers in Manhattan. These centers may be divided into those which are downtown (south of Central Park) and those which are uptown. Two of the centers are special service centers and are downtown, while the remainder of the centers are general service centers. There is a total of 7 service centers downtown.

    The percentage of the general service centers which are uptown is MOST NEARLY

    A. 56   B. 64   C. 69   D. 79

KEY (CORRECT ANSWERS)

1. A
2. D
3. B
4. C
5. D

6. A
7. C
8. A
9. B
10. D

11. D
12. D
13. B
14. C
15. A

16. B
17. C
18. C
19. D
20. B

21. A
22. C
23. D
24. A
25. B

TEST 2

DIRECTIONS: Each question or incomplete statement is followed by several suggested answers or completions. Select the one that BEST answers the question or completes the statement. *PRINT THE LETTER OF THE CORRECT ANSWER IN THE SPACE AT THE RIGHT.*

1. On January 1, a family was receiving supplementary monthly public assistance of $56 for food, $48 for rent, and $28 for other necessities. In the spring, their rent rose by 10%, and their rent allowance was adjusted accordingly.
   In the summer, due to the death of a family member, their allotments for food and other necessities were reduced by 1/7.
   Their monthly allowance check in the fall should be

   A. $124.80   B. $128.80   C. $132.80   D. $136.80

   1.____

2. Twice a month, a certain family receives a $170 general allowance for rent, food, and clothing expenses. In addition, the family receives a specific supplementary allotment for utilities of $192 a year, which is added to their semi-monthly check.
   If the general allowance alone is reduced by 5%, what will be the TOTAL amount of their next semi-monthly check?

   A. $161.50   B. $169.50   C. $170.00   D. $177.50

   2.____

3. If each clerk in a certain unit sees an average of 9 clients in a 7-hour day and there are 15 clerks in the unit, APPROXIMATELY how many clients will be seen in a 35-hour week?

   A. 315   B. 405   C. 675   D. 945

   3.____

4. The program providing federal welfare aid to the state and its cities is intended to expand services to public assistance recipients.
   All of the following services are included in the program EXCEPT

   A. homemaker/housekeeper services
   B. mental health clinics
   C. abortion clinics
   D. narcotic addiction control services

   4.____

5. The Department of Consumer Affairs is NOT concerned with regulation of

   A. prices
   B. product service guarantees
   C. welfare fraud
   D. product misrepresentation

   5.____

6. A plan to control the loss of welfare monies would likely contain all of the following EXCEPT

   A. identification cards with photographs of the welfare client
   B. individual cash payments to each member of a family
   C. computerized processing of welfare money records
   D. face-to-face interviews with the welfare clients

   6.____

7. The state law currently allows a woman to obtain an abortion 7._____

   A. only if it is intended to save her life
   B. if three doctors confirm the need for such treatment
   C. if it does not conflict with her religious beliefs
   D. upon her request, up to the 24th week of pregnancy

8. Under the city's public assistance program, allocations for payment of a client's rent and security deposits are given in check form directly to the welfare recipient and not to the landlord. 8._____
   This practice is used in the city MAINLY as an effort to

   A. increase the client's responsibility for his own affairs
   B. curb the rent overcharges made by most landlords in the city
   C. control the number of welfare recipients housed in public housing projects
   D. limit the number of checks issued to each welfare family

9. The city plans to save 100 million dollars a year in public assistance costs. 9._____
   To achieve this goal, the Human Resources Administration and the Department of Social Services may take any of the following steps EXCEPT

   A. tightening controls on public assistance eligibility requirements
   B. intensifying the investigations of relief frauds
   C. freezing the salaries of all agency employees for a one-year period
   D. cutting the services extended to public assistance clients

10. Recently, the state instituted a work relief program under which employable recipients of Home Relief and Aid to Dependent Children are given jobs to help work off their relief grants. 10._____
    Under the present work relief program, program recipients are NOT required to

    A. report to state employment offices every two weeks to pick up their welfare checks
    B. live within a two-mile radius of the job site to which they are referred
    C. respond to offers of part-time jobs in public agencies
    D. take job training courses offered through the State Employment Service

11. Of the following, the MOST inclusive program designed to help selected cities to substantially improve social, physical, and economic conditions in specially selected slum neighborhoods is known as the 11._____

    A. Model Cities Program
    B. Neighborhood Youth Corps Program
    C. Urban Renewal Program
    D. Emergency Employment Act

12. The crusade against environmental hazards in the United States is concentrated in urban areas MOSTLY on the problems of 12._____

    A. air pollution, sewage treatment, and noise
    B. garbage collection
    C. automobile exhaust fumes and street cleanliness
    D. recycling, reconstitution, and open space

Questions 13-16.

DIRECTIONS: Questions 13 through 16 are to be answered SOLELY on the basis of the information in the following passage.

City social work agencies and the police have been meeting at City Hall to coordinate efforts to defuse the tensions among teenage groups that they fear could flare into warfare once summer vacations begin. Police intelligence units, with the help of the District Attorneys' offices, are gathering information to identify gangs and their territories. A list of 3, 000 gang members has already been assembled, and 110 gangs have been identified. Social workers from various agencies like the Department of Social Services, Neighborhood youth Corps, and the Youth Board are out every day developing liaison with groups of juveniles through meetings at schools and recreation centers. Many street workers spend their days seeking to ease the intergang hostility, tracing potentially incendiary rumors, and trying to channel willing gang members into participation in established summer programs. The city's Youth Services Agency plans to spend a million dollars for special summer programs in ten main city areas where gang activity is most firmly entrenched. Five of the "gang neighborhoods" are clustered in an area forming most of southeastern Bronx, and it is here that most of the 110 identified gangs have formed. Special Youth Services programs will also be directed toward the Rockaway section of Queens, Chinatown, Washington Heights, and two neighborhoods in northern Staten Island noted for a lot of motorcycle gang activity. Some of these programs will emphasize sports and recreation, others vocational guidance or neighborhood improvement, but each program will be aimed at benefiting all youngsters in the area. Although none of the money will be spent specifically on gang members, the Youth Services Agency is consulting gang leaders, along with other teenagers, on the projects they would like developed in their area.

13. The above passage states that one of the steps taken by street workers in trying to defuse the tensions among teenage gangs is that of

    A. conducting summer school sessions that will benefit all neighborhood youth
    B. monitoring neighborhood sports competitions between rival gangs
    C. developing liaison with community school boards and parent associations
    D. tracing rumors that could intensify intergang hostilities

13._____

14. Based on the information given in the above passage on gangs and New York City's gang members, it is CORRECT to state that

    A. there are no teenage gangs located in Brooklyn
    B. most of the gangs identified by the police are concentrated in one borough
    C. there is a total of 110 gangs in New York City
    D. only a small percentage of gangs in New York City is in Queens

14._____

15. According to the above passage, one IMPORTANT aspect of the program is that

    A. youth gang leaders and other teenagers are involved in the planning
    B. money will be given directly to gang members for use on their projects
    C. only gang members will be allowed to participate in the programs
    D. the parents of gang members will act as youth leaders

15._____

16. Various city agencies are cooperating in the attempt to keep the city's youth *cool* during the summer school vacation period.
    The above passage does NOT specifically indicate participation in this project by the

    A. Police Department
    B. District Attorney's Office
    C. Board of Education
    D. Department of Social Services

Questions 17-19.

DIRECTIONS: Questions 17 through 19 are to be answered SOLELY on the basis of the information in the following passage.

It is important that interviewers understand to some degree the manner in which stereotyped thinking operates. Stereotypes are commonly held, but predominantly false, preconceptions about the appearance and traits of individuals of different racial, religious, ethnic, and subcultural groups. Distinct traits, physical and mental, are associated with each group, and membership in a particular group is enough, in the mind of a person holding the stereotype, to assure that these traits will be perceived in individuals who are members of that group. Conversely, possession of the particular stereotyped trait by an individual usually indicates to the holder of the stereotype that the individual is a group member. Linked to the formation of stereotypes is the fact that mental traits, either positive or negative, such as honesty, laziness, avariciousness, and other characteristics are associated with particular stereotypes. Either kind of stereotype, if held by an interviewer, can seriously damage the results of an interview. In general, stereotypes can be particularly dangerous when they are part of the belief patterns of administrators, interviewers, and supervisors, who are in a position to affect the lives of others and to stimulate or retard the development of human potential. The holding of a stereotype by an interviewer, for example, diverts his attention from significant essential facts and information upon which really valid assessments may be made. Unfortunately, it is the rare interviewer who is completely conscious of the real basis upon which he is making his evaluation of the people he is interviewing. The specific reasons given by an interviewer for a negative evaluation, even though apparently logical and based upon what, in the mind of the interviewer, are very good reasons, may not be the truly motivating factors. This is why the careful selection and training of interviewers is such an important responsibility of an agency which is attempting to help a great diversity of human beings.

17. Of the following, the BEST title for the above paragraph is

    A. POSITIVE AND NEGATIVE EFFECTS OF STEREOTYPED THINKING
    B. THE RELATIONSHIP OF STEREOTYPES TO INTERVIEWING
    C. AN AGENCY'S RESPONSIBILITY IN INTERVIEWING
    D. THE IMPACT OF STEREOTYPED THINKING ON PROFESSIONAL FUNCTIONS

18. According to the above passage, MOST interviewers

    A. compensate for stereotyped beliefs to avoid negatively affecting the results of their interviews
    B. are influenced by stereotypes they hold, but put greater stress on factual information developed during the interview
    C. are seldom aware of their real motives when evaluating interviewees
    D. give logical and good reasons for negative evaluations of interviewees

19. According to the above passage, which of the following is NOT a characteristic of stereotypes?

    A. Stereotypes influence estimates of personality traits of people.
    B. Positive stereotypes can damage the results of an interview.
    C. Physical traits associated with stereotypes seldom really exist.
    D. Stereotypes sometimes are a basis upon which valid personality assessments can be made.

Questions 20-25.

DIRECTIONS: Questions 20 through 25 are to be answered SOLELY on the basis of the information in the following passage.

The quality of the voice of a worker is an important factor in conveying to clients and co-workers his attitude and, to some degree, his character. The human voice, when not consciously disguised, may reflect a person's mood, temper, and personality. It has been shown in several experiments that certain character traits can be assessed with better than chance accuracy through listening to the voice of an unknown person who cannot be seen.

Since one of the objectives of the worker is to put clients at ease and to present an encouraging and comfortable atmosphere, a harsh, shrill, or loud voice could have a negative effect. A client who displays emotions of anger or resentment would probably be provoked even further by a caustic tone. In a face-to-face situation, an unpleasant voice may be compensated for to some degree by a concerned and kind facial expression. However, when one speaks on the telephone, the expression on one's face cannot be seen by the listener. A supervising clerk who wishes to represent himself effectively to clients should try to eliminate as many faults as possible in striving to develop desirable voice qualities.

20. If a worker uses a sarcastic tone while interviewing a resentful client, the client, according to the above passage, would MOST likely

    A. avoid the face-to-face situation
    B. be ashamed of his behavior
    C. become more resentful
    D. be provoked to violence

21. According to the above passage, experiments comparing voice and character traits have demonstrated that

    A. prospects for improving an unpleasant voice through training are better than chance
    B. the voice can be altered to project many different psychological characteristics
    C. the quality of the human voice reveals more about the speaker than his words do
    D. the speaker's voice tells the hearer something about the speaker's personality

22. Which of the following, according to the above passage, is a person's voice MOST likely to reveal?
    His

    A. prejudices   B. intelligence
    C. social awareness   D. temperament

23. It may be MOST reasonably concluded from the above passage that an interested and sympathetic expression on the face of a worker

   A. may induce a client to feel certain he will receive welfare benefits
   B. will eliminate the need for pleasant vocal qualities in the interviewer
   C. may help to make up for an unpleasant voice in the interviewer
   D. is desirable as the interviewer speaks on the telephone to a client

24. Of the following, the MOST reasonable implication of the above paragraph is that a worker should, when speaking to a client, control and use his voice to

   A. simulate a feeling of interest in the problems of the client
   B. express his emotions directly and adequately
   C. help produce in the client a sense of comfort and security
   D. reflect his own true personality

25. It may be concluded from the passage that the PARTICULAR reason for a worker to pay special attention to modulating her voice when talking on the phone to a client is that, during a telephone conversation,

   A. there is a necessity to compensate for the way in which a telephone distorts the voice
   B. the voice of the worker is a reflection of her mood and character
   C. the client can react only on the basis of the voice and words she hears
   D. the client may have difficulty getting a clear understanding over the telephone

KEY (CORRECT ANSWERS)

1. A
2. B
3. C
4. C
5. C

6. B
7. D
8. A
9. C
10. B

11. A
12. A
13. D
14. B
15. A

16. C
17. B
18. C
19. D
20. C

21. D
22. D
23. C
24. C
25. C

EXAMINATION SECTION
TEST 1

DIRECTIONS: Each question or incomplete statement is followed by several suggested answers or completions. Select the one that BEST answers the question or completes the statement. *PRINT THE LETTER OF IN THE CORRECT ANSWER THE SPACE AT THE RIGHT.*

1. Reports show that more men than women are physically handicapped MAINLY because

    A. women are instinctively more cautious than men
    B. men are more likely to have congenital deformities
    C. women tend to seek surgical remedies because of greater concern over personal appearance
    D. men have lower ability to recover from injury
    E. men are more likely to be exposed to hazardous conditions

    1.____

2. Of the following, the explanation married women give MOST frequently for seeking employment outside the home is that they wish to

    A. escape the drudgeries of home life
    B. develop secondary employment skills
    C. maintain an emotionally satisfying career
    D. provide the main support for the family
    E. supplement the family income

    2.____

3. Of the following home conditions, the one *most likely* to cause emotional disturbances in children is

    A. increased birthrate following the war
    B. disrupted family relationships
    C. lower family income than that of neighbors
    D. higher family income than that of neighbors
    E. overcrowded living conditions

    3.____

4. Casual unemployment, as distinguished from other types of unemployment, is traceable MOST readily to

    A. a decrease in the demand for labor as a result of scientific progress
    B. more or less haphazard changes in the demand for labor in certain industries
    C. periodic changes in the demand for labor in certain industries
    D. disturbances and disruptions in industry resulting from international trade barriers
    E. increased mobility of the population

    4.____

5. Labor legislation, although primarily intended for the benefit of the employee, MAY aid the employer by

    A. increasing his control over the immediate labor market
    B. prohibiting government interference with operating policies
    C. protecting him, through equalization of labor costs, from being undercut by other employers
    D. transferring to the general taxpayer the principal costs of industrial hazards of accident and unemployment
    E. increasing the pensions of civil service employees

    5.____

6. When employment and unemployment figures both decline, the MOST probable conclusion is that

   A. the population has reached a condition of equilibrium
   B. seasonal employment has ended
   C. the labor force has decreased
   D. payments for unemployment insurance have been increased
   E. industrial progress has reduced working hours

7. An individual with an I.Q. of 100 may be said to have demonstrated _____ intelligence.

   A. superior
   B. absolute
   C. substandard
   D. approximately average
   E. high average

8. While state legislatures differ in many respects, all of them are *most nearly* alike in

   A. provisions for retirement of members
   B. rate of pay
   C. length of legislative sessions
   D. method of selection of their members
   E. length of term of office

9. If a state passed a law in a field under Congressional jurisdiction and if Congress subsequently passed contrary legislation, the state provision would be

   A. regarded as never having existed
   B. valid until the next session of the state legislature, which would be obliged to repeal it
   C. superseded by the federal statute
   D. ratified by Congress
   E. still operative in the state involved

10. Power to pardon offenses committed against the people of the United States is vested in the

    A. Supreme Court of the United States
    B. United States District Courts
    C. Federal Bureau of Investigation
    D. United States Parole Board
    E. President of the United States

11. As distinguished from formal social control of an individual's behavior, an example of informal social control is that exerted by

    A. public opinion
    B. religious doctrine
    C. educational institutions
    D. statutes
    E. public health measures

12. The PRINCIPAL function of the jury in a jury trial is to decide questions of

    A. equity
    B. fact
    C. injunction
    D. contract
    E. law

13. Of the following rights of an individual, the one which usually depends on citizenship as distinguished from those given anyone living under the laws of the United States is the right to

    A. receive public assistance
    B. hold an elective office
    C. petition the government for redress of grievances
    D. receive equal protection of the laws
    E. be accorded a trial by jury

14. If the characteristics of a person were being studied by competent observers, it would be expected that their observations would differ MOST markedly with respect to their evaluation of the person's

    A. intelligence
    B. nutritional condition
    C. temperamental characteristics
    D. weight
    E. height

15. If there are evidences of dietary deficiency in families where cereals make up a major portion of the diet, the *most likely* reason for this deficiency is that

    A. cereals cause absorption of excessive quantities of water
    B. persons who concentrate their diet on cereals do not chew their food properly
    C. carbohydrates are deleterious
    D. other essential food elements are omitted
    E. children eat cereals too rapidly

16. Although malnutrition is generally associated with poverty, dietary studies of population groups in the United States reveal that

    A. malnutrition is most often due to a deficiency of nutrients found chiefly in high-cost foods
    B. there has been overemphasis of the casual relationship between poverty and malnutrition
    C. malnutrition is found among people with sufficient money to be well fed
    D. a majority of the population in all income groups is undernourished
    E. malnutrition is not a factor in the incidence of rickets

17. The organization which has as one of its primary functions the mitigation of suffering caused by famine, fire, floods, and other national calamities is the

    A. National Safety Council
    B. Salvation Army
    C. Public Administration Service
    D. American National Red Cross
    E. American Legion

18. The MAIN difference between public welfare and private social agencies is that in public agencies,

    A. case records are open to the public
    B. the granting of assistance cannot be sufficiently flexible to meet the varying needs of individual recipients
    C. only financial assistance may be provided
    D. all policies and procedures must be based upon statutory authorizations
    E. economical and efficient administration are stressed because their funds are obtained through public taxation

19. A recipient of relief who is in need of the services of an attorney but is unable to pay the customary fees, should *generally* be referred to the

    A. Small Claims Court
    B. Domestic Relations Court
    C. County Lawyers Association
    D. City Law Department
    E. Legal Aid Society

20. An injured workman should file his claim for workmen's compensation with the

    A. State Labor Relations Board
    B. Division of Placement and Unemployment Insurance
    C. State Industrial Commission
    D. Workmen's Compensation Board
    E. State Insurance Board

21. The type of insurance found MOST frequently among families such as those assisted by the Department of Social Services is

    A. accident   B. straight life
    C. endowment   D. industrial
    E. personal liability

22. Of the following items in the standard budget of the Department of Social Services, the one for which actual expenditures would be MOST constant throughout the year is

    A. fuel   B. housing
    C. medical care   D. clothing
    E. household replacements

23. The MOST frequent cause of "broken homes" is attributed to the

    A. temperamental incompatibilities of parents and in-laws
    B. extension of the system of children's courts
    C. psychopathic irresponsibility of the parents
    D. institutionalization of one of the spouses
    E. death of one or both spouses

24. In rearing children, the problems of the widower are usually greater than those of the widow, largely because of the

    A. tendency of widowers to impose excessively rigid moral standards
    B. increased economic hardship
    C. added difficulty of maintaining a desirable home
    D. possibility that a stepmother will be added to the household
    E. prevalent masculine prejudice against pursuits which are inherently feminine

24.____

25. Foster-home placement of children is often advocated in preference to institutionalization *primarily* because

    A. the law does not provide for local supervision of children's institutions
    B. institutions furnish a more expensive type of care
    C. the number of institutions is insufficient compared to the number of children needing care
    D. children are not well treated in institutions
    E. foster homes provide a more normal environment for children

25.____

KEY (CORRECT ANSWERS)

1.	E	11.	A
2.	E	12.	B
3.	B	13.	B
4.	B	14.	C
5.	C	15.	D
6.	C	16.	C
7.	D	17.	D
8.	D	18.	D
9.	C	19.	E
10.	E	20.	D

21. D
22. B
23. E
24. C
25. E

TEST 2

DIRECTIONS: Each question or incomplete statement is followed by several suggested answers or completions. Select the one that BEST answers the question or completes the statement. *PRINT THE LETTER OF THE CORRECT ANSWER IN THE SPACE AT THE RIGHT.*

1. Of the following, the category MOST likely to yield the greatest reduction in cost to the taxpayer under improved employment conditions is   1.____

   A. home relief, including aid to the homeless
   B. aid to the blind
   C. aid to dependent children
   D. old-age assistance

2. One of the MOST common characteristics of the chronic alcoholic is   2.____

   A. low intelligence level   B. wanderlust
   C. psychosis   D. egocentricity

3. Of the following factors leading toward the cure of the alcoholic, the MOST important is thought to be   3.____

   A. removal of all alcohol from the immediate environment
   B. development of a sense of personal adequacy
   C. social disapproval of drinking
   D. segregation from former companions

4. The Federal Housing Administration is the agency which   4.____

   A. insures mortgages made by lending institutions for new construction or remodeling of old construction
   B. provides federal aid for state and local government for slum clearance and housing for very low income families
   C. subsidizes the building industry through direct grants
   D. provides for the construction of low-cost housing projects owned and operated by the federal government

5. In comparing the advantages of foster home over institutional placement, it is generally agreed that institutional care is LEAST advisable for children   5.____

   A. who cannot sustain the intimacy of foster family living because of their experiences with their own parents
   B. who are socially well-adjusted or have had considerable experience in living with a family
   C. who have need for special facilities for observation, diagnosis, and treatment
   D. whose natural parents find it difficult to accept the idea of foster home placement because of its close resemblance to adoption

6. The school can play a vital part in detecting the child who displays overt symptomatic behavior indicative of social maladjustment CHIEFLY because the teacher has the opportunity to

    A. assume a pseudo-parental role in regard to discipline and punishment, thereby limiting the extent of the maladjusted child's anti-social behavior
    B. observe how the child relates to the group and what reactions are stimulated in him by his peer relationships
    C. determine whether the adjustment difficulties displayed by the child were brought on by the teacher herself or by the other students
    D. help the child's parents to resolve the difficulties in adjustment which are indicated by the child's reactions to the social pressures exerted by his peers

7. In treating juvenile delinquents, it has been found that there are some who make better social adjustment through group treatment than through an individual casework approach.
   In selecting delinquent boys for group treatment, the one of the following which is the MOST important consideration is that

    A. the boys to be treated in one group be friends or from the same community
    B. only boys who consent to group treatment be included in the group
    C. the ages of the boys included in the group vary as much as possible
    D. only boys who have not reacted to an individual casework approach be included in the group

8. Multi-problem families are generally characterized by various functional indicators.
   Of the following, the family which is *most likely* to be a multi-problem family is one which has

    A. unemployed adult family members
    B. parents with diagnosed character disorders
    C. children and parents with a series of difficulties in the community
    D. poor housekeeping standards

9. Multi-problem families generally have a complex history of intervention by a variety of social agencies.
   Of the following phases involved in planning for their treatment, the one which is MOST important to consider FIRST is the

    A. joint decision to limit any help to be given
    B. analysis of facts and definition of the problems involved
    C. determination of treatment priorities
    D. study of available community resources

10. The development of good public relations in the area for which the supervisor is responsible should be considered by the supervisor as

    A. not his responsibility as he is primarily responsible for his workers' services
    B. dependent upon him as he is in the best position to interpret the department to the community
    C. not important to the adequate functioning of the department
    D. a part of his method of carrying out his job responsibility as what his workers do affects the community

11. Of the following, the LEAST accurate statement concerning the relationship of public and private social agencies is that

    A. both have an important and necessary function to perform
    B. they are not to be considered as competing or rival agencies
    C. they are cooperating agencies
    D. their work is based on fundamentally different social work concepts

12. Of the following, the LEAST accurate statement concerning the worker-client relationship is that the worker should have the ability to

    A. express warmth of feeling in appropriate ways as a basis for a professional relationship which creates confidence
    B. feel appropriately in the relationship without losing the ability to see the situation in the perspective necessary to help the people immersed in it
    C. identify himself with the client so that the worker's personality does not influence the client
    D. use keen observation and perceive what is significant with a new range of appreciation of the meaning of the situation to the client

13. Of the following, the MOST fundamental psychological concept underlying case work in the public assistance field is that

    A. eligibility for public assistance should be reviewed from time to time
    B. workers should be aware of the prevalence of psychological disabilities among members of families on public assistance
    C. workers should realize the necessity of carrying out the policies laid down by the state office in order that state aid may be received
    D. in the process of receiving assistance, recipients should not be deprived of their normal status of self-direction

14. Of the following, the MOST comprehensive as well as the MOST accurate statement concerning the professional attitude of the social worker is that he should

    A. have a real concern for, and an intelligent interest in, the welfare of the client
    B. recognize that the client's feelings rather than the realities of his needs are of major importance to the client
    C. put at the client's service the worker's knowledge and sincere interest in him
    D. use his insight and understanding to make sound decisions about the client

15. The one of the following reasons for refusing a job which is LEAST acceptable, from the viewpoint of maintaining a client's continued rights to unemployment insurance benefits, is that

    A. acceptance of the job would interfere with the client's joining or retaining membership in a labor union
    B. there is a strike, lockout, or other industrial controversy in the establishment where employment is offered
    C. the distance from the place of employment to his home is greater than seems justified to the client
    D. the wages offered are lower than the prevailing wages in that locality

16. Experience pragmatically suggests that dislocation from cultural roots and customs makes for tension, insecurity, and anxiety. This holds for the child as well as the adolescent, for the new immigrant as well as the second-generation citizen.
Of the following, the MOST important implication of the above statement for a social worker in any setting is that

    A. anxiety, distress, and incapacity are always personal and can be understood best only through an understanding of the child's present cultural environment
    B. in order to resolve the conflicts caused by the displacement of a child from a home with one cultural background to one with another, it is essential that the child fully replace his old culture with the new one
    C. no treatment goal can be envisaged for a dislocated child which does not involve a value judgment which is itself culturally determined
    D. anxiety and distress result from a child's reaction to culturally oriented treatment goals

17. Accepting the fact that mentally gifted children represent superior heredity, the United States faces an important eugenic problem CHIEFLY because

    A. unless these mentally gifted children mature and reproduce more rapidly than the less intelligent children, the nation is heading for a lowering of the average intelligence of its people
    B. although the mentally gifted child always excels scholastically, he generally has less physical stamina than the normal child and tends to lower the nation's population physically
    C. the mentally subnormal are increasing more rapidly than the mentally gifted in America, thus affecting the overall level of achievement of the gifted child
    D. unless the mental level of the general population is raised to that of the gifted child, the mentally gifted will eventually usurp the reigns of government and dominate the mentally weaker

18. The form of psychiatric treatment which requires the LEAST amount of participation on the part of the patient is

    A. psychoanalysis   B. psychotherapy
    C. shock therapy   D. non-directive therapy

19. Tests administered by psychologists for the PRIMARY purpose of measuring intelligence are known as _____ tests.

    A. projective
    B. validating
    C. psychometric
    D. apperception

20. In recent years, there have been some significant changes in the treatment of patients in state psychiatric hospitals. These changes are PRIMARILY caused by the use of

    A. electric shock therapy
    B. tranquilizing drugs
    C. steroids
    D. the open-ward policy

21. The psychological test which makes use of a set of twenty pictures, each depicting a dramatic scene, is known as the

    A. Goodenough Test
    B. Thematic Apperception Test
    C. Minnesota Multiphasic Personality Inventory
    D. Healy Picture Completion Test

22. One of the MOST effective ways in which experimental psychologists have been able to study the effects on personality of heredity and environment has been through the study of

    A. primitive cultures
    B. identical twins
    C. mental defectives
    D. newborn infants

23. In hospitals with psychiatric divisions, the psychiatric function is PREDOMINANTLY that of

    A. the training of personnel in all psychiatric disciplines
    B. protection of the community against potentially dangerous psychiatric patients
    C. research and study of psychiatric patients so that new knowledge and information can be made generally available
    D. short-term hospitalization designed to determine diagnosis and recommendations for treatment

24. Predictions of human behavior on the basis of past behavior frequently are INACCURATE because

    A. basic patterns of human behavior are in a continual state of flux
    B. human behavior is not susceptible to explanation of a scientific nature
    C. the underlying psychological mechanisms of behavior are not completely understood
    D. quantitative techniques for the measurement of stimuli and responses are unavailable

25. Socio-cultural factors are being re-evaluated in casework practice as they influence both the worker and the client in their participation in the casework process.
Of the following factors, the one which is currently being studied MOST widely is the

   A. social class of worker and client and its significance in casework
   B. difference in native intelligence which can be ascribed to racial origin of an individual
   C. cultural values affecting the areas in which an individual functions
   D. necessity in casework treatment of the client's membership in an organized religious group

25.____

KEY (CORRECT ANSWERS)

1. A
2. D
3. B
4. A
5. B

6. B
7. B
8. C
9. B
10. D

11. D
12. C
13. D
14. C
15. C

16. C
17. A
18. C
19. C
20. B

21. B
22. B
23. D
24. C
25. C

EXAMINATION SECTION
TEST 1

DIRECTIONS: Each question or incomplete statement is followed by several suggested answers or completions. Select the one that BEST answers the question or completes the statement. *PRINT THE LETTER OF THE CORRECT ANSWER IN THE SPACE AT THE RIGHT.*

1. One day an elderly man asks you if he can apply for Social Security at the welfare office.
   Your response should be to
   A. tell him that it is foolish to think he can apply for Social Security at the welfare office
   B. take him back to his apartment because he is too old to be roaming the streets asking questions
   C. explain that Social Security is a federal program and direct him to the nearest Social Security office
   D. call his daughter and tell her that the family should take better care of their father

   1.____

2. One of your duties is to occasionally visit clients. On one occasion, you visit Mrs. B., who needs assistance in referral of her children for day care so that she may enter a job training program. She has postponed completing the referral.
   What should you do in this situation?
   A. Tell her that if she doesn't hurry there will be no room at the day care center and the training program will be closed
   B. Make the arrangements and tell Mrs. B. that she should do what you say
   C. Remember that all people who ask for help are not always ready to receive it and continue to allow Mrs. B. to complete the referral by herself
   D. The next time Mrs. B. asks for help, see that she gets it as slowly as possible

   2.____

3. Assume that you are trying to contact a community group to offer to meet with their representative to explain a new agency policy about intake procedures.
   In order to "get your message across," you should
   A. write a short concise letter explaining why you want to meet with them and when you will be available
   B. write a short letter stating only that it is important that they contact you in order to arrange a meeting
   C. ask a secretary to help you because you do not really like to write to groups
   D. call the agency rather than write since you know someone there

   3.____

2 (#1)

4. It is necessary for you to call the director of a head start center in order to discuss a training program for teaching aides. The operator asks who you are and what you wish to discuss with the director.
Your response should be to
   A. tell her that you would rather explain to the director and you want to speak to her immediately
   B. identify yourself, your department, and the nature of your business with the director
   C. hang up and try to call again when another operator is on duty
   D. tell your supervisor that the operator at the head start center is rude and you would rather not be asked to call there again

4.____

5. Mr. A. wants her children to go to summer camp. She has receive the request forms, but does not understand all of the questions and you are asked to help her complete them. She comes to the office at the appointed time.
Of the following, the action you should take is to
   A. tell her she has taken so long that maybe the children will not go to camp
   B. see her as quickly as possible, explain the questions to her, and help her in completing the forms
   C. help her, but tell her she will have to learn to read better and refer her to an evening school
   D. fill out the forms or her by yourself

5.____

6. Mrs. B. needs a referral to the cancer clinic. You contact the clinic and make arrangements for her visit. You go to her home to inform her about the time because she has no phone. She thanks you for your help and then offers you a piece of jewelry that appears to be rather expensive.
Of the following, the action you should take is to
   A. take the gift because you don't want to hurt her feelings
   B. tell her that she is foolish and should spend her money on herself
   C. explain to her that you are pleased with her thoughtfulness, but you are unable to accept the gift
   D. refuse the gift and get someone else to make referrals in the future because she is trying to pay you for your help

6.____

7. Mrs. C., a seemingly healthy, intelligent woman whose husband is disabled, and who works part-time, asks for help in getting homemaker services.
Of the following, the action you should take is to
   A. give Mrs. C. the necessary information and help her get the services
   B. tell Mrs. C. that you do not feel she needs these services since her husband is capable of helping
   C. make note of her request since you do not feel it is urgent
   D. refer her to a caseworker since she obviously needs help in defining her role as a woman

7.____

8. When you are interviewing clients, it is important to notice and record how they say what they say—angrily, nervously, or with "body English"—because these signs may

8.____

A. tell you that the client's words are the opposite of what the client feels and you may need to dig to find out what those feelings are
B. be the prelude to violent behavior which no aide is prepared to handle
C. show that the client does not really deserve serious consideration
D. be important later should you be asked to defend what you did for the client

9. You are recording a visit you have made with a client who was angry and abusive to you during the interview. At one point, you lost your temper and said some things that you immediately regretted. You are embarrassed to record that you lost your temper.
However, it would be desirable to record this MAINLY because
    A. you would feel guilty if you did not record it
    B. your supervisor might hear about it from the client, so it would be better to have it written down from your point of view
    C. your supervisor can use the information to help you to improve your skills
    D. it is agency policy to write down everything

10. Through one of your clients you learn that a day care program's hours have been extended. You confirm this information with the day care center.
It is then MOST important for you to
    A. make a note of this fact, since it will mean you have to change your schedule in working with the client
    B. add this information to your personal resource file so that you can refer other clients to the day dare program
    C. inform your supervisor of the new information so that it can be added to the central resource file
    D. ignore the information, since your client does not need to have her child in day care for any extra hours

11. You are sent to a meeting of day-care parents to explain the programs of your agency. One of the parents becomes very angry, saying that welfare departments treat people like animals.
You should remain as calm as possible and say to the parent that
    A. he is right, but you have no control over what your agency does
    B. he is disrupting the meeting and you have come to explain a program, not to listen to complaints
    C. you understand his feelings and that sometimes clients do not get the services they wish as quickly as possible; however, you will do whatever you can to assist him
    D. he should call your supervisor tomorrow and make an appointment to discuss his feelings

12. Assume that you receive a telephone call from a very angry father. His daughter took money from his wallet, and he wants the caseworker to control the daughter. He yells, screams, and swears at you.
What is the BEST way for you to respond?

A. Hang up because you are not responsible for his daughter's actions. He shouldn't scream and swear at you.
B. Remember to be courteous and polite at all times, never losing your temper
C. Transfer the call to the supervisor because you are concerned about the father's unreasonableness and do not want the responsibility of dealing with him
D. Tell him that behavior such as he is demonstrating is the reason his daughter steals from him

13. Mrs. D.'s son, aged 12, has been getting into difficulty in the neighborhood. At a community meeting, she asks your help in finding worthwhile activities for him. It is APPROPRIATE for you to respond to her because
    A. you should have knowledge of the social services available in the neighborhood and the activities they offer
    B. you have known Mrs. D. and her family for several years and know how much trouble she has had with her son
    C. it is your job to do what the caseworker assigns to you without question
    D. you are concerned about impressing Mrs. D with your knowledge

14. Several clients live in your neighborhood. They know that you work for the human resources administration. One day one of them tells you that there is a rumor that another client is pregnant and asks if this is true. You know from a past discussion with the caseworker that this client is pregnant.
    The BEST answer for you to give would be to
    A. tell her it is none of her business and if she wants to know, she should ask the caseworker
    B. ask her who told her that this client is pregnant
    C. explain that anything told to the agency is held in confidence and will not be shared with anyone else
    D. tell her you don't know, but will ask when you get back to the office and let her know later

15. The area senior citizens group asks for an agency representative to discuss old-age assistance and new SSI regulations. Your supervisor asks you to attend this meeting; however, you do not wish to go because you really do not feel that you work well with older people. In fact, you don't like them very much.
    What should be your response?
    A. Tell the supervisor that you cannot go because you have an appointment with the doctor that day
    B. Get another worker to go for you and assume his task while he is gone
    C. Explain to your supervisor what problems you have in working with old-age clients
    D. Go, because you should do the tasks that are assigned to you according to your job description

16. At a center where you are distributing literature about agency programs, a citizen comes up to you and begins to complain loudly about agency programs. What should be your response?
    A. Call the police and have the complainer removed from the center
    B. Tell him that you do not make policy; suggest that he go to the office and complain
    C. Remain as calm as possible and ask that he discuss the complaints with you calmly. If necessary, make an appointment with him
    D. Yell at him since this seems to be the way he relates to agency people

17. A community group is having a training program. You are sent to explain agency policy and answer questions.
    Providing this type of contact between the agency and community groups is PROPER because
    A. you like people and are a good public speaker
    B. it is the responsibility of the agency to cooperate with community groups in order to help the public to be well-informed about agency policy
    C. you were once in the same training program and understand the kind of people who are being trained
    D. once in a while everyone should have the opportunity to speak to a community group

18. While you are assisting in the intake area, a young man who is applying is cooperative but begins to ask you personal questions: your age, where you live, whether you have children, and other similar questions.
    You are disturbed by these questions, so you should
    A. tell him that agency policy does not allow you to answer personal questions and send him to another intake worker
    B. tell him it is your responsibility to ask questions, not his
    C. tell your supervisor that you do not want to work in intake because clients can get too nosy and you get nervous
    D. avoid answering personal questions and try to get him to return to the purpose of the interview

19. You are assigned to the reception area for the day. A mother arrives in the office with three small children. In a rage, she says that she does not have enough money to feed the children and demands that you find a home for them.
    The BEST action for you to take should be to
    A. call a security officer and have him remove her and the children from the office
    B. attempt to calm her down by listening to her, attend to the children's needs and call for a supervisor
    C. take the children from her and ask her to leave at once
    D. call the supervisor and security because it is their job to take care of abusive clients

20. Assume that you are interviewing a young unwed mother who has recently arrived in the city from Alabama. She is a likable girl and is very cooperative. However, it is difficult to understand the meaning of her conversation due to her accent and different use of words.
    You would like to establish a good relationship with her, so you should FIRST
    A. suggest that she go to evening school so that she can learn to speak like other people in the city
    B. tell her that you don't understand her sometimes and you would appreciate it if she would explain what she means
    C. take another worker with you on visits to help you in the interview
    D. try to find a worker in the agency who has a similar background and have the case handled by the worker

21. A man being interviewed is entitled to Medicaid, but he refuses to sign up for it because he says he cannot accept any form of welfare.
    Of the following, the BEST course of action for an aide to take FIRST is to
    A. try to discover the reason for his feeling this way
    B. tell him that he should be glad financial help is available
    C. explain that others cannot get help him if he will not help himself
    D. suggest that he speak to someone who is already on Medicaid

22. Of the following, the outcome of an interview by an aide depends MOS heavily on the
    A. personality of the interviewee
    B. personality of the aide
    C. subject matter of the questions asked
    D. interaction between aide and interviewee

23. Some patients being interviewed are PRIMARILY interested in making a favorable impression. The aide should be aware of the fact that such patients are more likely than other patients to
    A. try to anticipate the answers the interviewer is looking for
    B. answer all questions openly and frankly
    C. try to assume the role of interviewer
    D. be anxious to get the interview over as quickly as possible

24. The type of interview which an aide usually conducts is substantially different from most interviewing situations in all of the following aspects EXCEPT the
    A. setting   B. kinds of clients
    C. techniques employed   D. kinds of problems

25. During an interview, an aide uses a "leading question."
    This type of question is so-called because it generally
    A. starts a series of questions about one topic
    B. suggests the answer which the aide wants
    C. forms the basis for a following "trick" question
    D. sets, at the beginning, the tone of the interview

KEY (CORRECT ANSWERS)

1.	C		11.	C
2.	C		12.	B
3.	A		13.	A
4.	B		14.	C
5.	B		15.	C
6.	C		16.	C
7.	A		17.	B
8.	A		18.	D
9.	C		19.	B
10.	C		20.	B

21. A
22. D
23. A
24. C
25. B

TEST 2

DIRECTIONS: Each question or incomplete statement is followed by several suggested answers or completions. Select the one that BEST answers the question or completes the statement. *PRINT THE LETTER OF THE CORRECT ANSWER IN THE SPACE AT THE RIGHT.*

1. Miss Lally is an old-age assistance recipient. Her health is not good and it is important that she have three good meals each day. She follows these instructions except on Friday she refuses to eat meat because of her religious beliefs. She will not even substitute fish.
   You are very concerned about this, so you should
   A. tell your supervisor so that she will go to see Miss Lally and make her eat nourishing meals on Friday
   B. call her doctor and tell him so that he will see her and explain to her that fasting is not good for her health
   C. attempt to understand her value system and accept that it is possible that she is acting in good faith with her own values even though they may be harmful to her health
   D. explain to her how important it is that she eat meat each day in order to be in good health and enjoy the remaining years of her life

2. Theodore is a junkie. Every cent he can get his hands on legally or illegally is used to supply his habit. You are angry because the junkie is destroying himself and his family. You feel that the courts should punish him for his illegal acts.
   Of the following, the BEST action for you to take is to
   A. suggest to your supervisor that the income maintenance center reduce the family grant, taking out his portion
   B. help his wife to find another apartment for her and the children away from him
   C. call the local police to find out why they are doing nothing about this man's activities in the community
   D. reconsider your ideas about punishment, remembering that punishment alone will not help the man to change his behavior

3. You are regularly assigned to taking Sarah Jones and her young son to the clinic. She is a very warm, friendly woman and your relationship with her is good. However, she invited you to come for dinner on Sunday and to go to a school play with her. You would like to accept the invitations because you need weekend activities and you like her.
   What should be your PRIMARY consideration in coming to a decision?
   A. You need friends just as she does, so you should accept the invitations
   B. You are a worker and should not be seen with a client in public places
   C. Decide whether accepting the invitations will help to meet agency needs or will hamper the relationship you are expected to establish
   D. Tell her "no" because it is not a good policy to be on such friendly terms with clients

4. Martha's husband has been arrested in a drug raid and she is extremely anxious. Your supervisor asks that you visit her to determine ways in which the agency may help her. You visit and find her weeping; the house and the children have obviously been neglected.
   The BEST thing for you to do is to
   A. tell her to stop crying and help her to clean the apartment and the children
   B. remind her that her husband has been warned and now has to pay for not listening
   C. listen to her, allowing her to express her feelings of fear, loss, and grief, and reassure her of your concern
   D. listen to her but caution her that she is neglecting the home and children because of her anxiety and you may have to ask your supervisor to remove the children if she doesn't get any better

4.____

5. Mrs. Dwight's landlord is very slow in making repairs in her apartment. Each time you see her, she complains about this over and over again, calling her landlord names and threatening to report him to the city. She complains to any agency person she meets.
   Realizing that these complaints are not getting any action, you should
   A. avoid meeting with her because she is annoying
   B. suggest that she see a doctor because she is irrational and should get some help
   C. ask her what she would like to do about the problem and assist her in carrying out her plans
   D. ask the supervisor to see her because you do not have the skills to help her

5.____

6. In the day-to-day operations of the human resources administration, which of the following would you consider to be the PRIMARY function of the agency?
   A. Getting work done to meet city and federal deadlines
   B. Being sure that all of the clients who come to the agency are seen before closing time
   C. Delivering services to those persons who are eligible for assistance
   D. Making sure everyone gets his check on time

6.____

7. During the course of an interview you find it is necessary to arrange a special appointment for the client to return for a further interview. After checking your calendar, you tell the client the date she is to come back. The client, however, says she cannot see you on that date because she is to attend a rally at a community center in her neighborhood.
   Of the following, your BEST action should be to
   A. let her know that any other day is an inconvenience to you and remind her that the appointment is for her benefit
   B. forget about the special appointment and try to get along with the information you have
   C. explain to her the need for the appointment and ask when she can meet with you
   D. tell her that since the community center is not city-operated, she must keep her appointment with you

7.____

8. In working with community groups, it is important that you be able to define what a community is.
   Of the following definitions, which is the MOST appropriate?
   A community
   A. consists of a group of people living fairly close together in a more or less compact territory, who come together in their chief concerns
   B. is a particular section of a city designated on a census tract
   C. is that portion of a city which constitutes an election district
   D. is a section of a city or town in which a particular ethnic group conducts its social, business, and religious life

9. The agency has implemented a new policy regarding the intake procedure. You wish to explain and discuss this policy with as many community groups as possible. You make an initial contact by mail.
   In order to get your message across well, your letter should be
   A. short and as concise as possible explaining why you want to meet with them, and offer several possible times that you will be available
   B. short, explaining only that it is important that the groups contact you in order to arrange a meeting
   C. drafted by the center's secretary and sent to the usual groups
   D. put in the usual announcement form in the center's newsletter

10. A group of young welfare mothers want to form an organization that will provide babysitting services for mothers of children who are too young to enroll in a day care center.
    What should be your answer to them?
    A. Tell them to try to get the center to change its policy to include young children
    B. Arrange the time to meet with them to offer as much advice and support as possible, since most communities do need this service
    C. Suggest that it may be better that they spend their time taking care of their own children
    D. Ask a social worker to survey the community to determine if such a service is really needed at this time

11. New regulations have removed the disabled, blind, and old-age assistance cases from the public assistance caseload. Assistance in these categories is given directly by the federal government. A former client has not received his check. The chairman of the senior citizens committee calls and angrily demands that your agency do something in this man's behalf.
    In response, you should
    A. answer politely, explaining that your agency is not concerned about OAA clients
    B. arrange to meet with him in order to discuss the new policy
    C. refer him to the Social Security office covering the area where the client lives
    D. ask that he call again when he is calmer so that you may discuss this matter with him

12. A high school student from the community comes to see you about a homework assignment to write a report on your center.
    The BEST way to help him is to
    A. refer him to a social worker who has daily contact with clients in their homes
    B. contact the boy's teacher and find out why you were not warned of his coming
    C. explain your center's program and answer as many of his questions as you can
    D. give him literature about the welfare system in the city and state

13. Assume that the women's group of the Community Baptist Church has invited you to a Sunday afternoon service to celebrate the tenth anniversary of the pastor. The agency's relationship with the women is good in that they often offer their homes as emergency homes for adult clients.
    What should you do about the invitation?
    A. Do not attend but send them a note congratulating the pastor and explaining that agency personnel do not work on Sundays
    B. Ask a social worker who lives close to the church to go
    C. Accept the invitation if at all possible, attend the service and whatever social hour they may have afterwards
    D. Ignore the invitation since this function has little relationship to your job

14. Suppose that a person you are interviewing becomes angry at some of the questions you have asked, calls you meddlesome and nosy, and states that she will not answer those questions.
    Of the following, which is the BEST action for you to take
    A. Explain the reasons the questions are asked and the importance of the answers
    B. Inform the interviewee that you are only doing your job and advise her that she should answer your questions or leave your office
    C. Report to your supervisor what the interviewee called you and refuse to continue the interview
    D. End the interview and tell the interviewee she will not be serviced by your department

15. Suppose that during the course of an interview the interviewee demands in a very rude way that she be permitted to talk to your supervisor or someone in charge.
    Which of the following is probably the BEST way to handle this situation?
    A. Inform your supervisor of the demand and ask her to speak to the interviewee
    B. Pay no attention to the demands of the interviewee and continue the interview
    C. Report to your supervisor and tell her to get another interviewer for this interviewee
    D. Tell her you are the one "in charge" and that she should talk to you

16. Suppose that a worker asks a client to answer several required but rather personal questions about the family's health history. The client delays and seems embarrassed about giving the answers.
    Of the following, the MOST reasonable response to the client is one which
    A. shows an awareness of the client's efforts to hide something
    B. demonstrates the worker's qualifications for asking such questions
    C. allows this client to be excused from answering the questions
    D. convinces the client that his uneasiness in the situation is understood

17. A representative from a planned parenthood group comes to see you to get information for a community education program.
    You should
    A. check out this group to make sure it is not promoting zero population growth for minority groups
    B. develop a good relationship with him so as to provide better service to clients
    C. make sure they will not encourage unnecessary abortions
    D. refuse to see him

18. A member of a clerical training program is continually late to classes. He explains to you that he has a hard time getting up and asks that you report him on time because he needs to train for a job.
    What should your response be?
    A. Tell him that you get there on time and so should he
    B. Tell him that you do not lie for anyone
    C. Explain that it is your duty to keep accurate records and refer him to a counselor
    D. Tell him that you will cooperate with him but he has to try to do better

19. In a community meeting to explain a new agency policy, you find that the audience has no questions about the policy or your explanations.
    What would be the MOST appropriate response to the silence?
    A. Leave right away before they think of questions
    B. Thank the audience for their attention and assure them that you will be available if there are any questions later
    C. Ask several members in the audience if they understand the new policy
    D. Explain that the audience could not possibly understand all of the policy and they must have questions

20. Assume that you are confronted by an angry member of the public who has not been able to obtain the information he needs from your office. You do not know the answer to his question.
    The BEST thing for you to do would be to
    A. tell him to come back another time, after you have looked up the information
    B. check with your supervisor to find the correct answer

C. tell him to ask in another office, so that you will not lose time looking for the information
D. make up and answer to keep the man satisfied until the right answer is found

KEY (CORRECT ANSWERS)

1.	C	11.	C
2.	D	12.	C
3.	C	13.	C
4.	C	14.	A
5.	C	15.	A
6.	C	16.	D
7.	C	17.	B
8.	A	18.	C
9.	A	19.	B
10.	B	20.	B

EXAMINATION SECTION
TEST 1

DIRECTIONS: Each question or incomplete statement is followed by several suggested answers or completions. Select the one that BEST answers the question or completes the statement. *PRINT THE LETTER OF THE CORRECT ANSWER IN THE SPACE AT THE RIGHT.*

Questions 1-10.

DIRECTIONS: For each of the sentences given below, numbered 1 through 10, select from the following choices the MOST correct choice and print your choice in the space at the right. Select as your answer:
- A – if the statement contains an unnecessary word of expression
- B – if the statement contains a slang term or expression ordinarily not acceptable in government report writing
- C – if the statement contains an old-fashioned word or expression, where a concrete, plain term would be more useful
- D – if the statement contains no major faults

1. Every one of us should try harder. 1.____
2. Yours of the first instant has been received. 2.____
3. We will have to do a real snow job on him. 3.____
4. I shall contact him next Thursday. 4.____
5. None of us were invited to the meeting with the community. 5.____
6. We got this here job to do. 6.____
7. She could not help but see the mistake in the checkbook. 7.____
8. Don't bug the Director about the report. 8.____
9. I beg to inform you that your letter has been received. 9.____
10. This project is all screwed up. 10.____

Questions 11-15.

DIRECTIONS: Read the following Inter-office Memo. Then answer Questions 11 through 15 based ONLY on the memo.

INTER-OFFICE MEMORANDUM

To: Alma Robinson, Human Resources Aide
From: Frank Shields, Social Worker

    I would like to have you help Mr. Edward Tunney who is trying to raise his two children by himself. He needs to learn to improve the physical care of his children and especially of his daughter Helen, age 9. She is avoided and ridiculed at school because her hair is uncombed, her teeth not properly cleaned, her clothing torn, wrinkled and dirty, as well as shabby and poorly fitted. The teachers and school officials have contacted the Department and the social worker for two years about Helen. She is not able to make friends because of these problems. I have talked to Mr. Tunney about improvements for the child's clothing, hair, and hygiene. He tends to deny these things are problems, but is cooperative, and a second person showing him the importance of better physical care for Helen would be helpful.

    Perhaps you could teach Helen how to fix her own hair. She has all the materials. I would also like you to form your own opinion of the sanitary conditions in the home and how they could be improved.

    Mr. Tunney is expecting your visit and is willing to talk with you about ways he can help with these problems.

11. In the above memorandum, the Human Resources Aide is being asked to help Mr. Tunney to

    A. improve the learning habits of his children
    B. enable his children to make friends at school
    C. take responsibility for the upbringing of his children
    D. give attention to the grooming and cleanliness of his children

12. This case was brought to the attention of the social worker by

    A. government officials
    B. teachers and school officials
    C. the Department
    D. Mr. Tunney

13. In general, Mr. Tunney's attitude with regard to his children could BEST be described as

    A. interested in correcting the obvious problems, but unable to do so alone
    B. unwilling to follow the advice of those who are trying to help
    C. concerned, but unaware of the seriousness of these problems
    D. interested in helping them, but afraid of taking the advice of the social worker

14. Which of the following actions has NOT been suggested as a possible step for the Human Resources Aide to take?

    A. Help Helen to learn to care for herself by teaching her grooming skills
    B. Determine ways of improvement through information gathered on a home visit
    C. Discuss her own views on Helen's problems with school officials
    D. Ask Mr. Tunney in what ways he believes the physical care may be improved

15. According to the memo, the Human Resources Aide is ESPECIALLY being asked to observe and form her own opinions about   15.____

    A. the relationship between Mr. Tunney and the school officials
    B. Helen's attitude toward her classmates and teacher
    C. the sanitary conditions in the home
    D. the reasons Mr. Tunney is not cooperative with the agency

16. In one day, an aide receives 18 inquiries by phone and 27 inquiries in person. What percentage of the inquiries received that day were by phone?   16.____

    A. 33%   B. 40%   C. 45%   D. 60%

17. If the weekly pay checks for 5 part-time employees are: $129.32, $162.74, $143.67, $135.75, and $156.56, then the combined weekly income for the 5 employees is   17.____

    A. $727.84   B. $728.04   C. $730.84   D. $737.04

18. Suppose that there are 17 aides working in an office where many community complaints are received by telephone. In one ten-day period, 4250 calls were received. If the same number of calls were received each day, and the aides divided the work load equally, about how many calls did each aide respond to daily?   18.____

    A. 25   B. 35   C. 75   D. 250

19. Suppose that an assignment was divided among 5 aides. If the first aide spent 67 hours on the assignment, the second aide spent 95 hours, the third aide spent 52 hours, the fourth aide spent 78 hours, and the fifth aide spent 103 hours, what was the AVERAGE amount of time spent by each aide on the assignment?   19.____
    _____ hours.

    A. 71   B. 75   C. 79   D. 83

20. If there are 240 employees in a center and 1/3 are absent on the day of a bad snowstorm, how many employees were at work in the center on that day?   20.____

    A. 80   B. 120   C. 160   D. 200

KEY (CORRECT ANSWERS)

1.	D	11.	D
2.	C	12.	B
3.	B	13.	C
4.	D	14.	C
5.	D	15.	C
6.	B	16.	B
7.	D	17.	B
8.	B	18.	A
9.	C	19.	C
10.	B	20.	C

TEST 2

DIRECTIONS: Each question or incomplete statement is followed by several suggested answers or completions. Select the one that BEST answers the question or completes the statement. *PRINT THE LETTER OF THE CORRECT ANSWER IN THE SPACE AT THE RIGHT.*

1. Suppose that an aide takes 25 minutes to prepare a letter to a client. 1.____
   If the aide is assigned to prepare 9 letters on a certain day, how much time should she set aside for this task? _____ hours.

   A. 3 3/4   B. 4 1/4   C. 4 3/4   D. 5 1/4

2. Suppose that a certain center uses both Form A and Form B in the course of its daily 2.____
   work, and that Form A is used 4 times as often as Form B.
   If the total number of both forms used in one week is 750, how many times was Form A used?

   A. 100   B. 200   C. 400   D. 600

3. Suppose a center has a budget of $1092.70 from which 8 desks costing $78.05 apiece 3.____
   must be bought?
   How many ADDITIONAL desks can be ordered from this budget after the 8 desks have been purchased?

   A. 4   B. 6   C. 9   D. 14

4. When researching a particular case, a team of 16 aides was asked to check through 234 4.____
   folders to obtain the necessary information.
   If half the aides worked twice as fast as the other half, and the slow group checked through 12 folders each hour, about how long would it take to complete the assignment? _____ hours.

   A. $4\frac{1}{4}$ B. 5   C. 6   D. $6\frac{1}{2}$

5. The difference in the cost of two printers is $28.32. If the less expensive printer 5.____
   costs $153.61, what is the cost of the other printer?

   A. $171.93   B. $172.03   C. $181.93   D. $182.03

Questions 6-8.

DIRECTIONS: Questions 6 through 8 are to be answered on the basis of the following information contained on a sample page of a payroll book.

Emp. No.	Name of Employee	Hours Worked M	T	W	Th	F	Total Hours Worked	Pay PerHour	Total Wages
1	James Smith	8	8	8	8	8			$480.00
2	Gloria Jones	8	7 3/4	7		7 1/2		$16.00	$560.00
3	Robert Adams	6	6	7 1/2	7 1/2	8 3/4		$18.28	

6. The pay per hour of Employee No. 1 is   6._____

   A. $12.00   B. $13.72   C. $15.00   D. $19.20

7. The number of hours that Employee No. 2 worked on Friday is   7._____

   A. 4   B. 5 1/2   C. 4.63   D. 4 3/4

8. The total wages for Employee No. 3 is   8._____

   A. $636.92   B. $648.94   C. $661.04   D. $672.96

9. As a rule, the FIRST step in writing a check should be to   9._____

   A. number the check
   B. write in the payee's name
   C. tear out the check stub
   D. write the purpose of the check in the space provided at the bottom

10. If an error is made when writing a check, the MOST widely accepted procedure is to   10._____

    A. draw a line through the error and initial it
    B. destroy both the check and check stub by tearing into small pieces
    C. erase the error if it does not occur in the amount of the check
    D. write *Void* across both the check and check stub and save them

11. The check that is MOST easily cashed is one that is   11._____

    A. not signed   B. made payable to *Cash*
    C. post-dated   D. endorsed in part

12.   12._____

No. *103*	$ *142. 77*
May 14	
To *Alan Jacobs*	
For *Wages (5/6-5/10)*	
Bal. Bro't For'd	2340. 63
Amt. Deposited	205. 24
Total	
Amt. This Check	142. 77
Bal. Car'd For'd	

   The balance to be carried forward on the check stub above is
   A. $2,278.16   B. $1,992.62   C. $2,688.64   D. $2,403.10

13. The procedure for reconciling a bank statement consists of _____ the bank balance   13._____
    and _____ the checkbook balance.

    A. *adding* outstanding checks to; *subtracting* the service and check charges from
    B. *subtracting* the service charge from; *subtracting* outstanding checks from
    C. *subtracting* the service charge from; *adding* outstanding checks to
    D. *subtracting* outstanding checks from; *subtracting* the service and check charges from

14. An employee makes $15.70 an hour and receives time-and-a-half in overtime pay for every hour more than 40 in a given week. If the employee works 47 hours, the employee's total wages for that week would be

    A. $792.85   B. $837.90   C. $875.25   D. $1,106.85

15. A high-speed copier can make 25,000 copies before periodic service is required. Before this service is necessary, _____ copies of a 137-page document can be printed.

    A. 211   B. 204   C. 190   D. 178

16. An aide is typing a letter to the James Weldon Johnson Head Start Center. To be sure that a Mr. Joseph Maxwell reads it, an attention line is typed below the inside address. The salutation should, therefore, read:

    A. To Whom It May Concern: B. Dear Mr. Maxwell:
    C. Gentlemen: D. Dear Joseph:

17. When describing the advantages of the numeric filing system, it is NOT true that it

    A. is the most accurate of all methods
    B. allows for unlimited expansion according to the needs of the agency
    C. is a system useful for filing letters directly according to name or subject
    D. allows for cross-referencing

18. In writing a letter for your Center, the PURPOSE of the letter should usually be stated in

    A. the first paragraph. This assists the reader in making more sense of the letter.
    B. the second paragraph. The first paragraph should be used to confirm receipt of the letter being answered
    C. the last paragraph. The first paragraphs should be used to build up to the purpose of the letter.
    D. any paragraph. Each letter has a different purpose and the letter should conform to that purpose.

19. If you open a personal letter addressed to another aide by mistake, the one of the following actions which it would generally be BEST for you to take is to

    A. reseal the envelope or place the contents in another envelope and pass it on to the employee
    B. place the letter inside the envelope, indicate under your initials that it was opened in error and give it to the employee
    C. personally give the employee the letter without any explanation
    D. ignore your error, attach the envelope to the letter, and give it out in the usual manner

20. Of the following, the MAIN purpose of the head start program is to

    A. provide programs for pre-school development of children
    B. provide children between the ages of 6 and 12 with after-school activity
    C. establish a system for providing care for teenage youngsters with working parents
    D. supervise centers providing 24-hour child care

KEY (CORRECT ANSWERS)

1. A
2. D
3. B
4. D
5. C

6. A
7. D
8. B
9. A
10. D

11. B
12. D
13. D
14. A
15. D

16. C
17. C
18. A
19. B
20. A

EXAMINATION SECTION
TEST 1

DIRECTIONS: Each question or incomplete statement is followed by several suggested answers or completions. Select the one that BEST answers the question or completes the statement. *PRINT THE LETTER OF THE CORRECT ANSWER IN THE SPACE AT THE RIGHT.*

1. An interview is BEST conducted in private primarily because
   A. the person interviewed will tend to be less self-conscious
   B. the interviewer will be able to maintain his continuity of thought better
   C. it will insure that the interview is "off the record"
   D. people tend to "show off" before an audience

2. An interviewer can BEST establish a good relationship with the person being interviewed by
   A. assuming casual interest in the statements made by the person being interviewed
   B. taking the point of view of the person interviewed
   C. controlling the interview to a major extent
   D. showing a genuine interest in the person

3. An interviewer will be better able to understand the person interviewed and his problems if he recognizes that much of the person's behavior is due to motives
   A. which are deliberate
   B. of which he is unaware
   C. which are inexplicable
   D. which are kept under control

4. An interviewer's attention must be directed toward himself as well as toward the person interviewed.
   This statement means that the interviewer should
   A. keep in mind the extent to which his own prejudices may influence his judgment
   B. rationalize the statements made by the person interviewed
   C. gain the respect and confidence of the person interviewed
   D. avoid being too impersonal

5. More complete expression will be obtained from a person being interviewed if the interviewer can create the impression that
   A. the data secured will become part of a permanent record
   B. official information must be accurate in every detail
   C. it is the duty of the person interviewed to give accurate data
   D. the person interviewed is participating in a discussion of his own problems

6. The practice of asking leading questions should be avoided in an interview because the
   A. interviewer risks revealing his attitudes to the person being interviewed
   B. interviewer may be led to ignore the objective attitudes of the person interviewed
   C. answers may be unwarrantedly influenced
   D. person interviewed will resent the attempt to lead him and will be less cooperative

7. A good technique for the interviewer to use in an effort to secure reliable data and to reduce the possibility of misunderstanding is to
   A. use casual undirected conversation, enabling the person being interviewed to talk about himself, and thus secure the desired information
   B. adopt the procedure of using direct questions regularly
   C. extract the desired information from the person being interviewed by putting him on the defensive
   D. explain to the person being interviewed the information desired and the reason for needing it

8. You are interviewing a patient to determine whether she is eligible for medical assistance. Of the many questions that you have to ask her, some are routine questions that patients tend to answer willingly and easily. Other questions are more personal and some patients tend to resent being asked them and avoid answering them directly.
   For you to begin the interview with the more personal questions would be
   A. *desirable*, because the end of the interview will go smoothly and the patient will be left with a warm feeling
   B. *undesirable*, because the patient might not know the answers to the questions
   C. *desirable*, because you will be able to return to these questions later to verify the accuracy of the responses
   D. *undesirable*, because you might antagonize the patient before you have had a chance to establish rapport

9. While interviewing a patient about her family composition, the patient asks you whether you are married.
   Of the following, the MOST appropriate way for you to handle this situation is to
   A. answer the question briefly and redirect her back to the topic under discussion
   B. refrain from answering the question and proceed with the interview
   C. advise the patient that it is more important that she answer your questions than that you answer hers, and proceed with the interview
   D. promise the patient that you will answer her question later, in the hope that she will forget, and redirect her back to the topic under discussion

10. In response to a question about his employment history, a patient you are interviewing rambles and talks about unrelated matters.
    Of the following, the MOST appropriate course of action for you to take FIRST is to

A. ask questions to direct the patient back to his employment history
B. advise him to concentrate on your questions and not to discuss irrelevant information
C. ask him why he is resisting a discussion of his employment history
D. advise him that if you cannot get the information you need, he will not be eligible for medical assistance

11. Suppose that a person you are interviewing becomes angry at some of the questions you have asked, calls you meddlesome and nosy, and states that she will not answer those questions.
Of the following, which is the BEST action for you to take?
    A. Explain the reasons the questions are asked and the importance of the answers
    B. Inform the interviewee that you are only doing your job and advise her that she should answer your questions or leave the office
    C. Report to your supervisor what the interviewee called you and refuse to continue the interview
    D. End the interview and tell the interviewee she will not be serviced by your department

11._____

12. Suppose that during the course of an interview the interviewee demands in a very rude way that she be permitted to talk to your supervisor or someone in charge.
Which of the following is probably the BEST way to handle this situation?
    A. Inform your supervisor of the demand and ask her to speak to the interviewee
    B. Pay no attention to the demands of the interviewee and continue the interview
    C. Report to your supervisor and tell her to get another interviewer for this interviewee
    D. Tell her you are the one "in charge" and that she should talk to you

12._____

13. Of the following, the outcome of an interview by an aide depends MOST heavily on the
    A. personality of the interviewee
    B. personality of the aide
    C. subject matter of the questions asked
    D. interaction between aide and interviewee

13._____

14. Some patients being interviewed are primarily interested in making a favorable impression.
The aide should be aware of the fact that such patients are more likely than other patients to
    A. try to anticipate the answers the interviewer is looking for
    B. answer all questions openly and frankly
    C. try to assume the role of interviewer
    D. be anxious to get the interview over as quickly as possible

14._____

15. The type of interview which an aide usually conducts is substantially different from most interviewing situations in all of the following aspects EXCEPT the
    A. setting
    B. kinds of clients
    C. techniques employed
    D. kinds of problems

16. During an interview, an aide uses a "leading question."
    This type of question is so-called because it generally
    A. starts a series of questions about one topic
    B. suggests the answer which the aide wants
    C. forms the basis for a following "trick" question
    D. sets, at the beginning, the tone of the interview

17. Casework interviewing is always directed to the client and his situation.
    The one of the following which is the MOST accurate statement with respect to the proper focus of an interview is that the
    A. caseworker limits the client to concentration on objective data
    B. client is generally permitted to talk about facts and feelings with no direction from the caseworker
    C. main focus in casework interviews is on feelings rather than facts
    D. caseworker is responsible for helping the client focus on any material which seems to be related to his problems or difficulties

18. Assume that you are conducting a training program for the caseworkers under your supervision. At one of the sessions, you discuss the problem of interviewing a dull and stupid client who gives a slow and disconnected case history.
    The BEST of the following interviewing methods for you to recommend in such a case in order to ascertain facts is for the caseworker to
    A. ask the client leading questions requiring "yes" or "no" answers
    B. request the client to limit his narration to the essential facts so that the interview can be kept as brief as possible
    C. review the story with the client, patiently asking simple questions
    D. tell the client that unless he is more cooperative he cannot be helped to solve his problem

19. A recent development in casework interviewing procedure, known as multiple-client interviewing, consists of interviews of the entire family at the same time. However, this may not be an effective casework method in certain situations.
    Of the following, the situation in which the standard individual interview would be preferable is when
    A. family member derive consistent and major gratification from assisting each other in their destructive responses
    B. there is a crucial family conflict to which the members are reacting
    C. the family is overwhelmed by interpersonal anxieties which have not been explored
    D. the worker wants to determine the pattern of family interaction to further his diagnostic understanding

20. A follow-up interview was arranged for an applicant in order that he could furnish certain requested evidence. At this follow-up interview, the applicant still fails to furnish the necessary evidence.
    It would be MOST advisable for you to
    A. advise the applicant that he is now considered ineligible
    B. ask the applicant how soon he can get the necessary evidence and set a date for another interview
    C. question the applicant carefully and thoroughly to determine if he has misrepresented or falsified any information
    D. set a date for another interview and tell the applicant to get the necessary evidence by that time

20.____

KEY (CORRECT ANSWERS)

1.	A	11.	A
2.	D	12.	A
3.	B	13.	D
4.	A	14.	A
5.	D	15.	C
6.	C	16.	B
7.	D	17.	D
8.	D	18.	C
9.	A	19.	A
10.	A	20.	B

TEST 2

DIRECTIONS: Each question or incomplete statement is followed by several suggested answers or completions. Select the one that BEST answers the question or completes the statement. *PRINT THE LETTER OF THE CORRECT ANSWER IN THE SPACE AT THE RIGHT.*

1. In interviewing, the practice of anticipating an applicant's answers to questions is generally
   A. *desirable*, because it is effective and economical when it is necessary to interview large numbers of applicants
   B. *desirable*, because many applicants have language difficulties
   C. *undesirable*, because it is the inalienable right of every person to answer as he sees fit
   D. *undesirable*, because applicants may tend to agree with the answer proposed by the interviewer even when the answer is not entirely correct

   1.____

2. When an initial interview is being conducted, one way of starting is to explain the purpose of the interview to the applicant.
   The practice of starting the interview with such an explanation is generally
   A. *desirable*, because the applicant can then understand why the interview is necessary and what will be accomplished by it
   B. *desirable*, because it creates the rapport which is necessary to successful interviewing
   C. *undesirable*, because time will be saved by starting directly with the questions which must be asked
   D. *undesirable*, because the interviewer should have the choice of starting an interview in any manner he prefers

   2.____

3. For you to use responses such as "That's interesting," "Uh-huh," and "Good" during an interview with a patient is
   A. *desirable*, because they indicate that the investigator is attentive
   B. *undesirable*, because they are meaningless to the patient
   C. *desirable*, because the investigator is not supposed to talk excessively
   D. *undesirable*, because they tend to encourage the patient to speak freely

   3.____

4. During the course of a routine interview, the BEST tone of voice for an interviewer to use is
   A. authoritative   B. uncertain
   C. formal   D. conversational

   4.____

5. It is recommended that interviews which inquire into the personal background of an individual should be held in private.
   The BEST reason for this practice is that privacy
   A. allows the individual to talk freely about the details of his background
   B. induces contemplative thought on the part of the interviewed individual
   C. prevents any interruptions by departmental personnel during the interview
   D. most closely resembles the atmosphere of the individual's personal life

   5.____

2 (#2)

6. Assume that you are interviewing a patient to determine whether he has any savings accounts.
   To obtain this information, the MOST effective way to phrase your question would be:
   A. "You don't have any savings, do you?"
   B. "At which bank do you have a savings account?"
   C. "Do you have a savings account?"
   D. "May I assume that you have a savings account?"

6.____

7. You are interviewing a patient who is not cooperating to the extent necessary to get all required information. Therefore, you decide to be more forceful in your approach.
   In this situation, such a course of action is
   A. *advisable*, because such a change in approach may help to increase the patient's participation
   B. *advisable,* because you will be using your authority more effectively
   C. *inadvisable*, because you will not be able to change this approach if it doesn't produce results
   D. *inadvisable*, because an aggressive approach generally reduces the validity of the interview

7.____

8. You have attempted to interview a patient on two separate occasions, and both attempts were unsuccessful. The patient has been totally uncooperative and you sense a personal hostility toward you.
   Of the following, the BEST way to handle this type of situation would be to
   A. speak to the patient in a courteous manner and ask him to explain exactly what he dislikes about you
   B. inform the patient that you will not allow personality conflicts to disrupt the interview
   C. make no further attempt to interview the patient and recommend that he be billed in full
   D. discuss the problem with your supervisor and suggest that another investigator be assigned to try to interview the patient

8.____

9. At the beginning of an interview, a patient with normal vision tells you that he is reluctant to discuss his finances. You realize that it will be necessary in this case to ask detailed questions about his net income.
   When you begin this line of questioning, of the following, the LEAST important aspect you should consider is your
   A. precise wording of the question   B. manner of questioning
   C. tone of voice   D. facial expressions

9.____

10. A caseworker under your supervision has been assigned the task of interviewing a man who is applying for foster home placement for his two children. The caseworker seeks your advice as to how to question this man, stating that she finds the applicant to be a timid and self-conscious person who seems torn between the necessity of having to answer the worker's questions truthfully and the effect he thinks his answers will have on his application.

10.____

111

Of the following, the BEST method for the caseworker to use in order to determine the essential facts in this case is to
- A. assure the applicant that he need not worry since the majority of applications for foster home placement are approved
- B. delay the applicant's narration of the facts important to the case until his embarrassment and fears have been overcome
- C. ignore the statements made by the applicant and obtain all the required information from his friends and relatives
- D. inform the applicant that all statements made by him will be verified and are subject to the law governing perjury

11. Assume that a worker is interviewing a boy in his assigned group in order to help him find a job.
    At the BEGINNING of the interview, the worker should
    - A. suggest a possible job for the youth
    - B. refer the youth to an employment agency
    - C. discuss the youth's work history and skills with him
    - D. refer the youth to the manpower and career development agency

12. As part of the investigation to locate an absent father, you make a field visit to interview one of the father's friends. Before beginning the interview, you identify yourself to the friend and show him your official identification.
    For you to do this is, generally,
    - A. *good practice*, because the friend will have proof that you are authorized to make such confidential investigations
    - B. *poor practice*, because the friend may not answer your questions when he knows why you are interviewing him
    - C. *good practice*, because your supervisor can confirm from the friend that you actually made the interview
    - D. *poor practice*, because the friend may warn the absent father that your agency is looking for him

13. You are interviewing a client in his home as part of your investigation of an anonymous complaint that he has been receiving Medicaid fraudulently.
    During the interview, the client frequently interrupts your questions to discuss the hardships of his life and the bitterness he feels about his medical condition.
    Of the following, the BEST way for you to deal with these discussions is to
    - A. cut them off abruptly, since the client is probably just trying to avoid answering your questions
    - B. listen patiently, since these discussions may be helpful to the client and may give you information for your investigation
    - C. remind the client that you are investigating a complaint against him and he must answer directly
    - D. seek to gain the client's confidence by discussing any personal or medical problems which you yourself may have

14. While interviewing an absent father to determine his ability to pay child support, you realize that his answers to some of your questions contradict his answers to other questions.
    Of the following, the BEST way for you to try to get accurate information from the father is to
    A. confront him with his contradictory answers and demand an explanation from him
    B. use your best judgment as to which of his answers are accurate and question him accordingly
    C. tell him that he has misunderstood your questions and that he must clarify his answers
    D. ask him the same questions in different words and follow up his answer with related questions

14.____

15. Assume that an applicant, obviously under a great deal of stress, talks continuously and rambles, making it difficult for you to determine the exact problem and her need.
    In order to make the interview more successful, it would be BEST for you to
    A. interrupt the applicant and ask her specific questions in order to get the information you need
    B. tell the applicant that her rambling may be a basic cause of her problem
    C. let the applicant continue talking as long as she wishes
    D. ask the applicant to get to the point because other people are waiting for you

15.____

16. A worker must be able to interview clients all day and still be able to listen and maintain interest.
    Of the following, it is MOST important for you to show interest in the client because, if you appear interested,
    A. the client is more likely to appreciate your professional status
    B. the client is more likely to disclose a greater amount of information
    C. the client is less likely to tell lie
    D. you are more likely to gain your supervisor's approval

16.____

17. When you are interviewing clients, it is important to notice and record how they say what they say—angrily, nervously, or with "body English"—because these signs may
    A. tell you that the client's words are the opposite of what the client feels and you may need to dig to find out what those feeling are
    B. be the prelude to violent behavior which no aide is prepared to handle
    C. show that the client does not really deserve serious consideration
    D. be important later should you be asked to defend what you did for the client

17.____

18. The patient you are interviewing is reticent and guarded in responding to your questions. He is not providing the information needed to complete his application for medical assistance.
    In this situation, the one of the following which is the MOST appropriate course of action for you to take FIRST is to

18.____

A. end the interview and ask him to contact you when he is ready to answer your questions
B. advise the patient that you cannot end the interview until he has provided all the information you need to complete the application
C. emphasize to the patient the importance of the questions and the need to answer them in order to complete the application
D. advise the patient that if he answers your questions the interview will be easier for both of you

19. At the end of an interview with a patient, he describes a problem he is having with his teenage son, who is often truant and may be using narcotics. The patient asks you for advice in handling his son.
Of the following, the MOST appropriate action for you to take is to
A. make an appointment to see the patient and his son together
B. give the patient a list of drug counseling programs to which he may refer his son
C. suggest to the patient that his immediate concern should be his own hospitalization rather than his son's problem
D. tell the patient that you are not qualified to assist him but will attempt to find out who can

20. A MOST appropriate condition in the use of direct questions to obtain personal data in an interview is that, whenever possible,
A. the direct questions be used only as a means of encouraging the person interviewed to talk about himself
B. provision be made for recording the information
C. the direct questions be used only after all other methods have failed
D. the person being interviewed understands the reason for requesting the information

KEY (CORRECT ANSWERS)

1.	D	11.	C
2.	A	12.	A
3.	A	13.	B
4.	D	14.	D
5.	A	15.	A
6.	B	16.	B
7.	A	17.	A
8.	D	18.	C
9.	A	19.	D
10.	B	20.	D

READING COMPREHENSION
UNDERSTANDING AND INTERPRETING WRITTEN MATERIAL

EXAMINATION SECTION
TEST 1

DIRECTIONS: Each question or incomplete statement is followed by several suggested answers or completions. Select the one that BEST answers the question or completes the statement. *PRINT THE LETTER OF THE CORRECT ANSWER IN THE SPACE AT THE RIGHT.*

Questions 1-2.

DIRECTIONS: Questions 1 and 2 are to be answered SOLELY on the basis of the following passage.

    The new suburbia that is currently being built does not look much different from the old; there has, however, been an increase in the class and race polarization that has been developing between the suburbs and the cities for several generations now. The suburbs have become the home for an ever larger proportion of working-class, middle-class, and upper-class whites; the cities, for an even larger proportion of poor and non-white people. A great number of cities are 30 to 50 percent non-white in population, with more and larger ghettos than cities have ever had. Now, there is greater urban poverty on the one hand, and stronger suburban opposition to open housing and related policies to solve the cities' problems on the other hand. The urban crisis will worsen; and although there is no shortage of rational solutions, nothing much will be done about the crisis unless white America permits a radical change of public policy and undergoes a miraculous change of attitude towards its cities and their populations.

1. Which of the following statements is IMPLIED by the above passage?

   A. The percentage of non-whites in the suburbs is increasing.
   B. The policies of suburbanites have contributed to the seriousness of the urban crisis.
   C. The problems of the cities defy rational solutions.
   D. There has been a radical change in the appearance of both suburbia and the cities in the past few years.

2. Of the following, the title which BEST describes the passage's main theme is:

   A. THE NEW SUBURBIA
   B. URBAN POVERTY
   C. URBAN-SUBURBAN POLARIZATION
   D. WHY AMERICANS WANT TO LIVE IN THE SUBURBS

Questions 3-4.

DIRECTIONS: Questions 3 and 4 are to be answered selecting the BEST interpretation of the following paragraph.

One of the most familiar *type* dichotomies is Jung's introvert versus extrovert. Introverts are motivated by principles, extroverts by expediency; introverts are thinkers, extroverts are doers; and so on. Analysis of the way people react to principle versus expediency situations, however, has demonstrated that most people would have to be described as ambiverts (i.e., they exhibit both introverted and extroverted behavior depending upon the specific situation). Of course, some people behave in a more introverted way than others. A graphic representation of the number of persons exhibiting various degrees of such behavior along a continuum would approximate the familiar bell-shaped curve.

3. A. Extreme extroverts exhibit deviant behavior.
   B. The bell-shaped curve would indicate that there are slightly more introverts than extroverts.
   C. A continuum is used to determine whether a person is an introvert or an extrovert.
   D. There is really very little difference between an introvert, an extrovert, or an ambivert.

4. A. Extroverts are not thinkers, and introverts are not doers.
   B. Ambiverts *think* more than they *do*.
   C. Ambiverts outnumber introverts in the general society.
   D. Extroverts possess fewer principles than introverts.

5. The fundamental desires for food, shelter, family, and approval, and their accompanying instinctive forms of behavior, are among the most important forces in human life because they are essential to and directly connected with the preservation and the welfare of the individual as well as of the race.
   According to this statement,

   A. as long as human beings are permitted to act instinctively, they will act wisely
   B. the instinct for self-preservation makes the individual consider his own welfare rather than that of others
   C. racial and individual welfare depend upon the fundamental desires
   D. the preservation of the race demands that instinctive behavior be modified

6. The growth of our cities, the increasing tendency to move from one part of the country to another, the existence of people of different cultures in the neighborhood, have together made it more and more difficult to secure group recreation as part of informal family and neighborhood life.
   According to this statement,

   A. the breaking up of family and neighborhood ties discourages new family and neighborhood group recreation
   B. neighborhood recreation no longer forms a significant part of the larger community
   C. the growth of cities crowds out the development of all recreational activities
   D. the non-English-speaking people do not accept new activities easily

7. Sublimation consists in directing some inner urge, arising from a lower psychological level into some channel of interest on a higher psychological level. Pugnaciousness, for example, is directed into some athletic activity involving combat, such as football or boxing, where rules of fair play and the ethics of the game lift the destructive urge for combat into a constructive experience and offer opportunities for the development of character and personality.

According to this statement,

   A. the manner of self-expression may be directed into constructive activities
   B. athletic activities such as football and boxing are destructive of character
   C. all conscious behavior on high psychological levels indicates the process of sublimation
   D. the rules of fair play are inconsistent with pugnaciousness

Questions 8-9.

DIRECTIONS: Questions 8 and 9 are to be answered on the basis of the following passage.

Just why some individuals choose one way of adjusting to their difficulties and others choose other ways is not known. Yet what an individual does when he is thwarted remains a reasonably good key to the understanding of his personality. If his responses to thwart-ings are emotional explosions and irrational excuses, he is tending to live in an unreal world. He may need help to regain the world of reality, the cause-and-effect world recognized by generations of thinkers and scientists. Perhaps he needs encouragement to redouble his efforts. Perhaps, on the other hand, he is striving for the impossible and needs to substitute a worthwhile activity within the range of his abilities. It is the part of wisdom to learn the nature of the world and of oneself in relation to it and to meet each situation as intelligently and as adequately as one can.

8. The title that BEST expresses the idea of this paragraph is

   A. ADJUSTING TO LIFE
   B. ESCAPE FROM REALITY
   C. THE IMPORTANCE OF PERSONALITY
   D. EMOTIONAL CONTROL

9. The writer argues that all should

   A. substitute new activities for old
   B. redouble their efforts
   C. analyze their relation to the world
   D. seek encouragement from others

Questions 10-15.

DIRECTIONS: Questions 10 through 15 are to be answered SOLELY on the basis of the information given in the paragraph below.

The use of role-playing as a training technique was developed during the past decade by social scientists, particularly psychologists, who have been active in training experiments. Originally, this technique was applied by clinical psychologists who discovered that a patient appears to gain understanding of an emotionally disturbing situation when encouraged to act out roles in that situation. As applied in government and business organizations, the purpose of role-playing is to aid employees to understand certain work problems involving interpersonal relations and to enable observers to evaluate various reactions to them. Thus, for example, on the problem of handling grievances, two individuals from the group might be selected to act out extemporaneously the parts of subordinate and supervisor. When this situation is enacted by various pairs among the class and the techniques and results are discussed, the members of the group are presumed to reach conclusions about the most effective means of handling similar situations. Often the use of role reversal, where participants take parts different from their actual work roles, assists individuals to gain more insight into other people's problems and viewpoints. Although role-playing can be a rewarding training device, the trainer must be aware of his responsibilities. If this technique is to be successful, thorough briefing of both actors and observers as to the situation in question, the participants' roles, and what to look for, is essential.

10. The role-playing technique was FIRST used for the purpose of

    A. measuring the effectiveness of training programs
    B. training supervisors in business organizations
    C. treating emotionally disturbed patients
    D. handling employee grievances

11. When role-playing is used in private business as a training device, the CHIEF aim is to

    A. develop better relations between supervisor and subordinate in the handling of grievances
    B. come up with a solution to a specific problem that has arisen
    C. determine the training needs of the group
    D. increase employee understanding of the human relation factors in work situations

12. From the above passage, it is MOST reasonable to conclude that when role-playing is used, it is preferable to have the roles acted out by

    A. only one set of actors
    B. no more than two sets of actors
    C. several different sets of actors
    D. the trainer or trainers of the group

13. Based on the above passage, a trainer using the technique of role reversal in a problem of first-line supervision should assign a senior enforcement agent to play the part of a(n)

    A. enforcement agent
    B. senior enforcement agent
    C. principal enforcement agent
    D. angry citizen

14. It can be inferred from the above passage that a *limitation* of role-play as a training method is that

    A. many work situations do not lend themselves to role-play
    B. employees are not experienced enough as actors to play the roles realistically
    C. only trainers who have psychological training can use it successfully
    D. participants who are observing and not acting do not benefit from it

15. To obtain good results from the use of role-play in training, a trainer should give participants

    A. a minimum of information about the situation so that they can act spontaneously
    B. scripts which illustrate the best method for handling the situation
    C. a complete explanation of the problem and the roles to be acted out
    D. a summary of work problems which involve interpersonal relations

Questions 16-20.

DIRECTIONS: Questions 16 through 20 are to be answered SOLELY on the basis of the following passage.

The dynamics of group behavior may be summed up by saying that the individuals in a group respond to many lines of force arising out of their relationship with every other member of a group and with the group itself. In addition, each member of a group quite naturally brings with him all the things that have been *bugging* him. Then, the situation or the setting in which the group meets, as well as the circumstances related to the formation of the group, are active working forces exerting some X influence upon each member of the group. Lastly, all of this kinetic energy is at the control of the person seeking to lead the group into some kind of action. If he is to produce something meaningful with the members of a group, he must utilize this energy, contain it, dissipate it in some fashion, or be faced with difficulty.

This dynamic force inherent in any group can be harnessed by a supervisor with leadership qualities, but it must be controlled. It will not be contained by acting without consultation with group members, by refusing to accept suggestions coming from the group, or by refusing to explain or even give notice of contemplated actions. However, it can be controlled by placing the focus upon the members of the group, rather than upon the supervisor, and depending upon the leader-supervisor to provide as many participative experiences for group members as is commensurate with his own decision-making responsibilities. It is true that this is subordinate-centered leadership, but the supervisor can gain strength through permissive leadership without sacrificing basic responsibilities for effective planning and adequate control of operations.

16. Of the following titles, the one that MOST closely describes the reading selection is

    A. THE SUPERVISOR WITH DYNAMIC LEADERSHIP POTENTIAL
    B. DISSIPATION OF GROUP ENERGY
    C. CONTROLLING GROUP RELATIONSHIPS
    D. SACRIFICING BASIC RESPONSIBILITIES

17. According to the above passage, the setting in which the group meets

    A. can readily be modified either in whole or in part
    B. must be made meaningful in some fashion to foster skills development
    C. can provide the sole source of group dynamics
    D. is one of the forces exerting influence on group members

18. According to the above passage, the members of the group

    A. should control their formation and development
    B. should control the circumstances of their meeting
    C. are influenced by the forces creating the group
    D. dissipate meaningless energy

19. According to the above passage, the effective group leader

    A. controls the focus of the group
    B. focuses his control over the group
    C. controls group forces by focusing upon group members
    D. focuses the group's forces upon himself

20. According to the above passage, effective leadership consists in

    A. partially compromising decision-making responsibilities
    B. partially sacrificing some basic responsibilities
    C. sometimes cultivating permissive subordinates
    D. providing participation for members of the group consistent with decision-making imperatives

Questions 21-22.

DIRECTIONS: Questions 21 and 22 are to be answered SOLELY on the basis of the following passage.

This country was built on the puritanical belief that honest toil was the foundation of moral rectitude, the cement of society, and the uphill road to progress. Idleness was sin. As a result, we treat free time today as a conditional joy. We permit outselves to relax only as a reward for hard work or as the recreation needed to put us back into shape for the job. Thus, the aimless delightful play of children gives way in adult life to a serious dedication to golf, the game that is so good for business.

21. According to the above passage, during former times in this country respectable work was considered to be MOST NEARLY a

    A. way to improve health
    B. form of recreation
    C. developer of good character
    D. reward for leisure

22. According to the point of view presented in the above passage, it would be MOST reasonable to assume that an employer would consider an employee's vacation to be a time for the employee to

    A. determine his own leisure time priorities
    B. loaf and relax
    C. learn new recreational skills
    D. increase his effectiveness at work

Questions 23-24.

DIRECTIONS: Questions 23 and 24 are to be answered SOLELY on the basis of the following passage.

A recent study revealed some very concrete evidence concerning the relationship between avocations and mental health. A number of well-adjusted persons were surveyed as to the type, number, and duration of their hobbies. The findings were compared to those from a similar survey of mentally disturbed persons. In the well-adjusted group, both the number of hobbies and the intensity with which they were pursued were far greater than that of the mentally disturbed group.

23. According to the above passage, the study showed that 23.____
    A. well-adjusted people engage in hobbies more widely and deeply than do mentally disturbed people
    B. hobbies, if taken seriously, serve to keep most people mentally well
    C. mental patients should be taught hobbies as a part of their therapy
    D. the degree of interest in hobbies plays an important role in maintaining good mental health

24. In reference to the study mentioned in the above passage, it is MOST accurate to say that it appears to have 24.____
    A. been based on a carefully-structured, complex research design
    B. considered the variables of mental health and hobby involvement
    C. contained a general definition of mental health
    D. given evidence of a causal relationship between hobbies and mental health

25. Across the years, our social sense has decreed that every position of social leadership, every place of influence, every concentration of social power in the hands of an individual, every instrument or agency that has aggregated to itself the power to affect the common welfare, has become by that very fact a social trust that must be administered for the common good. In our moral world, the social obligations of power are real and unescapable. On the basis of this statement, it would be MOST correct to state that 25.____
    A. an individual engaged in private enterprise does not have the social responsibility of one who holds public office
    B. social leadership carries with it the obligation to administer for the public good
    C. in our moral world, the abuse of the power is real and unescapable
    D. social leadership depends upon the aggregation of power in the hands of an individual or in an agency that wields concentrated influence

KEY (CORRECT ANSWERS)

1. B
2. C
3. A
4. C
5. C

6. A
7. A
8. A
9. C
10. C

11. D
12. C
13. A
14. A
15. C

16. C
17. D
18. C
19. C
20. D

21. C
22. D
23. A
24. B
25. B

———

TEST 2

DIRECTIONS: Each question or incomplete statement is followed by several suggested answers or completions. Select the one that BEST answers the question or completes the statement. *PRINT THE LETTER OF THE CORRECT ANSWER IN THE SPACE AT THE RIGHT.*

Questions 1-9.

DIRECTIONS: Questions 1 through 9 are to be answered SOLELY on the basis of the following passage.

    The establishment of a procedure whereby the client's rent is paid directly by the Social Service agency has been suggested recently by many people in the Social Service field. It is believed that such a procedure would be advantageous to both the agency and the client. Under the current system, clients often complain that their rent allowances are not for the correct amount. Agencies, in turn, have had to cope with irate landlords who complain that they are not receiving rent checks until much later than their due date.

    The proposed new system would involve direct payment of the client's rent by the agency to the landlord. Clients would not receive a monthly rent allowance. Under one possible implementation of such a system, special rent payment offices would be set up in each borough and staffed by Social Service clerical personnel. Each office would handle all work involved in sending out monthly rent payments. Each client would receive monthly notification from the Social Service agency that his rent has been paid. A rent office would be established for every three Social Service centers in each borough. Only in cases where the rental exceeds $350 per month would payment be made and records kept by the Social Service center itself rather than a special rent office. However, clients would continue to make all direct contacts through the Social Service center.

    Files in the rent offices would be organized on the basis of client rental. All cases involving monthly rents up to, but not exceeding, $300 would be placed in salmon-colored folders. Cases with rents from $300 to $500 would be placed in buff folders, and those with rents exceeding $500, but less than $750 would be filed in blue folders. If a client's rental changed, he would be required to notify the center as soon as possible so that this information could be brought up-to-date in his folder and the color of his folder changed if necessary. Included in the information needed, in addition to the amount of rent, are the size of the apartment, the type of heat, and the number of flights of stairs to climb if there is no elevator.

    Discussion as to whether the same information should be required of clients residing in city projects was resolved with the decision that the identical system of filing and updating of files should apply to such project tenants. The basic problem that might arise from the institution of such a program is that clients would resent being unable to pay their own rent. However, it is likely that such resentment would be only a temporary reaction to change and would disappear after the new system became standard procedure. It has been suggested that this program first be experimented with on a small scale to determine what problems may arise and how the program can be best implemented.

1. According to the above passage, there a number of complaints about the current system of rent payments. Which of the following is a complaint expressed in the passage?   1._____

A. Landlords complain that clients sometimes pay the wrong amount for their rent.
B. Landlords complain that clients sometimes do not pay their rent on time.
C. Clients say that the Social Service agency sometimes does not mail the rent out on time.
D. Landlords say that they sometimes fail to receive a check for the rent.

2. Assume that there are 15 Social Service centers in Manhattan.
According to the above passage, the number of rent offices that should be established in that borough under the new system is

   A. 1   B. 3   C. 5   D. 15

3. According to the above passage, a client under the new system would receive

   A. a rent receipt from the landlord indicating that Social Services has paid the rent
   B. nothing since his rent has been paid by Social Services
   C. verification from the landlord that the rent was paid
   D. notices of rent payment from the Social Service agency

4. According to the above passage, a case record involving a client whose rent has changed from $310 to $540 per month should be changed from a _____ folder to a _____ folder.

   A. blue; salmon-colored   B. buff; blue
   C. salmon-colored; blue   D. yellow; buff

5. According to the above passage, if a client's rental is lowered because of violations in his building, he would be required to notify the

   A. building department   B. landlord
   C. rent payment office   D. Social Service center

6. Which one of the following kinds of information about a rented apartment is NOT mentioned in the above passage as being necessary to include in the client's folder?
The

   A. floor number, if in an apartment house with an elevator
   B. rental, if in a city project apartment
   C. size of the apartment, if in a two-family house
   D. type of heat, if in a city project apartment

7. Assume that the rent payment proposal discussed in the above passage is approved and ready for implementation in the city.
Which of the following actions is MOST in accordance with the proposal described in the above passage?

   A. Change over completely and quickly to the new system to avoid the confusion of having clients under both systems.
   B. Establish rent payment offices in all of the existing Social Service centers.
   C. Establish one small rent payment office in Manhattan for about six months.
   D. Set up an office in each borough and discontinue issuing rent allowances.

8. According to the above passage, it can be inferred that the MOST important drawback of the new system would be that once a program is started clients might feel

A. they have less independence than they had before
B. unable to cope with problems that mature people should be able to handle
C. too far removed from Social Service personnel to successfully adapt to the new requirements
D. too independent to work with the system

9. The above passage suggests that the proposed rent program be started as a pilot program rather than be instituted immediately throughout the city.
Of the following possible reasons for a pilot program, the one which is stated in the above passage as the MOST direct reason is that

A. any change made would then be only on a temporary basis
B. difficulties should be determined from small-scale implementation
C. implementation on a wide scale is extremely difficult
D. many clients might resent the new system

Questions 10-14.

DIRECTIONS: Questions 10 through 14 are to be answered SOLELY on the basis of the following passage.

PROCEDURE TO OBTAIN REIMBURSEMENT FROM DEPARTMENT OF HEALTH FOR CARE OF PHYSICALLY HANDICAPPED CHILDREN

Application for reimbursement must be received by the Department of Health within 30 days of the date of hospital admission in order that the Department of Hospitals may be reimbursed from the date of admission. Upon determination that patient is physically handicapped, as defined under Chapter 780 of the State Laws, the ward clerk shall prepare seven copies of Department of Health Form A-1 or A-2, Application and Authorization, and shall submit six copies to the institutional Collections Unit. The ward clerk shall also initiate two copies of Department of Health Form B-1 or B-2, Financial and Social Report, and shall forward them to the institutional Collections Unit for completion of Page 1 and routing to the Social Service Division for completion of the Social Summary on Page 2. Social Service Division shall return Form B-1 or B-2 to the institutional Collections Unit which shall forward one copy of Form B-1 or B-2 and six copies of Form A-1 or A-2 to Central Office Division of Collections for transmission to Bureau of Handicapped Children, Department of Health.

10. According to the above paragraph, the Department of Health will pay for hospital care for

A. children who are physically handicapped
B. any children who are ward patients
C. physically handicapped adults and children
D. thirty days for eligible children

11. According to the procedure described in the above paragraph, the definition of what constitutes a physical handicap is made by the

A. attending physician
B. laws of the State
C. Social Service Division
D. ward clerk

12. According to the above paragraph, Form B-1 or B-2 is   12.____
    A. a three page form containing detachable pages
    B. an authorization form issued by the Department of Hospitals
    C. completed by the ward clerk after the Social Summary has been entered
    D. sent to the institutional Collections Unit by the Social Service Division

13. According to the above paragraph, after their return by the Social Service Division, the institutional Collections Unit keeps   13.____
    A. one copy of Form A-1 or A-2
    B. one copy of Form A-1 or A-2 and one copy of Form B-1 or B-2
    C. one copy of Form B-1 or B-2
    D. no copies of Forms A-1 or A-2 or B-1 or B-2

14. According to the above paragraph, forwarding the *Application and Authorization* to the Department of Health is the responsibility of the   14.____
    A. Bureau for Handicapped Children
    B. Central Office Division of Collections
    C. Institutional Collections Unit
    D. Social Service Division

Questions 15-19.

DIRECTIONS: Questions 15 through 19 are to be answered SOLELY on the basis of the following *total annual income adjustment* rules for household income.

The basic annual income is to be calculated by multiplying the total of the current weekly salaries of all adults (age 21 or over) by 52.

Upward and downward adjustments must be made to the basic annual salary to arrive at the *total adjusted annual income* for the household.

UPWARD ADJUSTMENTS

1. Add one-half of total overtime payments in the previous two years.
2. Add that part of the earnings of any minor in the household that exceeded $3,000 in the previous 12 months.

DOWNWARD ADJUSTMENTS

1. Deduct one-third of all educational tuition payments for household members in the previous 12 months.
2. Deduct the expense of going to and from work in excess of $30 per week per household member. This adjustment is made on the basis of the previous 12 months and should be computed for each household member individually for each week in which excess travel expenses were incurred.
3. Deduct that part of child care expenses which exceeded $1,500 in the previous 12 months.

15. In Household A, the husband has a weekly salary of $585 and the wife has just had her salary increased from $390 to $420 per week. In the previous 12 months, each had a paid continuous vacation of four weeks; the husband had to travel to a secondary work location every fourth week. His travel costs during those weeks were $42 per week. In the previous 12 months, they had child care costs of $1,470.
What is the TOTAL annual adjusted income for the household?

    A. $52,116   B. $52,104   C. $51,828   D. $51,234

    15._____

16. In Household B, the husband has a weekly salary of $540. In the past year, he received overtime payments of $255. In the year before that, he received overtime payments of $1,221. His wife has just begun a job with a weekly salary of $330. As a result of this, annual child care expenses will be $2,130.
What is the TOTAL annual adjusted income for the household?

    A. $45,240   B. $45,348   C. $45,978   D. $46,824

    16._____

17. In Household C, the husband has a weekly salary of $555. The wife has a weekly salary of $390. They each had expenses of $33 per week when traveling to and from work in the previous 12 months. The husband had an annual paid vacation of five weeks, and the wife had an annual paid vacation of three weeks in the previous year. There is a daughter in college for whom annual tuition payments of $1,710 were made in the previous 12 months.
What is the TOTAL annual adjusted income for the household?

    A. $48,258   B. $48,282   C. $49,140   D. $50,022

    17._____

18. In Household D, the husband has a weekly salary of $465, the wife has a weekly salary of $330, and an adult daughter has a weekly salary of $285. The husband received overtime payments of $1,890 in the past year. In the year before that, he received no overtime payments. In the past year, there were weekly child care expenses of $210 per week for 47 weeks.
What is the TOTAL adjusted annual income for the household?

    A. $57,105   B. $48,735   C. $47,235   D. $46,845

    18._____

19. In Household E, the husband has a weekly salary of $615. The wife has a weekly salary of $195. During the past year, there were tuition payments of $255 per month for 10 months per year for children in grade school and annual tuition payments of $2,310 for a boy in high school. What is the TOTAL adjusted annual income for the household?

    A. $39,570   B. $39,690   C. $40,500   D. $42,120

    19._____

Questions 20-22.

DIRECTIONS: Questions 20 through 22 are to be answered SOLELY on the basis of the following paragraph.

Effective December 1, 2004, tenants thereafter admitted to public housing projects shall pay rents in accordance with Schedule DV if they are veterans of the Gulf War, and in accordance with Schedule D if they are not Gulf War veterans. However, all recipients of public assistance shall pay rents in accordance with Schedule DW. Tenants of public housing projects prior to the effective date of this change will continue to pay rent in accordance with Schedule C2 if they are veterans of the Iraqi War or the Gulf War, in accordance with

Schedule C if they are not such veterans, and in accordance with Schedule CW if they receive public assistance and if they are not eligible to use the C2 Schedule. In addition, effective December 1, 2004, when a tenant is accepted for assistance by the Department of Welfare, if such acceptance requires that the tenant pay a new rental as outlined above, the effective date of the new rental is to be the first of the month following the date that the tenant is accepted for assistance by the Department of Welfare instead of the first of the month following the date of application for public assistance.

20. John Jones, a Gulf War veteran, has been living in a public housing project since June 2003. He applied for public assistance on November 15, 2004 and was accepted for public assistance on December 17, 2004.
    If he continues to receive public assistance, his present rent should be based on the _____ Schedule.

    A. C2   B. CW   C. DV   D. DW

21. Jack Smith, who is not a veteran, moves into a public housing project in January 2006. If it should become necessary for him to apply for public assistance on February 10, 2006 and should he be accepted for such assistance on March 5, 2006, the rent that he pays in March 2006 should be based on the _____ Schedule.

    A. C   B. CW   C. D   D. DW

22. John Doe, a veteran of the Iraqi War, was admitted to a public housing project in August 2004. He applied for public assistance on February 1, 2005 and was accepted for such assistance on March 1, 2005.
    On April 1, 2005, his rent should

    A. change to the C2 Schedule
    B. remain on the C2 Schedule, as previously
    C. change to the CW Schedule
    D. remain on the CW Schedule, as previously

Questions 23-25.

DIRECTIONS: Questions 23 through 25 are to be answered SOLELY on the basis of the following paragraph.

It has been proposed that an act be passed to provide for family allowances in the form of cash payments, normally to mothers, for children under sixteen years of age. Allowances are supposed to be spent exclusively for the care and education of the children; otherwise, they may be discontinued. They would vary in amount according to the age of the child and would be conditional upon satisfactory school attendance and accomplishment. The allowance would be paid to all families, regardless of means, but income tax exemptions for dependents would be reduced in consequence. The act would also permit the withdrawal of children from school and their entrance into the labor market after completing eighth grade. However, there would be no financial advantage in sending a child to work since the allowances would approximate the child's net earnings. Proponents of this proposal claim as advantages that it would provide social justice by taking into account elements of family need not possible under any normal wage structure system, be simple to administer, encourage an increase in the birth rate, remove unwilling or incapable students from our middle schools, and provide financial aid to poor, large families without the stigma of public welfare.

23. According to the proposal, the one of the following factors which would be LEAST likely to cause a variation in the amount of the allowance to a family or cause a discontinuance of it is

    A. a change in family wealth
    B. poor school attendance record of a child
    C. a child's being left back
    D. use of the allowance money on a hobby of one of the parents

24. The LEAST accurate of the following statements concerning schooling under this proposal is:

    A. A 14-year-old girl attending the 6th grade of elementary school will not be permitted to leave school, even though her school work is unsatisfactory.
    B. A poor family will be encouraged to continue the schooling of their 15-year-old twins who are in the junior year of high school.
    C. A 14-year-old boy who has been graduated from elementary school, but whose school attendance has been unsatisfactory, will not be permitted to attend high school.
    D. The family of a 17-year-old high school senior who is an honor student will not receive an allowance.

25. College attendance of bright children of poor families may be aided by this proposal because

    A. such children will be assured of higher marks
    B. families are likely to be smaller and consequently parents will be better able to send their children to college
    C. more scholarships are likely to be offered by private colleges as a result of this proposal
    D. the financial subsidy granted for a child under 16 may help the family save money towards a college education

KEY (CORRECT ANSWERS)

1.	B	11.	B
2.	C	12.	D
3.	D	13.	C
4.	B	14.	B
5.	D	15.	A
6.	A	16.	C
7.	C	17.	B
8.	A	18.	B
9.	B	19.	C
10.	A	20.	A

21. C
22. B
23. A
24. C
25. D

ARITHMETICAL REASONING
EXAMINATION SECTION
TEST 1

DIRECTIONS: Each question or incomplete statement is followed by several suggested answers or completions. Select the one that BEST answers the question or completes the statement. *PRINT THE LETTER OF THE CORRECT ANSWER IN THE SPACE AT THE RIGHT.*

1. On January 1, a family was receiving supplementary monthly public assistance of $280 for food, $240 for rent, and $140 for other necessities. In the spring, their rent rose by 10%, and their rent allotment was adjusted accordingly. In the summer, due to the death of a family member, their allotments for food and other necessities were reduced by 1/7.
Their monthly allowance check in the fall should be
   A. $623   B. $644   C. $664   D. $684

2. Twice a month, a certain family receives a $340 general allowance for rent, food, and clothing expense. In addition, the family receives a specific supplementary allotment for utilities of $384 a year, which is added to their semi-monthly check.
If the general allowance alone is reduced by 5%, what will be the TOTAL amount of their next semi-monthly check?
   A. $323   B. $339   C. $340   D. $355

3. If each supervising clerk in a certain unit sees an average of 9 clients in a 7-hour day and there are 15 supervising clerks in the unit, APPROXIMATELY how many clients will be seen in a 35-hour week?
   A. 315   B. 405   C. 675   D. 945

4. In one day, an aide receives 18 inquiries by phone and 27 inquiries in person. What percentage of the inquiries received that day were by phone?
   A. 33%   B. 40%   C. 45%   D. 60%

5. If the weekly paychecks for 5 employees are $258.64, $325.48, $287.50, and $313.12, then the combined weekly income for the 5 employee is
   A. $1,455.68   B. $1,456.08   C. $1,462.68   D. $1,474.08

6. Suppose that there are 17 aides working in an office where many community complaints are received by telephone. In one ten-day period, 4,250 calls were received.
If the same number of calls were received each day and the aides divided the work load equally, about how many calls did each aide respond to daily?
   A. 25   B. 35   C. 75   D. 250

7. Suppose that an assignment was divided among 5 aides.
If the first aide spent 67 hours on the assignment, the second aide spent 95 hours, the third aide spent 52 hours, the fourth aide spent 78 hours, and the fifth aide spent 103 hours, what was the AVERAGE amount of time spent by each aide on the assignment? _____ hours.
   A. 71 B. 75 C. 79 D. 83

7.____

8. If there are 240 employees in a center and 1/3 are absent on the day of a bad snowstorm, how many employees were at work in the center on that day?
   A. 80 B. 120 C. 160 D. 200

8.____

9. Suppose that an aide takes 25 minutes to prepare a letter to a client.
If the aide is assigned to prepare 9 letters on a certain day, how much time should be set aside for this task? _____ hours.
   A. 3¾ B. 4¼ C. 4¾ D. 5¼

9.____

10. Suppose that a certain center uses both Form A and Form B in the course of its daily work and that Form A is used 4 times as often as Form B.
If the total number of both forms used in one week is 750, how many times was Form A used?
    A. 100 B. 200 C. 400 D. 600

10.____

11. Suppose a center has a budget of $2,185.40 from which 8 desks costing $156.10 apiece must be bought.
How many additional desks can be ordered from this budget after the 8 desks have been purchased?
    A. 4 B. 6 C. 9 D. 14

11.____

12. When researching a particular case, a team of 16 aides was asked to check through 234 folders to obtain the necessary information.
If half the aides worked twice as fast as the other half, and the slow group checked through 12 folders each hour, about how long would it take to complete the assignment? _____ hours.
    A. 4¼ B. 5 C. 6 D. 6½

12.____

13. The difference in the cost of two typewriters is $56.64.
If the less expensive typewriter costs $307.22, what is the cost of the other typewriter?
    A. $343.86 B. $344.06 C. $363.86 D. $364.06

13.____

14. At the start of a year, a family was receiving a public assistance grant of $382 twice a month, on the first and fifteenth of each month. On March 1, their rent allowance was decreased from $150 to $142 a month since they had moved to a smaller apartment. On August 1 their semi-monthly food allowance, which had been $80.40, was raised by 10%.
In that year, the TOTAL amount of money disbursed to this family was
    A. $4,544.20 B. $6,581.40 C. $9,088.40 D. $9,168.40

14.____

3 (#1)

15. It is discovered that a client has received double public assistance for 2 months by having been enrolled at two service centers of the Department of Social Services. The client should have received $168 twice a month instead of the double amount. He now agrees to repay the money by equal deductions from his public assistance check over a period of 12 months.
What will the amount of his NEXT check be?
   A. $112   B. $140   C. $154   D. $160

15.____

16. Suppose a study is being made of the composition of 3,550 families receiving public assistance. Of the first 1,050 families reviewed, 18% had four or more children.
If, in the remaining number of families, the percentage with four or more children is half as high as the percentage in the group already reviewed, then the percentage of families with four or more children in the entire group of families is MOST NEARLY
   A. 12   B. 14   C. 16   D. 17

16.____

17. Suppose that food prices have risen 13%, and an increase of the same amount has been granted in the food allotment given to people receiving public assistance.
If a family has been receiving $810 a month, 35% of which is allotted for food, then the TOTAL amount of public assistance this family receives per month will be changed to
   A. $805.42   B. $840.06   C. $846.86   D. $899.42

17.____

18. Assume that the food allowance is to be raised 5% in August but will be retroactive for four months to April.
The retroactive allowance is to be divided into equal sections and added to the public assistance checks for August, September, October, November, and December.
A family which has been receiving $840 monthly, 40% of which was allotted for food, will receive what size check in August?
   A. $853.44   B. $856.80   C. $861.00   D. $870.24

18.____

19. A blind client, who receives $210 public assistance twice a month, inherits 14 shares of stock worth $180 each. The client is required to sell the stock and spend his inheritance before receiving more public assistance.
Using his public assistance allowance as a guide, how many months are his new assets expected to last?
   A. 6   B. 7   C. 8   D. 12

19.____

20. The Department of Social Services has 16 service centers. These centers may be divided into those which are downtown and those which are uptown. Two of the centers are special service centers and are downtown, while the remainder of the centers are general service centers. There is a total of 7 service centers downtown.
The percentage of the general service centers which are uptown is MOST NEARLY
   A. 56   B. 64   C. 69   D. 79

20.____

133

21. For six months, a family lived in a 4-room apartment where they paid $380 a month. They made an intrasite move to a 4-room apartment where they paid $85 per room a month for six months.
Comparing the two six-month periods, the TOTAL amount of money the family saved by making the intrasite was
    A. $240   B. $290   C. $430   D. $590

22. To calculate a tenant's usable income, you should make Social Security deductions of 4.4 percent on salary up to a maximum of $9,000 and State Disability deductions of .5 percent on salary up to $3,000.
What does a tenant's combined deduction amount to if his annual salary is $13,400?
    A. $411.00   B. $568.60   C. $619.60   D. $700.00

23. If the temporary relocation expenses for housing are set at $18 per day for one adult and $10 per day for each additional person in a room, how much money is allowed for a woman and four children temporarily relocated in one room for a period of six days?
    A. $168   B. $348   C. $378   D. $518

24. According to relocation policy, a family relocating to private housing from federally-aided or certain other sites will be granted a relocation payment. This payment equals the difference between 1/5 of the family's yearly income and the scheduled yearly rent for a standard apartment for their size family.
Suppose a 2-person family whose yearly income is $12,900 has been unable to obtain public housing and so finds a one-bedroom private apartment. The scheduled rent for a one-bedroom apartment appropriate for their occupancy is $240 a month.
What payment will they receive?
    A. $240   B. $288   C. $300   D. $410

25. A family on a housing relocation site is paying $410 per month for rent. This represents 25% of their gross monthly income.
If the husband earns 4/5 of their total combined monthly income, how much does the wife earn per month?
    A. $328   B. $540   C. $1,280   D. $1,500

KEY (CORRECT ANSWERS)

1.	A		11.	B
2.	B		12.	D
3.	C		13.	C
4.	B		14.	D
5.	B		15.	B
6.	A		16.	A
7.	C		17.	C
8.	C		18.	D
9.	A		19.	A
10.	D		20.	B

21.	A
22.	A
23.	B
24.	C
25.	A

SOLUTIONS TO PROBLEMS

1. After spring, the rent allotment should be $(240+24) = $264. After the summer, the reduced allotment for food and other necessities should be $[(280+140) − 1/7(280+140)] = $(420-1/7(420)] = $(420-60) = $360. The monthly check in the fall including rent, food, and other necessities should be $360 + $264 = $624.

2. Amount of general allowance in the family's semi-monthly check = $340. Amount of utilities allotment in the family's semi-monthly check: ($\frac{384}{12}$ × ½) = $16. Amount of general allowance in family' semi-monthly check after a 5% reduction = $340 less 5% of $340 = $(340-17) = $3223. Total amount of the next month's semi-monthly check: Reduced general allowance + utilities allotment = $323 + $16 = $339.

3. During 7 hours, a total of (15)(9) = 135 clients can be seen. Thus, in 35 hours, a total of (135)(5) = 675 clients will be seen.

4. 18(18+27) = .40 = 40%

5. $258.64 + $325.48 + $287.34 + $271.50 + $313.12 = $1,456.08

6. 4250/10 = 425 calls per day. Then, 425/17 = 25

7. (67+95+52+78+103)/5 = 79 hours

8. Number present = (240)(2/3) = 160

9. (25)(9) = 225 min. = 3 hrs. 45 min. = 3 ¾ hours

10. Let x, 1/4x = number of forms A, B, respectively. Then, x + 1/4x = 750. Solving, x = 600

11. $2,185.40 − (8)($156.10) = $936.60. Then, $936.60 ÷ $156.10 = 6 desks

12. Since the slow group did 12 folders each hour, the faster group did 24 folders each hour. Then, 234/(12+24) = 6 ½ hrs.

13. Expensive typewriter costs $307.22 + $56.64 = $363.86

14. For months of January and February, the amount the family receives is $(382×2×2) = $1528
    For months of March through July, the family receives $(764-8) × 5 = $3780
    For months August through December, the family receives $(756+16.08) × 5 = $3860.40
    The total amount of money disbursed to this family is $1528 + $3780 + $3860.40 = $9,168.40

15. The overpayment for 2 months = ($168)(4) = $672. If this is paid back over 12 months, each month's amount is reduced by $672/12 = $56. Then, each check (semi-monthly) is reduced by $28. His next check will be $168 - $28 = $140

16. $(1050)(.18) + (2500)(.09) = 414$. Then, $414/3550 = 12\%$

17. $(\$810)(.35) = \$283.50$ originally allotted for food. The new food allotment = $(\$283.50)(1.13) = \$320.355$. The total assistance now = $\$810 - \$283.50 + \$320.355 = \$846.855$ or $\$846.86$

18. $(\$840)(.40) = \$336$ per month for food. The new food allowance = $(\$336)(1.05) = \$352.80$ per month. The difference of $\$16.80$ is retroactive to April, which means $(\$16.80)(9) = \$151.20$ additional money for August through December. Each check for these 5 months will be increased by $\$15.20/5 = 30.24$. Thus, the check in August = $\$840 + 30.24 = \$840 + 30.24 = \$870.24$

19. $(\$180)(14) = \$2520$. Then, $\$2520/\$420 = 6$ months

20. 5 general are downtown; 9 of 14 general are uptown; $9/14 \approx 64\%$

21. $(\$85)(4) = \$340$ per month. Savings per month = $\$380 - \$340 = \$40$ For six months, the savings = $\$240$

22. $(\$9000(.044) + (\$3000)(.005) = \$411$ total deductions

23. $(\$18+\$40)(6) = \$348$ relocation expenses

24. $(\$240)(12) - (1/5)(\$12,900) = \$300$ relocation payment

25. $\$410 \div .25 = \$1640$. The wife earns $(1640)(1/5) = \$328$ each month

TEST 2

DIRECTIONS: Each question or incomplete statement is followed by several suggested answers or completions. Select the one that BEST answers the question or completes the statement. *PRINT THE LETTER OF THE CORRECT ANSWER IN THE SPACE AT THE RIGHT.*

1. A project tenant who owns and drives a taxicab for living, reports for a three-month period an income of $6,250 after operating expenses of $1,300 have been considered. In addition, his tips are valued at 12% of his income before operating expenses.
   An estimate of his yearly income is MOST NEARLY
   A. $22,000 B. $23,000 C. $28,000
   D. $28,500 E. $29,000

   1.____

2. The maximum annual subsidy which can be paid by the State toward the operation of any low-rent housing project is the sum of the annual interest on the total original loan or building the project and 1% of the portion of the loan actually spent.
   If the original loan for a project was $8,000,000 at 1¾% interest, but only $7,500,000 was actually spent, then the MAXIMUM annual subsidy is
   A. $140,000 B. $145,000 C. $215,000
   D. $220,000 E. $271,250

   2.____

3. In 2020, the cost of repairs and maintenance at a certain housing project was $5,589 more than in 2019, representing an increase of 4.6%. A further increase at the same rate was anticipated for 2021.
   The cost of repairs and maintenance in 2021 was MOST NEARLY
   A. $127,100
   B. $132,700
   C. $132,900
   D. $133,000
   E. an amount which cannot be determined from the given data

   3.____

4. Each day a delivery truck used by the Housing Authority travels 25 miles from a project to a storehouse and 25 miles on the return trip. It travels at the rate of 30 miles per hour going to the storehouse and at the rate of 20 miles per hour returning.
   The average rate, in miles per hour, for the roundtrip is MOST NEARLY
   A. 24
   B. 25
   C. 26
   D. the square root of 600
   E. an amount which cannot be determined from the given data

   4.____

5. A report on the first 6,000 applications for apartments in a certain project containing 1,400 apartments indicated that those who were ineligible fell into four categories: 2,800 ineligible for reason A, 600 ineligible for reason B, 1,200 ineligible for reason C, and 400 ineligible for reason D.

   5.____

2 (#2)

If the same proportions continue for the remaining 21,500 applications, then the percentage of eligible applicants who can be given apartments in the project is MOST NEARLY
   A. 25   B. 30   C. 33   D. 40   E. 60

6. The number of applications for apartments in low-rent housing projects was 40,000 in 2019. The number of applications increased 5% in 2020, and increased again in 2021 by 6% over the 2,000 total.
The percentage by which the 2021 figures exceed the 2019 figures is
   A. 5.3   B. 6.0   C. 11.0   D. 11.3   E. 30.0

6.____

7. A rectangular lot, 75 feet by 11.0 feet, was purchased as part of a project site for $28,500.
The price per square foot of this lot is MOST NEARLY
   A. $2.85   B. $3.45   C. $3.95   D. $30.00   E. $30.95

7.____

8. It has been estimated that 125 kilowatt-hours of electricity are used each month in one average Housing Authority apartment at a cost of 14.8 cents per kilowatt-hour.
On this basis, the total cost of the electricity used in one year in a project containing 1,400 apartments is MOST NEARLY
   A. $20,000   B. $25,000   C. $200,000
   D. $250,000   E. $2,000,000

8.____

9. The walls and ceilings of 20 rooms are to be painted with the same kind of paint, each room being 15 feet long, 12 feet wide, and 10 feet high. Each room contains two windows, each 3 feet by 6 feet, and a door 3 feet by 8 feet, which are not to be painted. One gallon of paint covers 400 square feet of surface.
The number of gallons of paint needed is MOST NEARLY
   A. 33   B. 34   C. 35   D. 36   E. 75

9.____

10. A group of buildings is valued at $11,500,000. Assume that the cos of fire insurance for these buildings is 5.3 cents per $100 of valuation per year.
The cost of fire insurance for one year is MOST NEARLY
   A. $600   B. $6,000   C. $20,000
   D. $60,000   E. $2,000,000

10.____

11. Of the 15 employees in a certain unit, one-third earn $27,600 per year, three earn $32,600, one earns $46,400, and the rest earn $33,800.
The average salary of the employees of this unit is MOST NEARLY
   A. $31,000   B. $32,000   C. $33,000   D. $34,000   E. $35,000

11.____

12. Four pieces, each 2'8½" long, are cut from a piece of pipe 16½' long.
The length of the remaining piece of pipe is
   A. 6'8½"   B. 6'10"   C. 6'10⅜"   D. 6'11⅛"   E. 9'9½"

12.____

13. A tenant ears E dollars a month, spends S dollars a week, and saves the rest. The tenant's yearly savings can be expressed by
    A. 12(E-4S)   B. 12E – 52S   C. 12(E-S)
    D. 52(E-4S)   E. E - S

14. A unit of fifteen Housing Assistants has been assigned the job of interviewing applicants. Each interview takes 35 minutes, and an additional 10 minutes is needed for making entries and notes. The last interview each day is always scheduled so that it can be completed that day.
    The number of applicants who can be interviewed in a week, consisting of five 7-hour days, is MOST NEARLY
    A. 375   B. 525   C. 675   D. 700   E. 725

15. A review of the 14,000 applications for apartments in a certain project containing 1,200 apartments indicated that 4,800 applicants were eligible and 6,400 were ineligible. No decision could be reached on the remaining applications because certain necessary information was omitted by the applicants, but it was assumed that the proportion of eligible and ineligible applicants would remain the same as in those already decided.
    On the basis of these figures, the percentage of eligible applicants who can be given apartments in the project is
    A. under 17%   B. 17%   C. 20%
    D. 25%   E. 33 1/3%

16. An oil burner in a housing development burns 76 gallons of fuel oil per hour. At 9 A.M. on a very cold day, the superintendent asks the Housing Manager to put in an emergency order for more fuel oil. At that time, he reports that he has on hand 266 gallons. At noon, he again comes to the manager, notifying him that no oil has been delivered.
    The MAXIMUM amount of time that he can continue to furnish heat without receiving more oil is
    A. no more time   B. ½ hour   C. 1 hour
    D. 1½ hours   E. 2 hours

17. As a result of reports received by the Housing Authority concerning the reputed ineligibility of 756 tenants because of above-standard incomes, an intensive check of their employers has been ordered. Four housing assistants have been assigned to this task. At the end of 6 days at 7 hours each, they have checked on 336 tenants. In order to speed up the investigation, two more housing assistants are assigned to this point.
    If they worked at the same rate, the number of additional 7-hour days it would take to complete the job is MOST NEARLY
    A. 1   B. 3   C. 5   D. 7   E. 9

18. A municipal aide on a special trip is returning to his office from a point 17½ miles away, and makes the return trip to his office at an average speed of 25 miles an hour, except for a 15-minute stopover at one point to get a flat tire fixed. The time it should take him to reach his office is MOST NEARLY _____ minutes.
    A. 12   B. 22   C. 36   D. 42   E. 57

19. A district office has an assigned staff of 320 employees. Of this number, 25% are not available for duty due to illness, vacations, and other reasons. Of those who are available for duty, 1/8 are assigned to auditing and special projects, and the rest to handling the workload.
    The ACTUAL number of employees available for handling the workload is
    A. 350   B. 310   C. 270   D. 210   E. 180

20. Two dozen shuttlecocks and four badminton rackets are to be purchased for a playground. The shuttlecocks are priced at $3.60 each, and the rackets at $27.50 each. The playground receives a discount of 30% from these prices.
    The TOTAL cost of this equipment is
    A. $72.90   B. $114.30   C. $137.48   D. $186.00   E. $220.70

21. On January 1, a family was receiving public assistance allowance of $185 for food, $53 for clothing, $17.50 for utilities, and $22 for personal needs, all semi-monthly, and a monthly allowance of $550 for rent. On May 1, the rent allowance was increased by 12% but all other allowances remained the same for the rest of the year.
    The TOTAL amount of money granted this family during the year was
    A. $10,528   B. $13,262   C. $13,788
    D. $21,056   E. $27,676

22. It has been decided to make changes in food allotments to clients receiving public assistance to conform to changes in food costs. Of the food allowance, 30% is intended for meat, 30% for fruits and vegetables, 25% for groceries, and 15% for dairy products. Assume that meat prices have gone up 5%, and dairy prices have remained the same.
    For a family that has been receiving $400 per month for food, the new monthly food allowance will be
    A. $333   B. $375   C. $393   D. $403.50   E. $420

23. On January 1, a family was receiving a public assistance allowance of $195 for food, $63 for clothing, $27.50 for utilities, and $32 for personal needs, all semi-monthly, and a monthly allowance of $510 for rent. On June 1, the rent allowance was increased by 12%, but all other allowances remained the same for the rest of the year.
    The TOTAL amount of money granted this family during the year was
    A. $13,843.40   B. $14,107.20   C. $14,168.40
    D. $14,474.40   E. $16,886.80

5 (#2)

24. A member of a family receiving public assistance amounting to $600 monthly has obtained a part-time job, for which he is paid $40 a day. He is employed 3 days a week. His carfare costs $3.00 per day and his lunches $2.00 per day. Assume that there are $4^1/_3$ weeks per month. The Department of Welfare requires that net earnings be deducted from relief allowances.
The family's semi-monthly public assistance allowances should be reduced to
   A. $40.00   B. $72.50   C. $96.25   D. $123.75   E. $145.00

24._____

25. A couple living in a furnished room has been receiving a public assistance grant of $375 semi-monthly and has been paying a weekly rent of $75. The landlord has been granted a 12% increase in rent. Assume that a month consists of $4^1/_3$ weeks.
The amount of the new semi-monthly grant, including this rent increase, that the couple will receive will be MOST NEARLY
   A. $394.50   B. $397   C. $409   D. $514   E. $557

25._____

KEY (CORRECT ANSWERS)

1.	D		11.	B
2.	C		12.	A
3.	C		13.	B
4.	A		14.	C
5.	B		15.	C
6.	D		16.	B
7.	B		17.	C
8.	D		18.	E
9.	A		19.	D
10.	B		20.	C

21. C
22. C
23. C
24. B
25. A

SOLUTIONS TO PROBLEMS

1. For 3 months, income = $6,250 + (.12)($7550) = $7156. Then, annual income = ($7154)(4) = $28,624, closest to $28,500.

2. Maximum annual subsidy = ($8,000,000)(.0175) + (.01)($7,500,000) = $215,000

3. Cost in 2019 = $5589/.046 = $121,500. The cost in 2020 = $121,500 + $5589 = $127,089. This means the cost in 2021 = ($127,089)(1.046) = $132,900

4. Average rate = total distance/total time = (25+25) ÷ (25/30 + 25/20) = 24 mph

5. Out of 600, number of eligible = 6000 – 2800 – 600 – 1200 – 400 = 1000. Thus, for 27,500 applications, (1/6)(27,500) = 4583 would be eligible. Finally, 1400 ÷ 4583 ≈ 30%

6. Number of applications in 2020 = (40,000)(1.05) = 42,000. Number of applications in 2021 = (42,000)(1.06) = 44,520. Then, (44,520–40,000) ÷ 40,000 = 11.3%

7. $28,500 ÷ [(75×110)] = $3.45 per sq. ft.

8. Total cost = (125)(.148)(12)(1400) = $310,800; closest to choice D of $250,000

9. Painted area of each room = (2)(15)(10) + (2)(12)(10) + (15)(12) – (2)(3)(6) – (3)(8) = 660 sq. ft. So, (20)(660) = 13,200 sq. ft. to be painted in all rooms. Finally, 13,200/400 = 33 gallons of paint needed

10. Insurance cost = (.053)($11,500,000)/$100 = $6095, closest to $6000

11. [(5)($27,600) + (3)($32,600) + (1)($46,400) + (6)($33,800)]/15 = $32,233 closest to $32,000

12. 16½ - (4)(2'5³/₈") = 16'6" – 8'21½" = 16'6" – 9'9½" = 6'8½"

13. Annual savings = 12E – 52S

14. 7 ÷ ¾ = 9.$\overline{3}$, which means each interviewer can interview a maximum of 9 applicants each day. Then, (5)(9)(15) = 675 applicants

15. 4800/(4800+6400) = 3/7 eligible. On that assumption, there would be (3/7)(14,000) = 6000 eligible applicants. Then, 1200/6000 = 20%

16. 266 – (3)(76) = 38 gallons of oil left. Then, 38/76 = ½ hour

17. (6)(7)(4) = 168 hours to check on 336 tenants. This means 2 tenants require 1 man-hour. Now, (6)(7)(x days) = man-hours would be needed to check the remaining 420 tenants. This requires 210 man-hours. So, (6)(7)(x) = 210. Solving, x = 5

18. $\frac{17.5}{25}$ = .7 hr. = 42 min. Total time = 42 + 15 = 57 minutes.

19. Number available = 320[1−.25(1/8)(.75) = 210

20. Total cost = (.70)[(24)($3.60)+(4)(27.50)] = $137.48

21. From January through April, amount = (8)($185+$53+$17.50+$22) + (4)($550) = $4420. From May through December, amount = (16)($185+$53+17.50+$22) + (8)($550)(1.12) = $9368. Total annual amount = $4420 + $9368 = $13,788

22. Meat allowance = ($400)(.30)(1.10) = $132; fruit and vegetable allowance = ($400)(.30)(.80) = $96; grocery allowance = ($400)(.25)(1.05) = $105; dairy allowance = ($400)(.15) = $60. New monthly allowance = $132 + $96 + $105 + $.60 = $393

23. From January through May, amount = (10)($195+$63+$27.50+$32) + (5)($510) = $5725. From June through December, amount = (14)($195+$63+$27.50+$32) + (7)($510)(1.12) = $8443.40. Total annual amount = $5725 + $8443.40 = $14,168.40

24. Monthly assistance should be reduced to $600 − [(40)(3)($4\frac{1}{3}$) − ($5)(3)($4\frac{1}{3}$)] = $145. So, the semi-monthly amount is now $145/2 = $72.50

25. ($75)($4\frac{1}{3}$)/2 = original semi-monthly rent.
New semi-monthly rent = (162.50)(1.12) = $182. Since this represents an increase of $19.50, the new semi-monthly grant will be increased to $375 + $19.50 = $394.50

GLOSSARY OF LEGAL, MEDICAL, SOCIAL WORK TERMS

TABLE OF CONTENTS

	Page
Abandonment ... Advocacy	1
Affidavit ... Annual Review of Dependency Cases	2
Anomie ... Battery	3
Best Interests of the Child ... Caretaker	4
Cartilage ... Child Abuse	5
Child Abuse and Neglect	6
Child Abuse Prevention and Treatment Act ... Child Health Visitor	7
Child in Need of Supervision ... Child Welfare League of America	8
Child Welfare Resource Information Exchange ... Circumstantial Evidence	9
Civil Proceeding ... Community Organization	10
Community Support Systems	11
Compliance ... Corporal Punishment	12
Cortex ... Custody	13
Custody Hearing ... Denver Model	14
Dependency ... Discipline	15
Dislocation ... Due Process	16
Duodenum ... Evidence	17
Exhibit ... Expungement	18
Extravasated Blood ... Family Dynamics	19
Family Dysfunction ... Family Violence	20
Federal Regulations ... Fracture	21
Frontal ... Helpline	22
Hematemesis ... Hypovitaminosis	23
Identification of Child Abuse and Neglect ... Incest	24
Incidence ... Infanticide	25
Institutional Child Abuse and Neglect ... Juvenile Judge	27
Labeling ... Legal Rights of Persons Identified in Reports	28
Lesion ... Local Authority	29
Long Bone ... Maternal Characteristics Scale	30
Maternal-Infant Bonding ... Model Child Protection Act	31
Mondale Act ... National Center for the Prevention and Treatment of Child Abuse and Neglect	32
National Center on Child Abuse and Neglect ... National Committee for the Prevention of Child Abuse	33
National Register ... Nurturance	34
Occipital ... Parent Effectiveness Training	35
Parental Stress Services ... Pathognomonic	36
Perinatal ... Pre-trial Diversion	37

TABLE OF CONTENTS
(Continued)

Prevention of Child Abuse and Neglect ... Probation	38
Program Coordination ... Public Defender	39
Public Law 93-247 ... Regional Resource Center	40
Registry ... Res Ipsa Loquitor	41
Retina ... Self-Incrimination	42
Sentencing ... Social Assessment	43
Social History ... Societal Child Abuse and Neglect	44
Special Child ... State Authority	45
Status Offense ... Subdural Hematoma	46
Subpoena ... Surrogate Parent	47
Suspected Child Abuse and Neglect ... Trauma	48
Trauma X ... Vascular	49
Venereal Disease ... Willful	50
Witness ... X-Rays	51
ACRONYMS	52

GLOSSARY OF
Legal, Medical, Social Work Terms

ABANDONMENT
Act of a parent or caretaker leaving a child without adequate supervision or provision for his/her needs for an excessive period of time. State laws vary in defining adequacy of supervision and the length of time a child may be left alone or in the care of another before abandonment is determined. The age of the child also is an important factor. In legal terminology, "abandonment cases" are suits calling for the termination of parental rights.

ABDOMINAL DISTENTION
Swelling of the stomach area. The distention may be caused by internal injury or obstruction or by malnutrition.

ABRASION
Wound in which an area of the body surface is scraped of skin or mucous membrane.

ABUSE (See CHILD ABUSE AND NEGLECT)

ABUSED CHILD (See INDICATORS OF CHILD ABUSE AND NEGLECT)

ABUSED PARENT
Parent who has been abused as a child and who therefore may be more likely to abuse his/her own child.

ABUSER, PASSIVE (See PASSIVE ABUSER)

ACADEMY OF CERTIFIED SOCIAL WORKERS (ACSW)
Professional category identifying experienced social workers. Eligibility is determined by written examination following two years' full-time or 3,000 hours part-time paid post-Master's degree experience and continuous National Association of Social Workers (NASW) membership.

ACTING OUT
1) Behavior of an abusive parent who may be unconsciously and indirectly expressing anger toward his/her own parents or other significant person.
2) Aggressive or sexual behavior explained by some psychoanalytic theorists as carrying out fantasies or expressing unconscious feelings and conflicts.
3) Children's play or play therapy activities used as a means of expressing hitherto repressed feelings.

ACUTE CARE CAPACITY
Capacity of a community to respond quickly and responsibly to a report of a child abuse or neglect. It involves receiving the report and providing a diagnostic assessment including both a medical assessment and an evaluation of family dynamics. It also involves rapid intervention, including immediate protection of the child when needed and referral for long term care or service to the child and his/her family.

ADJUDICATION HEARING
Court hearing in which it is decided whether or not charges against a parent or caretaker are substantiated by admissible evidence. Also known as jurisdictional or evidentiary hearing.

ADMISSIBLE EVIDENCE
Evidence which may be legally and properly used in court. (See also EVIDENCE, EVIDENTIARY STANDARDS, EXPERT TESTIMONY)

ADVOCACY
Interventive strategy in which a helping person assumes an active role in assisting or supporting a specific child and/or family or a cause on behalf of children and/or families. This could involve finding and facilitating services for specific cases or developing new

services or promoting program coordination. The advocate uses his/her power to meet client needs or to promote causes.

AFFIDAVIT
Written statement signed in the presence of a Notary Public who "swears in" the signer. The contents of the affidavit are stated under penalty of perjury. Affidavits are frequently used in the initiation of juvenile court cases and are, at times, presented to the court as evidence.

AGAINST MEDICAL ADVICE (AMA)
Going against the orders of a physician. In cases of child abuse or neglect, this usually means the removal of a child from a hospital without the physician's consent.

AID TO FAMILIES WITH DEPENDENT CHILDREN (AFDC) (See SOCIAL SECURITY ACT)

ALLEGATION
An assertion, declaration, or statement of a party to a legal action, which sets out what he or she expects to prove. In a child abuse or neglect case, the allegation forms the basis of the petition or accusation containing charges of specific acts of maltreatment which the petitioner hopes to prove at the trial.

ALOPECIA
Absence of hair from skin areas where it normally appears; baldness.

AMERICAN ACADEMY OF PEDIATRICS (AAP)
P.O. Box 1034
Evanston, Illinois 60204
AAP is the pan-American association of physicians certified in the care of infants, children, and adolescents. It was founded in 1930 for the primary purpose of ensuring "the attainment of all children of the Americas of their full potential for physical, emotional, and social health." Services and activities of AAP include standards-setting for pediatric residencies, scholarships, continuing education, standards-setting for child health care, community health services, consultation, publications, and research.

AMERICAN HUMANE ASSOCIATION, CHILDREN'S DIVISION (AHA)
5351 S. Roslyn St.
Englewood, Colorado 80110
National association of individuals and agencies working to prevent neglect, abuse, and exploitation of children. Its objectives are to inform the public of the problem, to promote understanding of its causes, to advise on the identification and protection of abused and neglected children, and to assist in organizing new and improving existing child protection programs and services. Some of the programs and services of CDAHA include research, consultation and surveys, legislative guidance, staff development training and workshops, and publications. AHA includes an Animal Division in addition to the Children's Division.

AMERICAN PUBLIC WELFARE ASSOCIATION (APWA)
1125 Fifteenth St. N.W. Suite 300
Washington, D.C. 20005
APWA was founded in 1930 and has, from its inception, been a voluntary membership organization composed of individuals and agencies interested in issues of public welfare. National in scope, its dual purpose is to: 1) exert a positive influence on the shaping of national social policy, and 2) promote professional development of persons working in the area of public welfare. APWA sponsors an extensive program of policy analysis and research, testimony and consultation, publications, conferences, and workshops. It works for policies which are more equitable, less complex, and easier to administer in order that public welfare personnel can respond efficiently and effectively to the needs of persons they serve.

ANNUAL REVIEW OF DEPENDENCY CASES
Annual or other periodic reviews of dependency cases to determine whether continued

child placement or court supervision of a child is necessary. Increasingly required by state law, such reviews by the court also provide some judicial supervision of probation or casework services.

ANOMIE
A state of anomie is characterized by attitudes of aimlessness, futility, and lack of motivation and results from the breakdown or failure of standards, rules, norms, and values that ordinarily bind people together in some socially organized way.

ANOREXIA
Lack or loss of appetite for food.

APATHY-FUTILITY SYNDROME
Immature personality type often associated with child neglect and characterized by an inability to feel and to find any significant meaning in life. This syndrome, often arising from early deprivations in childhood, is frequently perpetuated from generation to generation within a family system. (Polansky)

APPEAL
Resort to a higher court in an attempt to have a decision or ruling of the lower court corrected or reversed because of some claimed error or injustice. Appeals follow several different formats. Occasionally, appeals will result in a rehearing of the entire case. Usually, however, appeals are limited to consideration of questions of whether the lower court judge correctly applied the law to the facts of the case.

ASSESSMENT
1) Determination of the validity of a reported case of suspected child abuse or neglect through investigatory interviews with persons involved. This could include interviews with the family, the child, school, and neighbors, as well as with other professionals and paraprofessionals having direct contact with the child or family.
2) Determination of the treatment potential and treatment plan for confirmed cases.

ASSAULT
Intentional or reckless threat of physical injury to a person. Aggravated assault is committed with the intention of carrying out the threat or other crimes. Simple assault is committed without the intention of carrying out the threat or if the attempt at injury is not completed. (See also BATTERY, SEXUAL ASSAULT)

ATROPHY
Wasting away of flesh, tissue, cell, or organ.

AVITAMINOSIS
Condition due to complete lack of one or more essential vitamins. (See also HYPOVITAMINOSIS)

BATTERED CHILD SYNDROME
Term introduced in 1962 by C. Henry Kempe, M.D., in the *Journal of the American Medical Association* in an article describing a combination of physical and other signs indicating that a child's internal and/or external injuries result from acts committed by a parent or caretaker. In some states, the battered child syndrome has been judicially recognized as an accepted medical diagnosis. Frequently this term is misused or misunderstood as the only type of child abuse and neglect. (See also CHILD ABUSE AND NEGLECT)

BATTERED WOMEN
Women who are victims of non-accidental physical and/or psychological injury inflected by a spouse or mate. There seems to be a relationship between child abuse and battered women, with both often occurring in the same family. (See also SPOUSE ABUSE)

BATTERY
Offensive contact or physical violence with a person without his/her consent, and which may or may not be preceded by a threat of assault. Because a minor cannot legally give consent, any such contact or violence against a child is considered battery. The action may be aggravated, meaning intentional, or it may be simple, meaning that the action was not intentional or did not cause

severe harm. Assault is occasionally used to mean attempted battery. (See also ASSAULT)

BEST INTERESTS OF THE CHILD
Standard for deciding among alternative plans for abused or neglected children. This is also known as the least detrimental alternative principle. Usually it is assumed that it is in the child's best interest and least detrimental if the child remains in the home, provided that the parents can respond to treatment. However, the parents' potential for treatment may be difficult to assess and it may not be known whether the necessary resources are available. A few authorities believe that except where the child's life is in danger, it is always in the child's best interest to remain in the home. This view reflects the position that in evaluating the least detrimental alternative and the child's best interest, the child's psychological as well as physical well-being must be considered. In developing a plan, the best interest of the child may not be served because of parents' legal rights or because agency policy and practice focuses on foster care. The best interest of the child and least detrimental alternative principles were articulated as a reaction to the overuse of child placement in cases of abuse and neglect. Whereas "best interest of the child" suggests that some placement may be justified, "least detrimental alternative" is stronger in suggesting that any placement or alternative can have some negative consequences and should be monitored.

BEYOND A REASONABLE DOUBT (See EVIDENTIARY STANDARDS)

BONDING
The psychological attachment of mother to child which develops during and immediately following childbirth. Bonding, which appears to be crucial to the development of a health parent/child relationship, may be studied during and immediately following delivery to help identify potential families-at-risk. Bonding is normally a natural occurrence but it may be disrupted by separation of mother and baby or by situational or psychological factors causing the mother to reject the baby at birth.

BRUISE (See INTRADERMAL HEMORRHAGE)

BURDEN OF PROOF
The duty, usually falling on the state as petitioner in a child maltreatment case, of producing evidence at a trial so as to establish the truth of the allegations against the parent. At the commencement of a trial, it is always up to the petitioner to first present evidence which proves their case. (See also EVIDENCE, EVIDENTIARY STANDARDS)

BURN
Wound resulting from the application of too much heat. Burns are classified by the degree of damage caused.
    1st degree: Scorching or painful redness of the skin.
    2nd degree: Formation of blisters.
    3rd degree: Destruction of outer layers of the skin.

BURN OUT (See staff burn out.)

CALCIFICATION
Formation of bone. The amount of calcium deposited can indicate via X-ray the degree of healing of a broken bone or the location of previous fractures which have healed prior to the X-ray.

CALLUS
New bone formed during the healing process of a fracture.

CALVARIUM
Dome-like portion of the skull.

CARETAKER
A person responsible for a child's health or welfare, including the child's parent, guardian, or other person within the child's own home; or a person responsible for a child's health or welfare in a relative's home, foster care home, or residential institution. A caretaker is responsible for meeting a child's

basic physical and psychological needs and for providing protection and supervision.

CARTILAGE
The hard connective tissue that is not bone but, in the unborn and growing child, may be the forerunner of bone before calcium is deposited in it.

CASE MANAGEMENT
Coordination of the multiplicity of services required by a child abuse and neglect client. Some of these services may be purchased from an agency other than the mandated agency. In general, the role of the case manager is not the provision of direct services but the monitoring of those services to assure that they are relevant to the client, delivered in a useful way, and appropriately used by the client. To do this, a case manager assumes the following responsibilities.
1) Ascertains that all mandated reports have been properly filed.
2) Informs all professionals involved with the family that reports of suspected child abuse or neglect have been made.
3) Keeps all involved workers apprised of new information.
4) Calls and chairs the intial case conference for assessment, disposition, and treatment plans; conference may include parents, physician, probation worker, police, public health nurse, private therapist, parent aide, protective service and welfare workers, or others.
5) Coordinates interagency follow-up.
6) Calls further case conferences as needed. (See also PURCHASE OF SERVICE)

CASEWORK
A method of social work intervention which helps an individual or family improve their functioning in society by changing both internal attitudes and feelings and external circumstances directly affecting the individual or family. This contrasts with community organization and other methods of social work intervention which focuses on changing institutions or society. Social casework relies on a relationship between the worker and client as the primary tool for effecting change.

CATEGORICAL AID
Government financial assistance given to individuals who are aged or disabled or to families with dependent children. The eligibility requirements and financial assistance vary for different categories of persons, according to the guidelines of the Social Security Act. (See also SOCIAL SECURITY ACT)

CENTRAL REGISTER
Records of child abuse reports collected centrally from various agencies under state law or voluntary agreement. Agencies receiving reports of suspected abuse check with the central register to determine whether prior reports have been received by other agencies concerning the same child or parents. The purposes of central registers may be to alert authorities to families with a prior history of abuse, to assist agencies in planning for abusive families, and to provide data for statistical analysis of child abuse. Due to variance in state laws for reporting child abuse and neglect, there are diverse methods of compiling these records and of access to them. Although access to register records is usually restricted, critics warn of confidentiality problems and the importance of expunging unverified reports. (See also EXPUNGEMENT)

CHILD
A person, also known as minor, from birth to legal age of maturity for whom a parent and/or caretaker, foster parent, public or private home, institution, or agency is legally responsible. The 1974 Child Abuse Prevention and Treatment Act defines a child as a person under 18. In some states, a person of any age with a developmental disability is defined as a child.

CHILD ABUSE (See CHILD ABUSE AND NEGLECT)

CHILD ABUSE AND NEGLECT (CAN)
All-inclusive term, as defined in the Child Abuse Prevention and Treatment Act, for "the physical or mental injury, sexual abuse, negligent treatment or maltreatment of a child under the age of eighteen by a person who is responsible for the child's welfare. There is agreement that some parental care and supervision is essential, there is disagreement as to how much is necessary for a minimally acceptable environment.

Child Abuse refers specifically to an act of commission by a parent or caretaker which is not accidental and harms or threatens to harm a child's physical or mental health or welfare. All 50 States have a child abuse reporting law with varying definitions of child abuse and varying provisions as to who must and may report, penalties for not reporting, and required agency action following the report. Factors such as the age of the child and the severity of injury are important in determining abuse.

Physical Abuse
Child abuse which results in physical injury, including fractures, burns, bruises, welts, cuts, and/or internal injuries. Physical abuse often occurs in the name of discipline or punishment, and ranges from a slap of the hand to use of objects such as straps, belts, kitchen utensils, pipes, etc. (See also BATTERED CHILD SYNDROME)

Psychological/Emotional Abuse
Child abuse which results in impaired psychological growth and development. Frequently occurs as verbal abuse or excessive demands on a child's performance and results in a negative self-image on the part of the child and disturbed child behavior. May occur with or without physical abuse.

Sexual Abuse
Child abuse which results in any act of a sexual nature upon or with a child. Most states define any sexual involvement of a parent or caretaker with a child as a sexual act and therefore abuse. The most common form is incest between fathers and daughters.

Verbal Abuse
A particular form of psychological/emotional abuse characterized by constant verbal harassment and denigration of a child. Many persons abused as children report feeling more permanently damaged by verbal abuse than by isolated or repeated experiences of physical abuse.

Child Neglect refers to an act of omission, specifically the failure of a parent or other person legally responsible for a child's welfare to provide for the child's basic needs and proper level of care with respect to food, clothing, shelter, hygiene, medical attention, or supervision. Most states have neglect and/or dependency statutes; however, not all states require the reporting of neglect. While there is agreement that some parental care and supervision is essential, there is disagreement as to how much is necessary for a minimally acceptable environment. Severe neglect sometimes occurs because a parent is apathetic, impulse-ridden, mentally retarded, depressed, or psychotic.

Educational Neglect
Failure to provide for a child's cognitive development. This may include failure to conform to state legal requirements regarding school attendance.

Medical Neglect
Failure to seek medical or dental treatment for a health problem or condition which, if untreated, could become severe enough to represent a danger to the child. Except among religious sects prohibiting medical treatment, medical neglect is usually only one part of a larger family problem.

Moral Neglect
Failure to give a child adequate guidance in developing positive social values, such as parents who allow or teach their children to steal.

Physical Neglect
Failure to provide for a child's basic survival needs, such as food, clothing, shelter, and supervision, to the extent that the failure represents a hazard to the child's health or safety. Determining neglect for lack of supervision depends upon the child's age and competence, the amount of unsupervised time, the time of day when the child is unsupervised, and the degree of parental planning for the unsupervised period. For a particular kind of physical neglect involving failure to feed a baby or small child sufficiently, see FAILURE TO THRIVE SYNDROME.

Psychological /Emotional Neglect
Failure to provide the psychological nurturance necessary for a child's psychological growth and development. It is usually very difficult to prove the cause and effect relationship between the parent's unresponsiveness and lack of nurturance and the child's symptoms, and many states do not include psychological or emotional neglect in their reporting laws.

CHILD ABUSE PREVENTION AND TREATMENT ACT (PUBLIC LAW 93-247)
Act introduced and promoted in Congress by then U.S. Senator Walter Mondale and signed into law on January 31, 1974. The act established the National Center on Child Abuse and Neglect in the HEW Children's Bureau and authorized annual appropriations of between $15 million and $25 million through Fiscal Year 1977, but it is anticipated that Congress will extend the act for several years. Actual appropriations have been less than authorized. The purpose of the National Center is to conduct and compile research, provide an information clearinghouse, compile and publish training materials, provide technical assistance, investigate national incidence, and fund demonstration projects related to prevention, identification, and treatment of child abuse and neglect. In the 1974 act, not more than 20% of the appropriated funds may be used for direct assistance to states, which must be in compliance with specific legislative requirements including, among others, reporting and investigation of suspected neglect as well as abuse, provision of multidisciplinary programs, and appointment of a *guardian ad litem* to represent the child in all judicial proceedings. The act emphasizes multidisciplinary approaches. It also provides for funding for parent self-help projects.

Many persons do not understand that this act is primarily to support research and demonstration projects. Much larger amounts of funding for the ongoing provisions of child abuse and neglect services are provided to states through Title IV-B and Title XX of the Social Security Act.

CHILD DEVELOPMENT
Pattern of sequential stages of interrelated physical, psychological, and social development in the process of maturation from infancy and total dependence to adulthood and relative independence. Parents need to understand the level of maturity consistent with each stage of development and should not expect a child to display a level of maturity of which the child is incapable at a particular stage. Abusive or neglectful parents frequently impair a child's healthy growth and development because they do not understand child development or are otherwise unable to meet the child's physical, social, and psychological needs at a given stage or stages of development.

CHILD HEALTH VISITOR
Professional or paraprofessional who visits a home shortly after the birth of a baby and periodically thereafter to identify current and potential child health and development and family stress problems and to facilitate use of needed community services. While currently operating in many European countries, child health visitor programs are rare in the U.S. because they are perceived as contrary to the right to privacy and parental rights. A universal mandatory child health visitor program has, however, been recommended by several

authorities as the most effective way to assure children's rights and prevent child abuse and neglect. Also known as Home Health Visitor.

CHILD IN NEED OF SUPERVISION
Juvenile who has committed a delinquent act and has been found by a children's court judge to require further court supervision, such as 1) probation, or 2) the transfer of custody of the child to a relative or public or private welfare agency for a period of time, usually not to exceed one year. Also known as Person in Need of Supervision (PINS) or Minor in Need of Supervision (MINS).

CHILD NEGLECT (See CHILD ABUSE AND NEGLECT)

CHILD PORNOGRAPHY
The obscene or pornographic photography, filming, or depiction of children for commercial purposes. Recent campaigns have begun to increase public awareness of this problem. Also as a result of public pressure against these materials, the federal government and some states are currently implementing special legislation to outlaw the sale and interstate transportation of pornographic materials that portray children engaged in explicit sexual acts.

CHILD PROSTITUTION
Legislation prohibiting the use of children as prostitutes is currently being implemented by the federal government and many states. The use of or participation by children in sexual acts with adults for reward or financial gain when no force is present.

CHILD PROTECTIVE SERVICES or CHILD PROTECTION SERVICES (CPS)
A specialized child welfare service, usually part of a county department of public welfare, legally responsible in most states for investigating suspected cases of child abuse and neglect and intervening in confirmed cases. Qualifications of CPS workers vary, with some counties employing CPS workers without prior human services training and others requiring at least a , Bachelor's degree in social work. With over 3,000 counties in the U.S., there are many kinds of CPS programs of varying quality. Common to most is the problem of insufficient staff overburdened with excessive caseloads. This plus the pressure of CPS work creates stress for many CPS staff. (See also STAFF BURNOUT, STAFF FLIGHT, and STAFF SATISFACTION)

CHILD WELFARE AGENCY
A public or voluntary agency providing service to children in their own homes and/or in day care, and which may be licensed to place children in foster homes, group homes, or institutions or into permanent adoptive homes. The number of children served annually by child welfare agencies in the U.S. is estimated to be over one million, the majority being served by public agencies. Payments for foster care represent well over half the total of child welfare agencies' expenditures.

Child welfare agencies which meet certain standards, including Standards for Protective Services, are accredited by the Child Welfare League of America. It is estimated that the majority of social workers employed by these accredited agencies hold a Master's degree. In public child welfare agencies, Master's degree social workers are a minority, with specific educational requirements varying from state to state. However, unlike many other fields of social work which share responsibility with other professions, child welfare is a domain for which social work has been accorded major responsibility. Believing that child protection is a public child welfare agency responsibility, few private agencies provide it.

CHILD WELFARE LEAGUE OF AMERICA (CWLA)
67 Irving Place
New York,
N.Y. 10003
Founded in 1920, the Child Welfare League of America is a privately supported, non-sectarian organization which is dedicated to the improvement of care and services for

deprived, neglected, and dependent children and their families. Its program is directed toward helping agencies and communities in the U.S. and Canada to provide essential social services to promote the well-being of children. CWLA is an advocate for children and families, a clearinghouse and forum for knowledge and experience of persons in the field, and a coordinating facility through which all concerned with child welfare can share their efforts. Programs of the League and its membership of over 300 affiliated public and private agencies include: accreditation of agencies, adoption services, conferences, consultation, training, library/information services, publications, personnel services, public affairs and legislative programs, standards development, and surveys.

CHILD WELFARE RESOURCE INFORMATION EXCHANGE

A project of the Children's Bureau of the Administration for Children, Youth and Families, HEW. It is a source for materials on exemplary programs, curricula, technologies, and methods which ahve brought more effective and efficient services to children. Its purpose is to improve the delivery of child welfare services by identifying successful programs, methods, research, and materials, and by assisting agencies in adapting them for their own use. The Exchange disseminates information it has gathered through abstracts, a bimonthly bulletin, regional workshops, and colloquia.

CHILDHOOD LEVEL OF LIVING SCALE (CLL)

Instrument used to measure the level of physical and emotional/cognitive care a child is receiving in his/her home. Rated are adequacy of food, clothing, furniture, etc., as well as evidence of affection, type of discipline, and cultural stimulation. The scale is designed to be used as a guide to assessing nurturance levels rather than as objective evidence of neglect.

CHILDREN-AT-RISK

May refer to the possibility that children in the custody of a state or county will get lost in a series of placements or for other reasons not be returned to their natural homes when these homes are no longer threatening to the children's welfare. May also refer to children in potentially abusive institutions, but usually refer to children in families-at-risk. (See also FAMILIES-AT-RISK)

CHILDREN'S DEFENSE FUND (CDF) 1520 New Hampshire Ave., N.W. Washington, D.C. 20036

A non-profit organization founded in 1973. Staff includes researchers, lawyers, and others dedicated to long-range and systematic advocacy on behalf of children. CDF works at federal, state, and local levels to reform policies and practices which harmfully affect large numbers of children. Activities include investigation and public information, litigation, monitoring of federal agencies, and technical assistance to local organizations. Program priorities are to assure the rights of children to proper education, adequate health care, comprehensive child care and family support services, fair and humane treatment in the juvenile justice system, and the avoidance of institutionalization.

CHILDREN'S RIGHTS

Rights of children as individuals to the protections provided in the Constitution as well as to the care and protection necessary for normal growth and development. Children's rights are actually exercised through adult representatives and advocates. The extent to which children's rights are protected varies according to the individual state laws providing for the identification and treatment of child abuse and neglect. An unresolved issue is the conflict between children's rights and parents' rights or rights to privacy. (See also PARENTS' RIGHTS)

CHIP FRACTURE (See FRACTURE)

CIRCUMSTANTIAL EVIDENCE (See EVIDENCE)

CIVIL PROCEEDING
Any lawsuit other than criminal prosecutions. Juvenile and family court cases are civil proceedings. Also called a civil action.

CLEAR AND CONVINCING EVIDENCE
(See EVIDENTIARY STANDARDS)

CLOTTING FACTOR
Material in the blood that causes it to coagulate. Deficiencies in clotting factors can cause profuse internal or external bleeding and/or bruising, as in the disease hemophilia. Bruises or bleeding caused by such a disease may be mistaken as resulting from abuse.

COLON
The large intestine.

COMMINUTED FRACTURE (See FRACTURE)

COMMISSION, ACTS OF
Overt acts by a parent or caretaker toward a child resulting in physical or mental injury, including but not limited to beatings, excessive disciplining, or exploitation. (See also CHILD ABUSE AND NEGLECT)

COMMISSIONER (See HEARING OFFICER)

COMMUNITY AWARENESS
A community's level of understanding of child abuse and neglect. Ideally, this should include knowledge about the extent and nature of the problem and how to use the local resources. In reality, community awareness tends to focus on reporting rather than treatment and prevention.

COMMUNITY COUNCIL FOR CHILD ABUSE AND NEGLECT
Community group, including both professionals and citizens, which attempts to develop and coordinate resources and/or legislation for the prevention, identification, and treatment of child abuse and neglect. It is often the name given to the program coordination component of the community team (see COMMUNITY TEAM).

COMMUNITY EDUCATION
Developed for public audiences, this type of local level education provides understanding about a problem or issue of community and/or societal relevance, and information about appropriate community resources and services available to deal with the problem or issue. Sponsored by a professional agency or citizens' group, community education is usually provided through an ongoing speaker's bureau, through periodic lecture and discussion meetings open to the general public or offered to special groups, and/or through the local media and other publicity devices.

With reference to child abuse and neglect, it is important to combine community education with public awareness. Generally, public awareness is geared only to reporting child abuse and neglect, and may communicate a punitive image toward parents who abuse or neglect their children without communicating an understanding of the problem.

COMMUNITY NEGLECT
Failure of a community to provide adequate support and social services for families and children, or lack of community control over illegal or discriminatory activities with respect to families and children.

COMMUNITY ORGANIZATION
A social work method of achieving change in human service organizations or service delivery and utilization through social planning and/or social action. This kind of intervention rests explicitly or implicitly on understanding the nature of the community or service system which is the target of change and on organizing members of the community or system to participate in the change process. Professional community organizers assist, but do not direct, community groups in developing community organization strategies of confrontation, collaboration, coalition,

etc. Since child abuse and neglect is a multidisciplinary, multiagency problem, community organization for coordination of services is imperative.

COMMUNITY SUPPORT SYSTEMS

Community resources such as schools, public health services, day care centers, welfare advocacy, whose utilization can aid in preventing family dysfunction and child abuse and neglect, and aid in treating identified cases of abuse and neglect.

COMMUNITY TEAM

Often used incorrectly to refer to a multidisciplinary professional group which only diagnoses and plans treatment for specific cases of child abuse and neglect. More accurately, a community team separates the diagnosis and treatment functions and provides a third component for education, training, and public relations. The community tream also includes a community task force or council, including citizens as well as professionals from various disciplines, which coordinates the three community team components and advocates for resources and legislation. Citizens on the community team also monitor the professionals and agency participants. For effective child abuse and neglect management, a community team should be established for every geographic area of 400,000 to 500,000 population, and should consist of the following components:

Identification/Diagnostic Team Component
The identification/diagnostic team component has primary responsibility for diagnosing actual cases of child abuse and neglect among those which are reported or otherwise come to their attention, providing acute care or crisis intervention for the child in immediate danger, and developing long-term treatment recommendations. This team should be multidisciplinary and should probably include a public health nurse, pediatrician, psychologist or psychiatrist, lawyer, law enforcement person, case aides, and a number of child protective services workers. The protective services workers on the diagnostic team undergo unusual physical and emotional fatigue, and they should have a two or three week break from this activity every several months. However, to further relieve this stress, the diagnostic team, and not the protective services workers alone, should make and be accountable for all decisions. To function effectively, this team must establish protocol, define roles of each team member, establish policies and procedures, and establish a network of coordination with acute care service agencies.

Long Term Treatment Component
The long term treatment component has responsibility to review treatment needs and progress of specific cases periodically, to establish treatment goals, to coordinate existing treatment services, and to develop new treatment programs. This component should include supervisors and workers from supportive and advocacy services as well as from adult, children, and family treatment programs. The community team must assure provision and use of this component.

Education, Training, and Public Relations Component
The education, training, and public relations component has responsibility for community and professional awareness and education. Professional education includes implementation and/or evaluation of ongoing training programs for professionals and paraprofessionals.

The interrelationship among these various components is diagrammed below:

A - Identification and Diagnosis
B - Long-Term Treatment
C - Education, Training, Public Relations

1 - Case Coordination
2 - Professional Training and Recruitment
3 - Public and Professional ducation, Professional Training
4 - Program Coordination

COMPLIANCE
1) The behavior of children who readily yield to demands in an attempt to please abusive or neglectful parents or caretakers.
2) A state child abuse and neglect law which conforms to requirements outlined in the Child Abuse Prevention and Treatment Act and further HEW regulations, and which therefore permits funding under this act for child abuse and neglect activities in the state. (See also CHILD ABUSE PREVENTION AND TREATMENT ACT)

COMPLAINT
1) An oral statement, usually made to the police, charging criminal, abusive, or neglectful conduct.
2) A district attorney's document which starts a criminal prosecution.
3) A petitioner's document which starts a civil proceeding. In juvenile or family court, the complaint is usually called a petition.
4) In some states, term used for a report of suspected abuse or neglect.

COMPOUND FRACTURE (See FRACTURE)

COMPREHENSIVE EMERGENCY SERVICES(CES)
A community system of coordinated services available on a 24-hour basis to meet emergency needs of children and/or families in crisis. Components of a CES system can include 24-hour protective services, homemaker services, crisis nurseries, family shelters, emergency foster care, outreach, and follow-up services.

CONCILIATION COURT (See COURTS)

CONCUSSION
An injury of a soft structure resulting from violent shaking or jarring; usually refers to a brain concussion.

CONFIDENTIALITY
Professional practice of not sharing with others information entrusted by a client or patient. Sometimes communications from parent to physician or social worker are made with this expectation but are later used in court, and many physicians and social workers are torn between legal vs. professional obligations. Confidentiality which is protected by statute is known as privileged communications. Confidentiality need not obstruct information sharing with a multidisciplinary team provided that the client is advised of the sharing and the team has articulated its own policy and guidelines on confidentiality. (See also PRIVILEGED COMMUNICATIONS)

CONGENITAL
Refers to any physical condition present at birth, regardless of its cause.

CONJUNCTIVA
Transparent lining covering the white of the eye and eyelids. Bleeding beneath the conjunctiva can occur spontaneously or from accidental or non-accidental injury.

CONTRAINDICATION
Reason for not giving a particular drug or prescribing a particular treatment, as it may do more harm than good.

CONTUSION
A wound producing injury to soft tissue without a break in the skin, causing bleeding into surrounding tissues.

CORPORAL PUNISHMENT
Physical punishment inflected directly upon the body. Some abusive parents mistakenly believe that corporal punishment is the only way to discipline children, and some child development specialists believe that almost all parents must occasionally resort to corporal punishment to discipline or train children. Other professionals believe that corporal punishment is never advisable. In a Supreme Court ruling (Ingraham vs. Wright, April 19, 1977), corporal punishment in the schools was upheld. The Supreme Court ruled that the cruel and unusual punishment clause of the Eighth Amendment does not apply to corporal punishment in the schools. (See also DISCIPLINE).

CORTEX
Outer layer of an organ or other body structure.

COURTS
Places where judicial proceedings occur. There is an array of courts involved with child abuse and neglect cases, partly because different states divide responsibility for certain proceedings among different courts, and also because tradition has established a variety of names for courts which perform similar functions. Child abuse reports can result in proceedings in any of the following courts:

Criminal Court
Usually divided into superior court, which handles felony cases, and municipal court, which handles misdemeanors and the beginning stages of most felony cases.

Domestic Relations Court
A civil court in which divorces and divorce custody hearings are held.

Family Court
A civil court which, in some states, combines the functions of domestic relations, juvenile, and probate courts. Establishment of family courts is often urged to reform the presently wasteful and poorly-coordinated civil court system. Under some proposals, family courts would also deal with criminal cases involving family relations, thus improving coordination in child abuse litigation.

Court of Conciliation
A branch of domestic relations courts in some states, usually staffed by counselors and social workers rather than by lawyers or judges, and designed to explore and promote reconciliation in divorce cases.

Juvenile Court
Juvenile court, which has jurisdiction over minors, usually handles cases of suspected delinquency as well as cases of suspected abuse or neglect. In many states, terminations of parental rights occur in juvenile court proceedings, but that is generally the limit of juvenile court's power over adults.

Probate Court
Probate court may handle cases of guardianship and adoption in addition to estates of deceased persons.

CRANIUM
The skull.

CRIMINAL PROSECUTION
The process involving the filing of charges of a crime, followed by arraignment and trial of the defendant. Criminal prosecution may result in fines, imprisonment, and/or probation. Criminal defendants are entitled to acquittal unless charges against them are proven beyond a reasonable doubt. Technical rules of evidence exclude many kinds of proof in criminal trials, even though that proof might be admissible in civil proceedings. Criminal defendants are entitled to a jury trial; in many civil proceedings concerning children, there is no right to a jury trial.

CRISIS INTERVENTION
Action to relieve a specific stressful situation or series of problems which are immediately threatening to a child's health and/or welfare. This involves alleviation of parental stress through provision of emergency services in the home and/or removal of the child from the home. (See also EMERGENCY SERVICES and COMPREHENSIVE EMERGENCY SERVICES)

CRISIS NURSERY
Facility offering short-term relief of several hours to several days' duration to parents temporarily unable or unwilling to care for their children. The primary purpose are child protection, stabilization of the home, and prevention of child abuse and neglect.

CUSTODY
The right to care and control of a child and the duty to provide food, clothing, shelter, ordinary medical care, education, and discipline for a child. Permanent legal custody

may be taken from a parent or given up by a parent by a court action (see TERMINATION OF PARENTAL RIGHTS). Temporary custody of a child may be granted for a limited time only, usually pending further action or review by the court. Temporary custody may be granted for a period of months or, in the case of protective or emergency custody, for a period of hours or several days.

Emergency Custody
The ability of a law enforcement officer, pursuant to the criminal code, to take temporary custody of a child who is in immediate danger and place him/her in the control of child protective services. A custody hearing must usually be held within 48 hours of such action. Also known as police custody.

Protective Custody
Emergency measure taken to detain a child, often in a hospital, until a written detention request can be filed. In some states, telephone communication with a judge is required to authorize protective custody. In other states, police, social workers, or doctors have statutory authority to detain minors who are in imminent danger. (See also DETENTION)

CUSTODY HEARING
Hearing, usually held in children's court, to determine who has the rights of legal custody of a minor. It may involve one parent against the other or the parents vs. a social service agency.

CYCLE OF CHILD ABUSE OR NEGLECT
(See
WORLD OF ABNORMAL REARING)

DAUGHTERS UNITED
Organization name sometimes used for self-help groups of daughters who have been sexually abused. Daughters United is one component of a model Child Sexual Abuse Treatment Program in Santa Clara County, California. (See also PARENTS UNITED)

DAY CARE
A structured, supervised place for children to go more or less regularly while parents work or attend school. Experts believe that family stress can be relieved by more extensive provision of day care services, and day care providers are increasingly concerned with identification and prevention of child abuse and neglect.

DAY TREATMENT
1) Program providing treatment as well as structured supervision for children with identified behavioral problems, including abused and neglected children, while they remain in their own, foster, or group homes. Day treatment services usually include counseling with families or caretakers with whom the children reside.
2) Treatment and structured activities for parents or entire families in a treatment setting from which they return to their own homes evenings and weekends.

DELINQUENCY
Behavior of a minor which would, in the case of an adult, constitute criminal conduct. In some states, delinquency also includes "waywardness" or disobedient behavior on the part of the child. In contrast to dependency cases, where the parent(s) rather than the minor is assumed responsible, delinquency cases assume that the minor has some responsibility for his/her behavior.

DENVER MODEL
A multidisciplinary hospital-community coalition which originated in Denver, Colorado, and which has become a model replicated by many other programs. The following diagram outlines the components:

TIME	PLACE	FUNCTION
	Community	Child is identified as suspected abuse or neglect.
24 hours	Hospital	Child is admitted to hospital.
	Hospital	Telephone report is made to protective services.
	Community	Home is evaluated by protective services.
72 hours	Both	Dispositional conference is held.
	Community	Court is involved if needed.
2 weeks	Both	Implement dispositional plan.
6-9 months	Community	Maintain case.
	Both	Long-term Treatment program is followed.
	Both	Child is returned home when home has been made safe.

DEPENDENCY

A child's need for care and supervision from a parent or caretaker. Often a legal term referring to cases of children whose natural parent(s) cannot or will not properly care for them or supervise them so that the state must assume this responsibility. Many states distinguish findings of dependency, for which the juvenile is assumed to have little or no responsibility, from findings of delinquency, in which the juvenile is deemed to be at least partially responsible for his/her behavior.

DETENTION

The temporary confinement of a person by a public authority. In a case of child abuse or neglect, a child may be detained pending a trial when a detention hearing indicates that it is unsafe for the child to remain in his/her own home. This is often called protective custody or emergency custody. The child may be detained in a foster home, group home, hospital, or other facility.

DETENTION HEARING

A court hearing held to determine whether a child should be kept away from his/her parents until a full trial of neglect, abuse, or delinquency allegations can take place. Detention hearings must usually be held within 24 hours of the filing of a detention request. (See also CUSTODY)

DETENTION REQUEST

A document filed by a probation officer, social worker, or prosecutor with the clerk of a juvenile or family court, asking that a detention hearing be held, and that a child be detained until the detention hearing has taken place. Detention requests must usually be filed within 48 hours of the time protective custody of the child begins. (See also CUSTODY)

DIAGNOSTIC TEAM (See COMMUNITY TEAM)

DIAPHYSIS

The shaft of a long bone.

DIFFERENTIAL DIAGNOSIS

The determination of which of two or more diseases or conditions a patient may be suffering from by systematically comparing and contrasting the clinical findings.

DIRECT EVIDENCE (See EVIDENCE)

DIRECT SERVICE PROVIDERS

Those groups and individuals who directly interact with clients and patients in the delivery of health, education, and welfare services, or those agencies which employs them. It includes, among others, policemen, social workers, physicians, psychiatrists, and clinical psychologists who see clients or patients.

DISCIPLINE

1) A branch of knowledge or learning or a particular profession, such as law, medicine, or social work.
2) Training that develops self-control, self-sufficiency, orderly conduct. Discipline is

often confused with punishment, particularly by abusive parents who resort to corporal punishment. Although interpretations of both "discipline" and "punishment" tend to be vague and often overlapping, there is some consensus that discipline has positive connotations and punishment is considered negatively. Some general comparisons between the terms are:

a) Discipline can occur before, during, and/or after an event; punishment occurs only after an event.
b) Discipline is based on respect for a child and his/her capabilities; punishment is based on behavior or events precipitating behavior.
c) Discipline implies that there is an authority figure; punishment implies power and dominance vs. submissiveness.
d) The purpose of discipline is educational and rational; the purpose of punishment is to inflict pain, often in an attempt to vent frustration or anger.
e) Discipline focuses on deterring future behavior by encouraging development of internal controls; punishment is a method of external control which may or may not alter future behavior.
f) Discipline can lead to extrapolation and generalized learning patterns; punishment may relate only to a specific event.
g) Discipline can strengthen interpersonal bonds and recognizes individual means and worth; punishment usually causes deterioration of relationships and is usually a dehumanizing experience.
h) Both discipline and punishment behavior patterns may be transmitted to the next generation.

According to legal definitions applying to most schools and school districts, to accomplish the purposes of education, a schoolteacher stands in the place of a parent and may exercise powers of control, restraint, discipline, and correction as necessary, provided that the discipline is reasonable. The Supreme Court has ruled that under certain circumstances, the schools may also employ corporal punishment. (See also CORPORAL PUNISHMENT)

DISLOCATION
The displacement of a bone, usually disrupting a joint, which may accompany a fracture or may occur alone.

DISPOSITION
The order of a juvenile or family court issued at a dispositional hearing which determines whether a minor, already found to be a dependent or delinquent child, should continue in or return to the parental home, and under what kind of supervision, or whether the minor should be placed out-of-home, and in what kind of setting: a relative's home, foster home, or institution. Disposition in a civil case parallels sentencing in a criminal case.

DISPOSITIONAL CONFERENCE
A conference, preferably multidisciplinary, in which the child, parent, family, and home diagnostic assessments are evaluated and decisions are made as to court involvement, steps needed to protect the child, and type of long-term treatment. This conference should be held within the first 72 hours after hospital admission or reporting of the case.

DISPOSITIONAL HEARING (See DISPOSITION)

DISTAL
Far; farther from any point of reference. Opposite of proximal.

DOMESTIC RELATIONS COURT (See COURTS)

DUE PROCESS
The rights of persons involved in legal proceedings to be treated with fairness. These rights include the right to adequate notice in advance of hearings, the right to notice of allegations of misconduct, the right to assis-

tance of a lawyer, the right to confront and cross-examine witnesses, and the right to refuse to give self-incriminating testimony. In child abuse or neglect cases, courts are granting more and more due process to parents in recognition of the fact that loss of parental rights, temporarily or permanently, is as serious as loss of liberty. However, jury trials and presumptions of innocence are still afforded in very few juvenile or family court cases.

DUODENUM
The first portion of the small intestine which connects it to the stomach.

EARLY AND PERIODIC SCREENING, DIAGNOSIS, AND TREATMENT (EPSDT)
Program enacted in 1967 under Medicaid (Title 19 of the Social Security Act), with early detection of potentially crippling or disabling conditions among poor children as its goal. The establishment of EPSDT was a result of studies indicating that physical and mental defects were high among poor children and that early detection of the problems and prompt receipt of health care could reduce the consequences and the need for remedial'services in later life. Although a recent study by the Children's Defense Fund has indicated that existing health systems are not adequate to facilitate the goals of EPSDT, the program has uncovered many previously undetected or untreated health problems among those children whom it has been able to reach.

EARLY INTERVENTION
Programs and services focusing on prevention by relieving family stress before child abuse and neglect occur; for example, helplines, Head Start, home health visitors, EPSDT, crisis nurseries.

ECCHYMOSIS (See INTRADERMAL HEMORRHAGE)

EDEMA
Swelling caused by an excessive amount of fluid in body tissue. It often follows a bump or bruise but may also be caused by allergy, malnutrition, or disease.

EMERGENCY CUSTODY (See CUSTODY)

EMERGENCY SERVICES
The focus of these services is protection of a child and prevention of further maltreatment through availability of a reporting mechanism on a 24-hour basis and immediate intervention. This intervention could include hospitalization of the child, assistance in the home including homemakers, or removal of the child from the home to a shelter or foster home. (See also COMPREHENSIVE EMERGENCY SERVICES)

EMOTIONAL ABUSE (See CHILD ABUSE AND NEGLECT)

EMOTIONAL NEGLECT (See CHILD ABUSE AND NEGLECT)

ENCOPRESIS
Involuntary passage of feces.

ENURESIS
Involuntary passage of urine.

EPIPHYSIS
Growth center near the end of a long bone.

EVIDENCE
Any sort of proof submitted to the court for the purpose of influencing the court's decision. Some special kinds of evidence are:

Circumstantial
Proof of circumstances which may imply another fact. For example, proof that a parent kept a broken appliance cord may connect the parent to infliction of unique marks on a child's body.

Direct
Generally consisting of testimony of the type such as a neighbor stating that he/she saw the parent strike the child with an appliance cord.

Hearsay
Second-hand evidence, generally consisting of testimony of the type such as, "I heard him say. . . ." Except in certain cases, such evidence is usually excluded because it is considered unreliable and because the person making the original statement cannot be cross-examined.

Opinion
Although witnesses are ordinarily not permitted to testify to their beliefs or opinions, being restricted instead to reporting what they actually saw or heard, when a witness can be qualified as an expert on a given subject, he/she can report his/her conclusions, for example, "Based upon these marks, it is my opinion as a doctor that the child must have been struck with a flexible instrument very much like this appliance cord." Lawyers are sometimes allowed to ask qualified experts "hypothetical questions," in which the witness is asked to assume the truth of certain facts and to express an opinion based on those "facts." (See also EXPERT TESTIMONY)

Physical
Any tangible piece of proof such as a document, X-ray, photograph, or weapon used to inflict an injury. Physical evidence must usually be authenticated by a witness who testifies to the connection of the evidence (also called an exhibit) with other facts in the case.

Evidentiary Standards
State laws differ in the quantum of evidence which is considered necessary to prove a case of child maltreatment. Three of the most commonly used standards are:

Beyond a Reasonable Doubt (the standard required in all criminal court proceedings). Evidence which is entirely convincing or satisfying to a moral certainty. This is the strictest standard of all.

Clear and Convincing Evidence. Less evidence than is required to prove a case beyond a reasonable doubt, but still an amount which would make one confident of the truth of the allegations.

Preponderance of the Evident (the standard in most civil court proceedings). Merely presenting a greater weight of credible evidence than that presented by the opposing party. This is the easiest standard of proof of all.

EXHIBIT
Physical evidence used in court. In a child abuse case, an exhibit may consist of X-rays, photographs of the child's injuries, or the actual materials presumably used to inflict the injuries. (See also EVIDENCE)

EXPERT TESTIMONY
Witnesses with various types of expertise may testify in child abuse or neglect cases; usually these expert witnesses are physicians or radiologists. Experts are usually questioned in court about their education or experience which qualifies them to give professional opinions about the matter in question. Only after the hearing officer determines that the witness is, in fact, sufficiently expert in the subject matter may that witness proceed to state his/her opinions. (See also EVIDENCE)

EXPERT WITNESS (See EXPERT TESTIMONY)

EXPLOITATION OF CHILDREN
1) Involving a child in illegal or immoral activities for the benefit of a parent or caretaker. This could include child pornography, child prostitution, sexual abuse, or forcing a child to steal.
2) Forcing workloads on a child in or outside the home so as to interfere with the health, education, and well-being of the child.

EXPUNGEMENT

Destruction of records. Expungement may be ordered by the court after a specified number of years or when the juvenile, parent, or defendant applies for expungement and shows that his/her conduct has improved. Expungement also applies to the removal of an unverified report of abuse or neglect that has been made to a central registry. (See also CENTRAL REGISTRY)

EXTRAVASATED BLOOD
Discharge or escape of blood into tissue.

FAILURE TO THRIVE SYNDROME (FTT)
A serious medical condition most often seen in children under one year of age. An FTT child's height, weight, and motor development fall significantly short of the average growth rates of normal children. In about 10% of FTT cases, there is an organic cause such as serious heart, kidney, or intestinal disease, a genetic error of metabolisin, or brain damage. All other cases are a result of a disturbed parent-child relationship manifested in severe physical and emotional neglect of the child. In diagnosing FTT as child neglect, certain criteria should be considered:
1) The child's weight is below the third percentile, but substantial weight gain occurs when the child is properly nurtured, such as when hospitalized.
2) The child exhibits developmental retardation which decreases when there is adequate feeding and appropriate stimulation.
3) Medical investigation provides no evidence that disease or medical abnormality is causing the symptoms.
4) The child exhibits clinical signs of deprivation which decrease in a more nurturing environment.
5) There appears to be a significant environmental psychosocial disruption in the child's family.

FAMILIES ANONYMOUS
1) Name used by the National Center for the Prevention and Treatment of Child Abuse and Neglect at Denver for self-help groups for abusive parents. These groups operate in much the same way as the more widely-known Parents Anonymous. (See also PARENTS ANONYMOUS)
2) Self-help groups for families of drug abusers.

FAMILIES-AT-RISK
May refer to families evidencing high potential for child abuse or neglect because of a conspicuous, severe parental problem, such as criminal behavior, substance abuse, mental retardation, or psychosis. More often refers to families evidencing high potential for abuse or neglect because of risk factors which may be less conspicuous but multiple. These include: 1) environmental stress such as unemployment or work dissatisfaction; social isolation; anomie; lack of child care resources; I and/or 2) family stress such as marital discord; chronically and/or emotionally immature parent with a history of abuse or neglect as a child; unwanted pregnancy; colicky, hyperactive, or handicapped baby or child; siblings a year or less apart; sudden changes in family due to illness, separation, or death; parentla ignorance of child care and child development. Increasingly, the maternal-infant bonding process at childbirth is evaluated and used as one means to identify families-at-risk. Families thus identified should be offered immediate and periodic assistance.

FAMILY
Two or more persons related by blood, marriage, or mutual agreement who interact and provide one another with mutual physical, emotional, social, and/or economic care. Families can be described as "extended," with more than one generation in a household; or "nuclear," with only parent(s) and child(ren). Families can also be described as "mixed" or "multiracial"; "multi-parent," as in a commune or collective; or "single-parent." These types are not mutually exclusive.

FAMILY COURT (See COURTS)

FAMILY DYNAMICS
Interrelationships between and among individual family members. The evaluation of family dynamics is an important factor in the

identification, diagnosis, and treatment of child abuse and neglect.

FAMILY DYSFUNCTION
Ineffective functioning of the family as a unit or of individual family members in their family role because of physical, mental, or situational problems of one or more family members. A family which does not have or use internal or external resources to cope with its problems or fulfill its responsibilities to children may be described as dysfunctional. Child abuse and neglect is evidence of family dysfunction.

FAMILY IMPACT STATEMENT
Report which assesses the effect of existing and proposed legislation, policies, regulations, and practices on family life. The purpose is to promote legislation and policies which work for, not against, healthy family life. At the federal level, this activity is being developed by the Family Impact Seminar, George Washington University Institute for Educational Leadership (1001 Connecticut Ave., N.W., Suite 732, Washington, D.C. 20036).

FAMILY LIFE EDUCATION
Programs focusing on educating, enlightening, and supporting individuals and families regarding aspects of family life; for example, child development classes, communication skills workshops, sex education courses, or money management courses. Family life education might well be part of every child abuse and neglect prevention program, and may be part of the treatment program for abusive or neglectful parents who lack this information.

FAMILY PLANNING
Information and counseling provided to assist in controlling family size and spacing of children, including referrals to various agencies such as Planned Parenthood.

As a condition of receiving federal funding for AFDC (see SOCIAL SECURITY ACT), states are required to offer family planning services to applicants designated as "appropriate." Family planning should be part of a child abuse and neglect prevention program.

FAMILY POLICY
Generally refers to public social and economic policies that centrally affect families. There is considerable confusion about the term, with some persons believing that family policy should mean more direct policies affecting families, such as family planning policies. There is much more agreement that we should look at the impact of numerous policies on families, and that these should include a wide range of governmental policies. (See also FAMILY IMPACT STATEMENT)

FAMILY SHELTER
A 24-hour residential care facility for entire families. The setting offers around-the-clock care, and often provides diagnosis and comprehensive treatment on a short-term basis. In child abuse and neglect, a family shelter is used primarily for crisis intervention.

FAMILY SYSTEM
The concept that families operate as an interacting whole and are an open system, so that many factors in the environment affect the functioning of family members and the interaction among members. It is also conceptualized that the behavior of the family as an interacting unit has an effect on a number of factors in the outer environment.

FAMILY VIOLENCE
Abusive or aggressive behavior between parents, known as wife battering or spouse abuse; between children, known as sibling abuse; and/or between parents and children within a family, usually child abuse. This behavior is related to factors within the structure of a family system and/or society; for example, poverty, models of violent behavior displayed via mass media, stress due to excessive numbers of children, values of dominance and submissiveness, and attitudes toward discipline and punishment. It may also occur as a result of alcoholism or other substance abuse.

The terms family violence and domestic violence are sometimes used interchangeably but some persons exclude child abuse from the definition of domestic violence and limit it to violence between adult mates or spouses.

FEDERAL REGULATIONS

Guidelines and regulations developed by departments or agencies of the federal government to govern programs administered or funded by those agencies. Regulations specify policies and procedures outlined in a more general way in public laws or acts. Proposed federal regulations, or changes in existing regulations, are usually published in the *Federal Register* for public review and comment. They are subsequently published in the final form adopted by the governing agency.

FEDERAL STANDARDS (See STANDARDS)

FELONY

A serious crime for which the punishment may be imprisonment for longer than a year and/or a fine greater than $1,000. Distinguished from misdemeanor or infraction, both of lesser degree.

FIFTH AMENDMENT

The Fifth Amendment to the U.S. Constitution guarantees a defendant that he/she cannot be compelled to present self-incriminating testimony.

FONTANEL

The soft spots on a baby's skull where the bones of the skull have not yet grown together.

FORENSIC MEDICINE

That branch of the medical profession concerned with establishing evidence for legal proceedings.

FOSTER CARE

A form of substitute care for children who need to be removed from their own homes. Usually this is a temporary placement in which a child lives with a licensed foster family or caretaker until he/she can return to his/her own home or until reaching the age of majority. Foster care all too often becomes a permanent method of treatment for abused or neglected children. Effective foster care ideally includes service to the child, service to the natural parents, service to the foster parents, and periodic review of the placement.

FOSTER GRANDPARENTS

Retired persons or senior citizens who provide nurturance and support for children to whom they are not related, including abused and neglected children, by babysitting or taking them for recreational outings. This enables parents to have some respite and allows retired or older persons an opportunity to become involved in community activities. Sometimes foster grandparents are volunteers and sometimes they are paid by an agency program.

FOUNDED REPORT

Any report of suspected child abuse or neglect made to the mandated agency which is confirmed or verified. Founded reports outnumber unfounded reports.

FRACTURE

A broken bone, which is one of the most common injuries found among battered children. The fracture may occur in several ways:

Chip Fracture
A small piece of bone is flaked from the major part of the bone.

Comminuted Fracture
Bone is crushed or broken into a number of pieces.

Compound Fracture
Fragment(s) of broken bone protrudes through the skin, causing a wound.

Simple Fracture
Bone breaks without wounding the surrounding tissue.

Spiral Fracture

Twisting causes the line of the fracture to encircle the bone like a spiral staircase.

Torus Fracture
A folding, bulging, or buckling fracture. See diagram on next page for names and locations of the major bones of the human skeleton.

FRONTAL
Referring to the front of the head; the forehead.

FUNDASCOPIC EXAM
Opthalmic examination to determine if irregularities or internal injuries to the eye exist.

GATEKEEPERS
Professionals and the agencies which employ them who are in frequent or periodic contact with families or children and who are therefore in an advantageous position to spot individual and family problems, including child abuse and neglect, and make appropriate referrals for early intervention or treatment.

GLUTEAL
Related to the buttocks, which are made up of the large gluteus maximus muscles.

GONORRHEA (See VENEREAL DISEASE)

GRAND ROUNDS
Hospital staff meetings for presentation and discussion of a particular case or medical problem.

GUARDIAN
Adult charged lawfully with the responsibility for a child. A guardian has almost all the rights and powers of a natural parent, but the relationship is subject to termination or change. A guardian may or may not also have custody and therefore actual care and supervision of the child.

GUARDIAN AD LITEM (GAL)
Adult appointed by the court to represent the child in a judicial proceeding. The *guardian ad litem* may be, but is not necessarily, an attorney. Under the Child Abuse Prevention and Treatment Act, a state cannot qualify for federal assistance unless it provides by statute "that in every case involving an abused or neglected child which results in a judicial proceeding a *guardian ad litem* shall be appointed to represent the child in such proceedings." Some states have begun to allow a GAL for children in divorce cases.

HEAD START
A nationwide comprehensive program for disadvantaged preschool children, funded by the HEW Administration for Children, Youth and Families to meet the educational, nutritional, and health needs of the children and to encourage parent participation in their children's development.

Through federal policy instructions (see *Federal Register,* January 26, 1977), all Head Start staff are mandated to report suspected cases of child abuse and neglect. These policy instructions supersede individual child abuse and neglect reporting laws in states which do not include Head Start staff as mandated reporters.

HEARING
Judicial proceeding where issues of fact or law are tried and in which both parties have a right to be heard. A hearing is synonymous with a trial.

HEARING OFFICER
A judge or other individual who presides at a judicial proceeding. The role of judge is performed in some juvenile court hearings by referees or commissioners, whose orders are issued in the name of the supervising judge. Acts of a referee or commissioner may be undone after the supervising judge has conducted a rehearing in the case.

HELPLINE
Usually a telephone counseling, information, and referral service characterized by caller anonymity, late hour availability, and the use

of trained volunteers as staff. The goal is usually early intervention in any kind of family stress, as well as crisis intervention in child abuse and neglect. Helplines relieve social isolation and offer ways of ventilating stress which are not destructive. Unlike hotlines, helplines generally cannot report cases of child abuse and neglect since they do not know the caller's name. Instead, the helpline attempts to have the caller himself/herself seek professional assistance and/or maintain a regular calling relationship for support and as an alternative to violent behavior. Helplines appear to be very cost effective in the preventive of child abuse and neglect. Major disadvantages are lack of visual cues to problems and limited opportunity for follow-up services. (See also HOTLINE)

HEMATEMESIS
Vomiting of blood from the stomach, often resulting from internal injuries.

HEMATOMA
A swelling caused by a collection of blood in an enclosed space, such as under the skin or the skull.

HEMATUREA
Blood in the urine.

HEMOPHILIA
Hereditary blood clotting disorder characterized by spontaneous or traumatic internal and external bleeding and bruising.

HEMOPTYSIS
Spitting or coughing blood from the windpipe or lungs.

HEMORRHAGE
The escape of blood from the vessels; bleeding.

HOME HEALTH VISITOR (See CHILD HEALTH VISITOR)

HOME START
A nationwide home-based program funded by the HEW Administration for Children, Youth and Families to strengthen parents as educators of their own children.

HOMEMAKER SERVICES
Provision of assistance, support, and relief for parents who may be unable or unwilling to fulfill parenting functions because of illness or being overwhelmed with parenting responsibilities. A homemaker is placed in a home on an hourly or weekly basis and assists with housekeeping and child care while demonstrating parenting skills and providing some degree of nurturance for parents and children.

HOSPITAL HOLD
Hospitalization for further observation and protection of a child suspected of being abused or neglected. This usually occurs when a suspected case is discovered in an emergency room. In most cases, holding the child is against the wishes of the parent or caretaker. (See also CUSTODY)

HOTLINE
Twenty-four hour statewide or local answering service for reporting child abuse or neglect and initiating investigation by a local agency. This is often confused with a helpline. (See also HELPLINE)

HYPERACTIVE
More active than is considered normal.

HYPERTHERMIA
Condition of high body temperature.

HYPHEMA
Hemorrhage within the anterior chamber of the eye, often appearing as a bloodshot eye. The cause could be a blow to the head or violent shaking.

HYPOACTIVE
Less active than is considered normal.

HYPOTHERMIA
Condition of low body temperature.

HYPOVITAMINOSIS

Condition due to the deficiency of one or more essential vitamins. (See also AVITAMINOSIS)

IDENTIFICATION OF CHILD ABUSE AND NEGLECT
Diagnosis or verification of child abuse and neglect cases by mandated agency workers or a diagnostic team following investigation of suspected child abuse and neglect (see INDICATORS OF CHILD ABUSE AND NEGLECT). Identification of child abuse and neglect therefore depends not only on professional diagnostic skill but also on the extent to which the public and professionals report suspected cases. Public awareness campaigns are important to effect identification, but at the same time it is important to have sufficient staff in the mandated agency to handle all the reports a public awareness campaign may generate (see COMMUNITY AWARENESS and COMMUNITY EDUCATION). More reporting and therefore identification will also occur as states strengthen their reporting laws so as to extend the number of persons who must report and penalize them more heavily if they don't. It is generally agreed that to date the identification of child abuse and neglect represents only a small proportion of the actual incidence of the problem. It is also generally agreed that a greater degree of identification occurs in minority and low income groups because these persons are more visible to agencies and professionals required to report. The incidence is probably as high in upper socio-economic groups, but identification is more difficult, particularly because private physicians generally dislike to report.

ILEUM
Final portion of the small intestine which connects with the colon.

IMMUNITY, LEGAL
Legal protection from civil or criminal liability.
1) Child abuse and neglect reporting statutes often confer immunity upon persons mandated to report, giving them an absolute defense to libel, slander, invasion of privacy, false arrest, and other lawsuits which the person accused of the act might file. Some grants of immunity are limited only to those persons who report in good faith and without malicious intent.
2) Immunity from criminal liability is sometimes conferred upon a witness in order to obtain vital testimony. Thereafter, the witness cannot be prosecuted with the use of information he/she disclosed in his/her testimony. If an immunized witness refuses to testify, he/she can be imprisoned for contempt of court.

IMPETIGO
A highly contagious, rapidly spreading skin disorder which occurs principally in infants and young children. The disease, characterized by red blisters, may be an indicator of neglect and poor living conditions.

IMPULSE-RIDDEN MOTHER
Term often used to describe one kind of neglectful parent who demonstrates restlessness, aggressiveness, inability to tolerate stress, manipulativeness, and craving for excitement or change. This parent may have a lesser degree of early deprivation than the apathetic-futile parent, but lacks self-control over strong impulses and/or has not learned limit-setting.

IN CAMERA
Any closed hearing before a judge in his chambers is said to be *in camera*.

IN LOCO PARENTIS
"In the place of a parent." Refers to actions of a guardian or other non-parental custodian.

INCEST
Sexual intercourse between persons who are closely related. Some state laws recognize incest only as sexual intercourse among consaguineous, or blood, relations; other states recognize incest as sexual relations between a variety of family members related by blood and/or law. In the U.S., the prohibition against incest is specified by many states' laws as well as by cultural tradition, with state laws

usually defining incest as marriage or sexual relationships between relatives who are closer than second, or sometimes even more distant, cousins. While incest and sexual abuse are sometimes thought to be synonymous, it should be realized that incest is only one aspect of sexual abuse. Incest can occur within families between members of the same sex, but the most common form of incest is between father and daughters. It is generally agreed that incest is much more common than the number of reported cases indicates. Also, because society has not until the present done much about this problem, professionals have generally not had adequate training to deal with it, and the way the problem is handled may prove more traumatic for a child victim of incest than the incest experience itself. It should be noted that sexual relations between relatives may be defined as incest, but that in cest is not considered child sexual abuse unless a minor is involved. (See also CHILD ABUSE AND NEGLECT, SEXUAL ABUSE, SEXUAL MISUSE)

INCIDENCE
The extent to which a problem occurs in a given population. No accurate or complete data is available on the actual incidence of child abuse and neglect in the U.S. because major studies have not been able to obtain data from some states or have found the data not to be comparable. For continuing efforts to solve this problem, see NATIONAL STUDY ON CHILD ABUSE AND NEGLECT REPORTING. Informed estimates of incidence range from 600,000 to one million cases of child abuse and neglect per year in this country. It is generally agreed that child neglect is four to five or more times more common than child abuse. Incidence of actual child abuse and neglect should not be confused with the number of reported cases in a central registry, since the latter include reports of suspected but unconfirmed cases. On the other hand, it is generally agreed that because of insufficient reporting, the number of actual cases coming to the attention of local agencies is but a small proportion of the actual number of cases in the population. (See also CENTRAL REGISTRY and IDENTIFICATION OF CHILD ABUSE AND NEGLECT)

INDICATED CHILD ABUSE AND NEGLECT
1) In some state statutes, "indicated" child abuse and neglect means a confirmed or verified case.
2) Medically, "indicated" means a probable case.

INDICATORS OF CHILD ABUSE AND NEGLECT
Signs or symptoms which, when found in various combinations, point to possible abuse or neglect. See chart on next page for common indicators of child abuse and neglect.

INDICTMENT
The report of a grand jury charging an adult with criminal conduct. The process of indictment by secret grand jury proceedings bypasses the filing of a criminal complaint and the holding of a preliminary hearing in municipal court, so that prosecution begins immediately in superior court.

INFANTICIDE
The killing of an infant or many infants. Until modern times, infanticide was an accepted method of population control. It often took the form of abandonment. A few primitive cultures still practice infanticide.

Indicators of Child Abuse and Neglect

CATEGORY	CHILD'S APPEARANCE	CHILD'S BEHAVIOR	CARETAKER'S BEHAVIOR
Physical Abuse	—Bruises and welts (on the face, lips, or mouth; in various stages of healing; on large areas of the torso, back, buttocks, or thighs; in unusual patterns, clustered, or reflective of the instrument used to inflict them; on several different surface areas). —Burns (cigar or cigarette burns; glove or sock-like burns or doughnut shaped burns on the buttocks or genitalia indicative of immersion in hot liquid; rope burns on the arms, legs, neck or torso; patterned burns that show the shape of the item (iron, grill, etc.) used to inflict them). —Fractures (skull, jaw, or nasal fractures; spiral fractures of the long (arm and leg) bones; fractures in various states of healing; multiple fractures; any fracture in a child under the age of two). —Lacerations and abrasions (to the mouth, lip, gums, or eye; to the external genitalia). —Human bite marks.	—Wary of physical contact with adults. —Apprehensive when other children cry. —Demonstrates extremes in behavior (e.g., extreme aggressiveness or withdrawal). —Seems frightened of parents. —Reports injury by parents.	—Has history of abuse as a child. —Uses harsh discipline inappropriate to child's age, transgression, and condition. —Offers illogical, unconvincing, contradictory, or no explanation of child's injury. —Seems unconcerned about child. —Significantly misperceives child (e.g., sees him as bad, evil, a monster, etc.). —Psychotic or psychopathic. —Misuses alcohol or other drugs. —Attempts to conceal child's injury or to protect identity of person responsible.
Neglect	—Consistently dirty, unwashed, hungry, or inappropriately dressed. —Without supervision for extended periods of time or when engaged in dangerous activities. —Constantly tired or listless. —Has unattended physical problems or lacks routine medical care. —Is exploited, overworked, or kept from attending school. —Has been abandoned.	—Is engaging in delinquent acts (e.g., vandalism, drinking, prostitution, drug use, etc.). —Is begging or stealing food. —Rarely attends school.	—Misuses alcohol or other drugs. —Maintains chaotic home life. —Shows evidence of apathy or futility. —Is mentally ill or of diminished intelligence. —Has long-term chronic illnesses. —Has history of neglect as a child.
Sexual Abuse	—Has torn, stained, or bloody underclothing. —Experience pain or itching in the genital area. —Has bruises or bleeding in external genitalia, vagina, or anal regions. —Has venereal disease. —Has swollen or red cervix, vulva, or perineum. —Has semen around mouth or genitalia or on clothing. —Is pregnant.	—Appears withdrawn or engages in fantasy or infantile behavior. —Has poor peer relationships. —Is unwilling to participate in physical activities. —Is engaging in delinquent acts or runs away. —States he/she has been sexually assaulted by parent/caretaker.	—Extremely protective or jealous of child. —Encourages child to engage in prostitution or sexual acts in the presence of caretaker. —Has been sexually abused as a child. —Is experiencing marital difficulties. —Misuses alcohol or other drugs. —Is frequently absent from the home.
Emotional Maltreatment	—Emotional maltreatment, often less tangible than other forms of child abuse and neglect, can be indicated by behaviors of the child and the caretaker.	—Appears overly compliant, passive, undemanding. —Is extremely aggressive, demanding, or rageful. —Shows overly adaptive behaviors, either inappropriately adult (e.g., parents other children) or inappropriately infantile (e.g., rocks constantly, sucks thumb, is enuretic). —Lags In physical, emotional, and intellectual development. Attempts suicide.	—Blames or belittles child. —Is cold and rejecting. —Withholds love. —Treats siblings unequally. —Seems unconcerned about child's problem.

INSTITUTIONAL CHILD ABUSE AND NEGLECT

1) Abuse and neglect as a result of social or institutional policies, practices, or conditions. The rather widespread practice of detaining children in adult jails is one example. Usually refers to specific institutions or populations, but may also be used to mean societal abuse or neglect. (See also SOCIETAL ABUSE AND NEGLECT)

2) Child abuse and neglect committed by an employee of a public or private institution or group home against a child in the institution or group home.

INTAKE

Process by which cases are introduced into an agency. Workers are usually assigned to interview persons seeking help in order to determine the nature and extent of the problem(s). However, in child abuse and neglect, intake of reports of suspected cases is usually by telephone and an interview with the reporting person is not required. Child abuse and neglect workers who do intake must be skilled in getting as much information as possible from the reporter in order to determine whether the situation is an emergency requiring instant attention.

INTERDISCIPLINARY TEAM (See COMMUNITY TEAM)

INTRADERMAL HEMORRHAGE

Bleeding within the skin; bruise. Bruises are common injuries exhibited by battered children, and are usually classified by size:

Petechiae
Very small bruise caused by broken capillaries. Petechiae may be traumatic in nature or may be caused by clotting disorders.

Purpura
Petechiae occurring in groups, or a small bruise (up to 1 cm. in diameter).

Ecchymosis
Larger bruise.

INVOLUNTARY CLIENT

Person who has been referred or court-ordered for services but who has not asked for help. Most abusive and neglectful parents are initially involuntary clients and may not accept the need for services. They may deny that there is a problem and resist assistance. Motivation for change may be minimal or nonexistent; however, skillful workers have demonstrated that motivation can be developed and treatment can be effective.

INVOLUNTARY PLACEMENT

Court-ordered assignment of custody to an agency and placement of a child, often against the parents' wishes, after a formal court proceeding, or the taking of emergency or protective custody against the parents' wishes preceding a custody hearing. (See also CUSTODY)

JEJUNUM

Middle portion of the small intestine between the duodenum and the ileum.

JURISDICTION

The power of a particular court to hear cases involving certain categories of persons or allegations. Jurisdiction may also depend upon geographical factors such as the county of a person's residence. (See also COURTS)

JURY

Group of adults selected by lawyers who judge the truth of allegations made in a legal proceeding. Trial by jury is available in all criminal cases, including cases of suspected child abuse and neglect. Very few juvenile, probate, or domestic relations court cases can be tried before a jury and are instead decided by the presiding judge.

JUVENILE COURT (See COURTS)

JUVENILE JUDGE

Presiding officer of a juvenile court. Often in a juvenile court, there are several other hearing officers of lesser rank, usually called referees or commissioners. (See also HEARING OFFICER)

LABELING
The widespread public and professional practice of affixing terms which imply serious or consistent deviance to the perpetrators and/or victims of child abuse and neglect; for example, "child abuser." Since deviance may suggest that punishment is warranted, this kind of labeling decreases the possibility of treatment. This is unfortunate, because experts agree that 80% or 85% of all child abuse and neglect cases have the potential for successful treatment. Such labeling may also make parents see themselves in a negative, despairing way, and discourage them from seeking assistance.

LABORATORY TESTS
Routine medical tests used to aid diagnosis. Those particularly pertinent to child abuse are:

Partial Thromboplastin Time (PTT) Measures clotting factors in the blood.

Prothrombin Time (PT)
Measures clotting factors in the blood.

Urinalysis
Examination of urine for sugar, protein, blood, etc.

Complete Blood Count (CBC)
Measure and analysis of red and white blood cells.

Rumpel-Leede (Tourniquet) Test
Measures fragility of capillaries and/or bruisability.

LACERATION
A jagged cut or wound.

LATCH KEY CHILDREN
Working parents' children who return after school to a home where no parent or caretaker is present. This term was coined because these children often wear a house key on a chain around their necks.

LATERAL
Toward the side.

LAY THERAPIST (See PARENT AIDE)

LEAST DETRIMENTAL ALTERNATIVE
(See
BEST INTEREST OF THE CHILD)

LEGAL RIGHTS OF PERSONS IDENTIFIED IN REPORTS
Standards for legal rights stress the need for all persons concerned with child abuse and neglect to be aware of the legal rights of individuals identified in reports and to be committed to any action necessary to enforce these rights. According to the National Center on Child Abuse and Neglect *Revision to Federal Standards on the Prevention and Treatment of Child Abuse and Neglect (Draft)*, these rights include the following:
1. Any person identified in a report as being suspected of having abused or neglected a child should be informed of his/her legal rights.
2) The person responsible for the child's welfare should receive written notice and be advised of his her legal rights when protective custody authority is exercised.
3) A child who is alleged to be abused or neglected should have independent legal representation in a child protection proceeding.
4) The parent or other person responsible for a child's welfare who is alleged to have abused or neglected a child should be entitled to legal representation in a civil or criminal proceeding.
5) The local child protective services unit should have the assistance of legal counsel in all child protective proceedings.
6) Each party should have the right to appeal protective case determinations.
7) Any person identified in a child abuse or neglect report should be protected from unauthorized disclosure of personal information contained in the report.

LESION
Any injury to any part of the body from any cause that results in damage or loss of structure or function of the body tissue involved. A lesion may be caused by poison, infection, dysfunction, or violence, and may be either accidental or intentional.

LIABILITY FOR FAILURE TO REPORT
State statutes which require certain categories of persons to report cases of suspected child abuse and/or neglect are often enforced by the imposition of a penalty, fine and/or imprisonment, for those who fail to report. Recent lawsuits have provided what may become an even more significant penalty for failure to report: when a report should have been made and a child comes to serious harm in a subsequent incident of abuse or neglect, the person who failed to report the initial incident may be held civilly liable to the child for the damages suffered in the subsequent incident. Such damages could amount to many thousands of dollars. (See also MANDATED REPORTERS)

LICENSING PARENTHOOD
Proposed method of assuring adequate parenting skills. Various proposals have been developed, including mandatory parenthood education in high school, with a certificate upon completion. Serious advocates compare the process with certification of driving capability by driver's licenses. Many consider the proposal unworkable.

LOCAL AUTHORITY
Local authority refers to two groups: 1) the social service agency (local agency) designated by the state department of social services (state department) and authorized by state law to be responsible for local child abuse and neglect prevention, identification, and treatment efforts, and 2) the community child protection coordinating council (community council). The standards on local authority, as specified in the National Center on Child Abuse and Neglect *Revision to Federal Standards on the Prevention and Treatment of Child Abuse and Neglect (Draft)*, include:

Administration and Organization
1. The local agency should establish a distinct child protective services unit with sufficient and qualified staff.
2. The local agency in cooperation with the state department should allocate sufficient funds and provide adequate administrative support to the local unit.
3. The local agency should initiate the establishment of a community council which is to be representative of those persons providing or concerned with child abuse and neglect prevention, identification, and treatment services.

Primary Prevention
4. The local unit and the community council should work together to establish formalized needs assessment and planning processes.

Secondary and Tertiary Prevention
5. The local unit and the community council should work together to develop a comprehensive and coordinated service delivery system for children-at-risk and families-at-risk to be presented in an annual plan.
6. The local unit and the community council should develop standards on the care of children which represent the minimum expectations of the community and provide the basis for the local unit's operational definitions and referral guidelines.
7. The local unit and the community council should establish a multidisciplinary child abuse and neglect case consultation team.
8. The local unit should provide or arrange for services to assist families who request help for themselves in fulfilling their parenting responsibilities.
9. The local unit should ensure that reports of child abuse and neglect can be received on a twenty-four hour, seven days per week basis.

10 The intake services worker should intervene immediately if a report is considered an emergency; otherwise, intervention should take place within seventy-two hours.
11 The intake services worker should ensure the family's right to privacy by making the assessment process time-limited.
12 The treatment services worker should develop an individualized treatment plan for each family and each family member.
13 The treatment services worker should arrange for, coordinate, and monitor services provided to a family.

Resource Enhancement

14 The agency and the community council should assist in the training of the local unit and other community service systems.
15 The agency should promote internal agency coordination.
16 The local unit should implement community education and awareness.
17 The agency should participate in or initiate its own research, review, and evaluation studies.

(See also STATE AUTHORITY)

LONG BONE
General term applied to the bones of the leg or the arm.

LONG TERM TREATMENT
Supportive and therapeutic services over a period of time, usually at least a year, to restore the parent(s) of an abused or neglected child and/or the child himself/herself to adequate levels of functioning and to prevent recurrence of child abuse or neglect.

LUMBAR
Pertaining to the part of the back and sides between the lowest ribs and the pelvis.

MALNUTRITION
Failure to receive adequate nourishment. Often exhibited in a neglected child, malnutrition may be caused by inadequate diet (either lack of food or insufficient amounts of needed vitamins, etc.) or by a disease or other abnormal condition affecting the body's ability to properly process foods taken in.

MALTREATMENT
Actions that are abusive, neglectful, or otherwise threatening to a child's welfare. Frequently used as a general term for child abuse and neglect.

MANDATED AGENCY
Agency designated by state statutes as legally responsible for receiving and investigating reports of suspected child abuse and neglect. Usually, this agency is a county welfare department or a child protective services unit within that department. Police or sheriffs departments may also be mandated agencies. (See also STATE AUTHORITY and LOCAL AUTHORITY)

MANDATED REPORTERS or MANDATORY REPORTERS
Persons designated by state statutes who are legally liable for not reporting suspected cases of child abuse and neglect to the mandated agency. The persons so designated vary according to state law, but they are primarily professionals, such as pediatricians, nurses, school personnel, and social workers, who have frequent contact with children and families.

MARASMUS
A form of protein-calorie malnutrition occurring in infants and children. It is characterized by retarded growth and progressive wasting away of fat and muscle, but it is usually accompanied by the retention of appetite and mental alertness.

MATERNAL CHARACTERISTICS SCALE
Instrument designed to study personality characteristics of rural Appalachian mothers and the level of care they were providing their children. The purpose of this scale is to

sharpen caseworkers' perception of "apathetic-futile" or "impulse-ridden" mothers' personality characteristics for evaluation, diagnosis, and formulation of a treatment plan in cases of child neglect. Some authorities believe this scale has not been adequately validated.

MATERNAL-INFANT BONDING (See BONDING)

MEDIAL
Toward the middle or mid-line.

MEDICAID, TITLE 19 (See SOCIAL SECURITY ACT)

MEDICAL MODEL
Conceptualizing problems in terms of diagnosis and treatment of illness. With respect to child abuse and neglect, the medical model assumes an identifiable and therefore treatable cause of the abuse and/or neglect and focuses on identification and treatment in a medical or other health setting. For child abuse and neglect, some advantages of the medical model are financial support by the hospital, clinic, medical community; accessibility of medical services to the abused or neglected child; involvement of the physicians; and visibility and public acceptance. Possible disadvantages are overemphasis on physical abuse; overemphasis on physical diagnosis to the detriment of total treatment; and isolation from other professional and community resources. (Kempe)

MEDICAL NEGLECT (See CHILD ABUSE AND NEGLECT)

MENKES KINKY HAIR SYNDROME
Rare, inherited disease resulting in brittle bones and, eventually, death. It is found in infants and, because of the great number of fractures the child may exhibit, can be mistaken for child abuse.

MENTAL INJURY
Injury to the intellectual or psychological capacity of a child as evidenced by observable and substantial impairment in his/her ability to function within a normal range of performance and behavior, with due regard to his/her culture. The Child Abuse Prevention and Treatment Act and some state statutes include mental injury caused by a parent or caretaker as child abuse or neglect.

MESENTERY
Membrane attaching various organs to the body wall.

METABOLISM
The sum of all physical and chemical processes which maintain the life of an organism.

METAPHYSIS
Wider part of a long bone between the end and the shaft.

MINIMALLY ACCEPTABLE ENVIRONMENT
The emotional climate and physical surroundings necessary for children to grow physically, mentally, socially, and emotionally.

MINOR (See CHILD)

MIRANDA RULE
Legal provision that a confession is inadmissible in any court proceeding if the suspect was not forewarned of his/her right to remain silent before the confession was disclosed. (See also FIFTH AMENDMENT)

MISDEMEANOR
A crime for which the punishment can be no more than imprisonment for a year and/or a fine of $1,000. A misdemeanor is distinguished from a felony, which is more serious, and an infraction, which is less serious.

MODEL CHILD PROTECTION ACT
Guide for development of state legislation concerning child abuse and neglect and intended to enable legislators to provide a

comprehensive and workable law which will aid in resolving the problem. A draft *Model Child Protection Act* has been developed and is available from the National Center on Child Abuse and Neglect.

MONDALE ACT (See CHILD ABUSE PREVENTION AND TREATMENT ACT)

MONGOLIAN SPOTS
A type of birthmark that can appear anywhere on a child's body, most frequently on the lower back. These dark spots usually fade by age five. They can be mistaken for bruises.

MORAL NEGLECT (See CHILD ABUSE AND NEGLECT)

MORIBUND
Dying or near death.

MOTHERS ANONYMOUS
Original name of Parents Anonymous. (See PARENTS ANONYMOUS)

MULTIDISCIPLINARY TEAM
A group of professionals and possibly paraprofessionals representing a variety of disciplines who interact and coordinate their efforts to diagnose and treat specific cases of child abuse and neglect. A multidisciplinary group which also addresses the general problem of child abuse and neglect in a given community is usually described as a community team, and it will probably consist of several multidisciplinary teams with different functions (see COMMUNITY TEAM). Multidisciplinary teams may include, but are not limited to, medical, child care, and law enforcement personnel, social workers, psychiatrists and/or psychologists. Their goal is to pool their respective skills in order to formulate accurate diagnoses and to provide comprehensive coordinated treatment with continuity and follow-up for both parent(s) and child or children. Many multidisciplinary teams operate according to the Denver Model (see DENVER MODEL). Multidisciplinary teams may also be referred to as cross-disciplinary teams, interdisciplinary teams, or SCAN teams (see SCAN TEAM). However, the Child Abuse Prevention and Treatment Act uses the term "multidisciplinary team."

NATIONAL ASSOCIATION OF SOCIAL WORKERS (NASW)
1425 H St., N.W.
Washington, D.C. 20005
A national organization of professional social workers who are enrolled in or have completed baccalaureate, master's, or doctoral programs in social work education. Members must subscribe to the NASW Code of Ethics, and NASW provides a policy for adjudication of grievances in order to protect members and promote ethical practices.

NATIONAL CENTER FOR CHILD ADVOCACY (NCCA)
P.O. Box 1182
Washington, D.C. 20013
The National Center for Child Advocacy is part of the Children's Bureau of the Administration for Children, Youth and Families within the Office of Human Development Services of HEW. NCCA supports research, demonstration, and training programs and provides technical assistance to state and local agencies with the goal of increasing and improving child welfare services. These services include in-home support to families, such as parent education and homemaker services; foster care, adoption, and child protective services; and institutional care of children. A major project of NCCA is the Child Welfare Resource Information Exchange. (See also CHILD WELFARE RESOURCE INFORMATION EXCHANGE)

NATIONAL CENTER FOR THE PREVENTION AND TREATMENT OF CHILD ABUSE AND NEGLECT
1205 Oneida St.
Denver, Colorado 80220
This center, which is affiliated with the Department of Pediatrics of the University of Colorado Medical School, was established in

the fall of 1972 to provide more extensive and up-to-date education, research, and clinical material to professionals working in the area of child abuse and neglect. The center's multidisciplinary staff has provided leadership in formulating the views that child abuse and neglect is symptomatic of troubled family relationships; that treatment must consider the needs of all family members; and that outreach to isolated, non-trusting families and the multidisciplinary approach are necessary. Funded by the State of Colorado, the HEW Administration for Children, Youth and Families, and private foundations, the center's work includes education, consultation and technical assistance, demonstration programs for treatment, program evaluation, and research. This center also serves as the HEW Region VIII Resource Center.

NATIONAL CENTER ON CHILD ABUSE AND NEGLECT (NCCAN)
P.O. Box 1182
Washington, D.C. 20013
Office of the federal government located within the Children's Bureau of the Administration for Children, Youth and Families (formerly the Office of Child Development), which is part of the Office of Human Development Services of HEW. Established in 1974 by the Child Abuse Prevention and Treatment Act, the functions of NCCAN are to:

1) Compile, analyze, and publish an annual summary of recent and current research on child abuse and neglect.
2) Develop and maintain an information clearinghouse on all programs showing promise of success for the prevention, identification, and treatment of child abuse and neglect.
3) Compile and publish training materials for personnel who are engaged or intend to engage in the prevention, identification, and treatment of child abuse and neglect.
4) Provide technical assistance to public and nonprofit private agencies and organizations to assist them in planning, improving, developing, and carrying out programs and activities relating to the prevention, identification, and treatment of child abuse and neglect.
5) Conduct research into the causes of child abuse and neglect, and into the prevention, identification, and treatment thereof.
6) Make a complete and full study and investigation of the national incidence of child abuse and neglect, including a determination of the extent to which incidents of child abuse and neglect are increasing in number or severity.
7) Award grants to states whose child abuse and neglect legislation complies with federal legislation.

NCCAN is authorized to establish grants and contracts with public and private agencies and organizations to carry out the above activities. Grants and contracts may also be used to establish demonstration programs and projects which, through training, consultation, resource provision, or direct treatment, are designed to prevent, identify, and treat child abuse and neglect. (See also CHILD ABUSE PREVENTION AND TREATMENT ACT and REGIONAL RESOURCE CENTER)

NATIONAL CLEARINGHOUSE ON CHILD NEGLECT AND ABUSE (NCCNA) (See NATIONAL STUDY ON CHILD NEGLECT AND ABUSE REPORTING)

NATIONAL COMMITTEE FOR THE PREVENTION OF CHILD ABUSE
111 E. Wacker Drive
Suite 510
Chicago, Illinois 60601
The National Committee originated in Chicago in 1972 in response to increasing national incidence of deaths due to child abuse. It was formed to help prevent child abuse, which was defined as including non-accidental injury, emotional abuse, neglect, sexual abuse, and exploitation of children, at a time when most programs focused on identification and treatment. The commit-

tee's goals are to:
1) Stimulate greater public awareness of the problem.
2) Encourage public involvement in prevention and treatment.
3) Provide a national focal point for advocacy to prevent child abuse.
4) Facilitate communication about programs, policy, and research related to child abuse prevention.
5) Foster greater cooperation between existing and developing resources for child abuse prevention.

Activities of the committee include a national media campaign, publications, conference, research, and the establishment of state chapters of the committee.

NATIONAL REGISTER
Often confused with the National Study on Child Neglect and Abuse Reporting (National Clearinghouse), which compiles statistics on incidence of child abuse and neglect. A national register, which does not exist at this time, would operate in much the same way and with the same purposes as a state-level central register, but would collect reports of abuse and neglect nationwide. Collecting reports on a national scale would be highly problematic because of variance in state reporting laws and definitions of abuse and neglect. (See also CENTRAL REGISTER and NATIONAL STUDY ON CHILD NEGLECT AND ABUSE REPORTING)

NATIONAL STUDY ON CHILD NEGLECT AND ABUSE REPORTING
Formerly the National Clearinghouse on Child Neglect and Abuse, the National Study is funded by the National Center on Child Abuse and Neglect, Children's Bureau, HEW and is being conducted by the Children's Division of the American Humane Association. The study has been established to systematically collect data from official state sources on the nature, incidence, and characteristics of child abuse and neglect. Participating states receive reports generated from their own data on a quarterly basis so that they can monitor their own reporting mechanisms. At this time, about 40 states are submitting detailed incidence data to the study. It is hoped that the National Study will be able to produce accurate data on the national incidence of child abuse and neglect.

NEEDS ASSESSMENT
A formal or informal evaluation of what services are needed by abused and neglected children and their families within a specified geographical area or within another given population.

NEGLECT (See CHILD ABUSE AND NEGLECT)

NEGLECTED CHILD (See INDICATORS OF CHILD ABUSE AND NEGLECT)

NEGLIGENCE
Failure to act. May apply to a parent, as in child neglect, or to a person who by state statute is mandated to report child abuse and neglect but who fails to do so. Negligence lawsuits arising from failure to report are increasing, and any failure to obey the statutes proves negligence. Lawsuits claiming damages for negligence are civil proceedings.

NETWORKING
Formal or informal linkages of individuals, families, or other groups with similar social, education, medical, or other service needs with the public or private agencies, organizations, and/or individuals who can provide such services in their locale. Formal agreements are usually written and spell out under what circumstances a particular agency, group, or individual will provide certain services. Informal agreements are apt to be verbal and relate to a particular family or case.

NURTURANCE
Affectionate care and attention provided by a parent, parent substitute, or caretaker to promote the well-being of a child and encour-

age healthy emotional and physical development. Nurturance may also be needed by adults with inadequate parenting skills, or who were themselves abused or neglected as children, as a model for developing more positive relationships with their own children and as a way of strengthening their own self-esteem.

OCCIPITAL
Referring to the back of the head.

OMISSION, ACTS OF
Failure of a parent or caretaker to provide for a child's physical and/or emotional well-being. (See also CHILD ABUSE AND NEGLECT)

OSSIFICATION
Formation of bone.

OSTEOGENESIS IMPERFECTA
An inherited condition in which the bones are abnormally brittle and subject to fractures, and which may be mistakenly diagnosed as the result of child abuse.

OUTREACH
The process in which professionals, paraprofessionals, and/or volunteers actively seek to identify cases of family strees and potential or actual child abuse and neglect by making services known, accessible, and unthreatening. Effective outreach providing early intervention is important for the prevention of child abuse and neglect.

PA BUDDY
Term used by Parents Anonymous for a person who functions like a parent aide in relation to a Parents Anonymous member. (See also PARENTS ANONYMOUS and PARENT AIDE)

PARAPROFESSIONAL
Volunteer or agency employee trained to a limited extent in a particular profession. Since paraprofessionals are usually close in age, race, nationality, religion, or lifestyle to the clientele, they often have a greater likelihood of developing a trusting relationship with a client than do some professionals. The role of the paraprofessional in protective service work is usually to provide outreach or nurturance and advocacy for the family, often as a case aide or parent aide. (See also PARENT AIDE)

PARENS PATRIAE
"The power of the sovereign." Refers to the state's power to act for or on behalf of persons who cannot act in their own behalf; such as, minors, incompetents, or some developmentally disabled.

PARENT
Person exercising the function of father and/or mother, including adoptive, foster, custodial, and surrogate parents as well as biological parents.

PARENT AIDE
A paraprofessional, either paid or voluntary, who functions primarily as an advocate and surrogate parent for a family in which child abuse or neglect is suspected or has been confirmed. The Parent Aide particularly serves the mother by providing positive reinforcement, emotional support, and nurturance, and by providing or arranging transportation, babysitting, etc., as necessary. Rather than serving as a homemaker, nutrition aide, or nurse, the parent aide's function is more like a friend to the family. Parent aides may also be referred to as case aides, lay therapists, or visiting friends.

PARENT EFFECTIVENESS TRAINING (PET)
An educational program developed by Dr. Thomas Gordon and presented in his book, *Parent Effectiveness Training* (New York, Peter H. Wyden, Inc., 1970). The program, taught by trained and certified PET instructors, focuses on improving communication between parents and children by teaching listening skills and verbal expression techniques to parents. The PET course has proven useful for parents who are motivated to change, who are able to give it a consider-

able amount of time, and who can afford the relatively high tuition. For these and other reasons, PET has not proven particularly useful in child abuse and neglect treatment, especially when used as the only mode of treatment.

PARENTAL STRESS SERVICES

Services aimed at relieving situational and/or psychological parental stress in order to relieve family dysfunction and to prevent parents from venting rage or frustration on their children. Service usually begins via a telephone helpline and may include home visits. Workers are usually trained volunteers or paraprofessionals who focus on providing warmth, nurturance, friendship, and resource referrals to the distressed parent. Some parental stress services promote development and use of Parents Anonymous chapters for their clients. Parental Stress Services may refer to specific programs such as in Chicago, Illinois, or Oakland, California, although there is no organizational linkage between them, or this may be a functional description of services provided within a larger agency program.

PARENTING SKILLS

A parent's competencies in providing physical care, protection, supervision, and psychological nurturance appropriate to a child's age and stage of development. Some parents, particularly those whose own parents demonstrated these skills, have these competencies without formal training, but adequacy of these skills may be improved through instruction.

PARENTS ANONYMOUS

22330 Hawthorne Blvd., #208
Torrance, California 90505
Self-help group for parents who want to stop physical, psychological, sexual, or verbal abuse of their children. Because members do not need to reveal their full names, they feel free to share concerns and provide mutual support. Members are accountable to the group for their behavior toward their children, and the group functions like a family in supporting members' efforts to change. With chapters in every state, over 800 in all, Parents Anonymous has been formally evaluated as an effective method for treating child abuse. Unlike most other self-help groups with anonymous members, Parents Anonymous requires that each chapter have an unpaid professional sponsor who attends all meetings to facilitate discussion, provide a role model, and suggest appropriate community resources for members' problems. The Child Abuse Prevention and Treatment Act provides for funding of self-help groups, and Parents Anonymous is one of the few self-help organizations which has received funding from the federal government.

PARENTS' RIGHTS

Besides the rights protected by the Constitution for all adults, society accords parents the right to custody and supervision of their own children, including, among others, parents' rights to make decisions about their children's health care. This plus parents' rights to privacy may complicate investigations of suspected child abuse and neglect and treatment of confirmed cases. Parents' rights may be cited in court in order to prevent the state from taking custody of a child who is in danger in his/her own home. (See also CHILDREN'S RIGHTS)

PARENTS UNITED

Organization name sometimes used for self-help groups of parents in families in which sexual abuse has occurred. Begun in 1972, Parents United is one component of a model Child Sexual Abuse Treatment Program in Santa Clara County, California. (See also DAUGHTERS UNITED)

PASSIVE ABUSER

Parent or caretaker who does not intervene to prevent abuse by another person in the home.

PATHOGNOMONIC

A sign or symptom specifically distinctive or characteristic of a disease or condition from which a diagnosis may be made.

PERINATAL
Around the time of birth, both immediately before and afterward.

PERIOSTEAL ELEVATION
The ripping or tearing of the surface layer of a bone (periosteum) and the resultant hemorrhage, occuring when a bone is broken.

PERITONITIS
Inflammation of the membrane lining the abdomen (peritoneum); caused by infection.

PERJURY
Intentionally inaccurate testimony. Perjury is usually punishable as a felony, but only if the inaccuracy of the testimony and the witness's knowledge of the inaccuracy can be proven.

PETECHIAE (See INTRADERMAL HEMORRHAGE)

PETITION
Document filed in juvenile or family court at the beginning of a neglect, abuse, and/or delinquency case. The petition states the allegations which, if true, form the basis for court intervention.

PETITIONER
Person who files a petition. In juvenile and family court practice, a petitioner may be a probation officer, social worker, or prosecutor, as variously defined by state laws.

PHYSICAL ABUSE (See CHILD ABUSE AND NEGLECT)

PHYSICAL NEGLECT (See CHILD ABUSE AND NEGLECT)

PLEA BARGAINING
Settlement of a criminal prosecution, usually by the reduction of the charge and/or the penalty, in return for a plea of guilty. Plea bargains are sometimes justified by congested court calendars. They are attacked as devices which weaken the intended effect of penal statutes and which reduce the dignity of the criminal justice system. Far more than half of all criminal prosecutions in this country are resolved by plea bargaining.

POLICE HOLD (See CUSTODY)

POLYPHAGIA
Excessive or voracious eating.

PREDICTION OF CHILD ABUSE AND NEGLECT
There are no evaluation instruments or criteria to predict absolutely that child abuse or neglect will occur in specific families. Recently, experts have developed instruments and methods of evaluating the bonding process at childbirth in order to identify families where because of incomplete or inadequate bonding, it can be expected that without further appropriate intervention, child abuse or neglect may occur. Besides bonding, many other indicators can be used to identify families-at-risk for child abuse and neglect, but these factors are rarely sufficiently conclusive to enable absolute prediction. (See also BONDING and FAMILIES-AT-RISK)

PREPONDERANCE OF EVIDENCE (See EVIDENTIARY STANDARDS)

PRESENTMENT
The notice taken or report made by a grand jury of an offense on the basis of the jury's knowledge and without a bill of indictment. (See also INDICTMENT)

PRE-TRIAL DIVERSION
Decision of the district attorney not to issue charges in a criminal case where those charges would be provable. The decision is usually made on the condition that the defendant agrees to participate in rehabilitative services. In child abuse cases, this usually involves cooperation with child protective services and/or voluntary treatment, such as Parents Anonymous.

PREVENTION OF CHILD ABUSE AND NEGLECT
Elimination of the individual and societal causes of child abuse and neglect.

Primary Prevention
Providing societal and community policies and programs which strengthen all family functioning so that child abuse and neglect is less likely to occur.

Secondary Prevention
Intervention in the early signs of child abuse and neglect for treatment of the presenting problem and to prevent further problems from developing.

Tertiary Prevention
Treatment after child abuse and neglect has been confirmed.

Primary, and to varying degrees secondary and tertiary, prevention requires:

1) Breaking the tendency in the generational cycle wherein the abused or neglected child is likely to become the abusive or neglectful parent.
2) Helping a parent cope with a child who has special problems or special meaning to a parent.
3) Helping families cope with long term and immediate situational or interpersonal stress.
4) Linking families to personal and community sources of help to break their social isolation.
5) Eliminating or alleviating violence in our society, particularly sanctioned violence such as corporal punishment in the schools.

A major problem in preventing child abuse and neglect is the stigma attached to the problem and to receiving services from a county protective service agency. Therefore, prevention programs must include community education and outreach. Another problem is that stress is pervasive in our society, and ways must be found both to reduce it and deal with it if child abuse and neglect is to be prevented. (See also EARLY INTERVENTION)

PRIMA FACIE
A latin term approximately meaning "at first sight," "on the first appearance," or "on the face of it." In law, this term is used in the context of a "prima facie case." That is, the presentation of evidence at a trial which has been sufficiently strong to prove the allegations unless contradicted and overcome by other evidence. In a child maltreatment case, the allegations of maltreatment will be considered as proven unless the parent presents rebutting evidence.

PRIVILEGED COMMUNICATIONS
Confidential communications which are protected by statutes and need not or cannot be disclosed in court over the objections of the holder of the privilege. Lawyers are almost always able to refuse to disclose what a client has told them in confidence. Priests are similarly covered. Doctors and psychotherapists have generally lesser privileges, and their testimony can be compelled in many cases involving child abuse or neglect. Some social workers are covered by such statutes, but the law and practice vary widely from state to state. (See also CONFIDENTIALITY)

PROBABLE CAUSE
A legal standard used in a number of contexts which indicates a reasonable ground for suspicion or belief in the existence of certain facts. Facts accepted as true after a reasonable inquiry which would induce a prudent and cautious person to believe them. Also-Please note that the definitions on page 28 of EVIDENTIARY STANDARDS are incorrect. A suggested alternative follows:

PROBATE COURT (See COURTS)

PROBATION
Allowing a convicted criminal defendant or a juvenile found to be delinquent to remain at liberty, under a suspended sentence of imprisonment, generally under the supervi-

sion of a probation officer and under certain conditions. Violation of a condition is grounds for revocation of the probation. In a case of child abuse or neglect, a parent or caretaker who is convicted of the offense may be required, as part of his/her probation, to make certain promises to undergo treatment and/or to improve the home situation. These promises are made as a condition of the probation in which the child is returned home and are enforced with the threat of revocation of parental rights.

PROGRAM COORDINATION
Interagency of intra-agency communication for policy, program, and resource development for an effective service delivery system in a given locality. Program coordination for child abuse and neglect is usually implemented through a community council or community task force or planning committee under the direction of a program coordinator. The functions of these groups are:
1) Comprehensive planning, including identifying gaps and duplication in service and funding policies.
2) Developing interagency referral policies.
3) Educating members to new and/or effective approaches to child abuse and neglect.
4) Problem sharing.
5) Facilitating resolution of interagency conflicts.
6) Providing a forum where differing professional and agency expertise can be pooled.
7) Generating and lobbying for needed legislation.

(See also COMMUNITY TEAM)

PROTECTIVE CUSTODY (See CUSTODY)

PROTOCOL
A set of rules or guidelines prescribing procedures and responsibilities. Originally used primarily in medical settings, establishment of protocols is an increasingly important goal of the child abuse and neglect community team.

PROXIMAL
Near; closer to any point of reference; opposed to distal.

PSYCHOLOGICAL ABUSE (See CHILD ABUSE AND NEGLECT)

PSYCHOLOGICAL NEGLECT (See CHILD ABUSE AND NEGLECT)

PSYCHOLOGICAL PARENT
Adult who, on a continuing day-to-day basis, fulfills a child's emotional needs for nurturance through interaction, companionship, and mutuality. May be the natural parent or another person who fulfills these functions.

PSYCHOLOGICAL TESTS
Instruments of various types used to measure emotional, intellectual, and personality characteristics. Psychological tests should always be administered and interpreted by qualified personnel. Such tests have been used to determine potential for abuse or neglect, effects of abuse or neglect, or psychological makeup of parent or children.

PSYCHOTIC PARENT
A parent who suffers a major mental disorder where the individual's ability to think, respond emotionally, remember, communicate, interpret reality, or behave appropriately is sufficiently impaired so as to interfere grossly with his/her capacity to meet the ordinary demands of life. The term "psychotic" is neither very precise nor definite. However, the parent who is periodically psychotic or psychotic for extended periods and who abuses his/her children has a poor prognosis; permanent removal of the children is often recommended in this situation. It is estimated that well under 10% of all abusive or neglectful parents are psychotic.

PUBLIC AWARENESS (See COMMUNITY AWARENESS)

PUBLIC DEFENDER
Person paid with public funds to plead the cause of an indigent defendant.

PUBLIC LAW 93-247 (See CHILD ABUSE PREVENTION AND TREATMENT ACT)

PUNISHMENT
Infliction of pain, loss, or suffering on a child because the child has disobeyed or otherwise antagonized a parent or caretaker. Abusive parents may inflect punishment without cause, or may inflict punishment, particularly corporal punishment, in the belief that it is the only way to discipline children. Many parents confuse the difference between discipline and punishment. These differences are delineated under DISCIPLINE. (See also CORPORAL PUNISHMENT)

PURCHASE OF SERVICE
Provision for diagnosis and/or treatment of child abuse and neglect by an agency other than the mandated agency using mandated agency funds. The mandated agency subcontracts with the provider agency for specific services with specific clients, but the mandated agency retains statutory responsibility for the case. (See also CASE MANAGEMENT)

PURPURA (See INTRADERMAL HEMORRHAGE)

RADIOLUCENT
Permitting the passage of X-rays without leaving a shadow on the film. Soft tissues are radiolucent; bones are not.

RAREFACTION
Loss of density. On an X-ray photograph, an area of bone which appears lighter than normal is in a state of rarefaction, indicating a loss of calcium.

RECEIVING HOME
A family or group home for temporary placement of a child pending more permanent plans such as return to his/her own home, foster care, or adoption.

RECIDIVISM
Recurrence of child abuse and neglect. This happens relatively frequently because child protective service agencies heretofore have been mandated and staffed only to investigate and provide crisis intervention and not to provide treatment. Most cases where child abuse or neglect results in a child's death have been previously known to a child protection agency.

REFEREE (See HEARING OFFICER)

REGIONAL RESOURCE CENTER
With respect to child abuse and neglect, a regional resource center was funded as a demonstration project in each of the ten HEW regions under the 1974 Child Abuse Prevention and Treatment Act. These resource centers vary in program emphasis, but they all function to some degree as extensions of the National Center on Child Abuse and Neglect in Washington to help NCCAN fulfill the aims of the Child Abuse Prevention and Treatment Act (see NATIONAL CENTER ON CHILD ABUSE AND NEGLECT and CHILD ABUSE PREVENTION AND TREATMENT ACT). Besides regional centers, there are also state resource centers in Arizona, Maryland, New York, and North Carolina; and two national resource centers, operated by the Education Commission of the States and the National Urban League. The regional resource centers are:

Region I (Connecticut, Maine, Massachusetts, New Hampshire, Rhode Island, Vermont)
Judge Baker Guidance Center
295 Longwood Ave.
Boston, Massachusetts 02115
Region II (New Jersey, Puerto Rico, Virgin Islands)
College of Human Ecology Cornell University
MVR Hall
Ithaca, New York 14853
Region III (Pennsylvania, Virginia, Delaware, West Virginia, District of Columbia)
Institute for Urban Affairs and Research
Howard University

2900 Van Ness St., N.W.
Washington, D.C. 20008
Region IV (Alabama, Florida, Georgia, Kentucky, Mississippi, South Carolina, Tennessee)
Regional Institute of Social Welfare Research
P.O. Box 152
Heritage Building
468 N. Milledge Ave.
Athens, Georgia 30601
Region V (Illinois, Indiana, Michigan, Minnesota, Ohio, Wisconsin)
Midwest Parent-Child Welfare Resource Center
Center for Advanced Studies in Human Services
School of Social Welfare
University of Wisconsin-Milwaukee
Milwaukee, Wisconsin 53201
Region VI (Arkansas, Louisiana, New Mexico, Oklahoma, Texas)
Center for Social Work Research
School of Social Work
University of Texas at Austin
Austin, Texas 78712
Region VII (Iowa, Kansas, Missouri, Nebraska)
Institute of Child Behavior and Development
University of Iowa
Oakdale, Iowa 53219
Region VIII (Colorado, Montana, North Dakota, South Dakota, Utah, Wyoming)
National Center for the Prevention and Treatment of Child Abuse and Neglect
University of Colorado Medical Center
1205 Oneida St.
Denver, Colorado 80220
Region IX (California, Hawaii, Nevada, Guam, Trust Territories of the Pacific, American Samoa)
Department of Special Education
California State University
5151 State University Dr.
Los Angeles, California 90033
Region X (Alaska, Idaho, Oregon, Washington)
Northwest Federation for Human Services
157 Yesler Way, #208
Seattle, Washington 98104

REGISTRY (See CENTRAL REGISTER and NATIONAL REGISTER)

REHEARING
After a juvenile court referee or commissioner has heard a case and made an order, some states permit a dissatisfied party to request another hearing before the supervising judge of juvenile court. This second hearing is called a rehearing. If the original hearing was not recorded by a court reporter, the rehearing may have to be granted. If a transcript exists, the judge may read it and either grant or deny the rehearing.

REPARENTING
Usually describes a nurturing process whereby parents who have not received adequate nurturance during their own childhoods are provided with emotional warmth and security through a surrogate parent such as a parent aide. Abusive and neglectful parents are thus given an opportunity to identify with more positive role models.

REPORTING LAWS
State laws which require specified categories of persons, such as professionals involved with children, and allow other persons, to notify public authorities of cases of suspected child abuse and, sometimes, neglect. All 50 states now have reporting statutes, but they differ widely with respect to types of instances which must be reported, persons who must report, time limits for reporting, manner of reporting (written, oral, or both), agencies to which reports must be made, and the degree of immunity conferred upon reporters.

RES IPSA LOQUITOR
Latin expression meaning "the thing speaks for itself." It is a doctrine of law which, when applied to criminal law, means that evidence can be admitted which is acceptable despite the fact that no one actually saw what occurred, only the results. An example in

criminal law would be admitting into evidence in a child abuse case the medical reports of the injured child victim which reflect multiple broken bones and the doctor's opinion that said injuries could not have been caused by an accident. The court using the *res ipsa loquitor* doctrine can convict the person having had exclusive custody of the child without any direct testimony as to how, when, where, or why the injuries were inflicted.

RETINA
Inside lining of the eye. Injury to the head can cause bleeding or detachment of the retina, possible causing blindness.

RICKETS
Condition caused by a deficiency of vitamin D, which disturbs the normal development of bones.

ROLE REVERSAL
The process whereby a parent or caretaker seeks nurturance and/or protection from a child rather than providing this for the child, who frequently complies with this reversal. Usually this process develops as a result of unfulfilled needs of the parent or caretaker.

SACRAL AREA
Lower part of the back.

SCAN TEAM
Suspected Child Abuse and Neglect team which has as its objective the assessment of a child and his/her family to determine if abuse and/or neglect has occurred and what treatment is indicated. The team usually includes a pediatrician, a social worker, and a psychiatrist or psychologist, but other professionals are often involved as well. A SCAN team or unit is generally located in a hospital or outpatient facility. (See also MULTIDISCIPLINARY TEAM and DENVER MODEL)

SCAPEGOATING
Casting blame for a problem on one who is innocent or only partially responsible; for example, a parent or caretaker abusing or neglecting a child as punishment for family problems unrelated to the child.

SCURVY
Condition caused by a deficiency of vitamin C (ascorbic acid) and characterized by weakness, anemia, spongy gums, and other symptoms.

SEALING
In juvenile court or criminal court practice, the closing of records to inspection by all but the defendant or minor involved. Sealing is provided by statute in some states and may be done after proof is made that the defendant or minor has behaved lawfully for a specified period of years. Note that juvenile court records are never public, as are the records of most other courts; access to juvenile court records is theoretically very restricted, even before sealing. (See also EXPUNGEMENT)

SEIZURES
Uncontrollable muscular contractions, usually alternating with muscular relaxation and generally accompanied by unconsciousness. Seizures, which vary in intensity and length of occurrence, are the result of some brain irritation which has been caused by disease, inherited condition, fever, tumor, vitamin deficiency, or injury to the head.

SELF-HELP GROUP
Groups of persons with similar, often stigmatized, problems who share concerns and experiences in an effort to provide mutual help to one another. Usually these groups are self-directed. (See also PARENTS ANONYMOUS)

SELF-INCRIMINATION
The giving of a statement, in court or during an investigation, which subjects the person giving the statement to criminal liability. (See also DUE PROCESS, FIFTH AMENDMENT, IMMUNITY, and MIRANDA RULE)

SENTENCING
The last stage of criminal prosecution in which a convicted defendant is ordered imprisoned, fined, or granted probation. This is equivalent in a criminal case, to the disposition in a juvenile court case.

SEQUELAE
After-effects; usually medical events following an injury or disease. In child abuse and neglect, sequelae is used to refer to psychological consequences of abusive acts and also the perpetuation of maltreatment behavior across generations, as well as specific aftereffects such as brain damage, speech impairment, and impaired physical and/or psychological growth.

SERVICES
(See EARLY INTERVENTION, EMERGENCY SERVICES, PREVENTION OF CHILD ABUSE AND NEGLECT, SUPPORTIVE SERVICES, TREATMENT OF CHILD ABUSE AND NEGLECT)

SEXUAL ABUSE
In order to encompass all forms of child sexual abuse and exploitation within its mandate, the National Center on Child Abuse and Neglect has adopted the following tentative definition of child sexual abuse: contacts or interactions between a child and an adult when the child is being used for the sexual stimulation of the perpetrator or another person. Sexual abuse may also be committed by a person under the age of 18 when that person is either significantly older than the victim or when the perpetrator is in a position of power or control over another child. (See also CHILD ABUSE AND NEGLECT)

SEXUAL ASSAULT
Unlawful actions of a sexual nature committed against a person forcibly and against his/her own will. Various degrees of sexual assault are established by state law and are distinguished by the sex of the perpetrator and/or victim, the amount of force used, the amount and type of sexual contact, etc. Sexual abuse is one form of sexual assault wherein the perpetrator is known by the victim and is usually a member of the family. (See also CHILD ABUSE AND NEGLECT)

SEXUAL EXPLOITATION
A term usually used in reference to sexual abuse of children for commercial purposes; such as child prostitution, sexual exhibition, or the production of pornographic materials. (See also CHILD PORNOGRAPHY, CHILD PROSTITUTION)

SEXUAL MISUSE
Alternative term for sexual abuse, but particularly reflects the point of view that sexual encounters with children, if properly handled, need not be as harmful as is usually assumed. Its implication is that children are not necessarily harmed by so-called sexually abusive acts themselves, but rather the abuse results from damage generated by negative social and cultural reactions to such acts. (See also CHILD MISUSE AND NEGLECT, INCEST, SEXUAL ABUSE)

SEXUALLY TRANSMISSIBLE DISEASE (STD) (See VENEREAL DISEASE)

SIMPLE FRACTURE (See FRACTURE)

SITUATIONAL CHILD ABUSE AND NEGLECT
Refers to cases of child abuse and particularly child neglect where the major causative factors cannot be readily eliminated because they relate to problems over which the parents have little control. (See also APATHY-FUTILITY SYNDROME)

SKELETAL SURVEY
A series of X-rays that studies all bones of the body. Such a survey should be done in all cases of suspected abuse to locate any old, as well as new, fractures which may exist.

SOCIAL ASSESSMENT (See ASSESSMENT)

SOCIAL HISTORY
1) Information compiled by a social worker about factors affecting a family's past and present level of functioning for use in diagnosing child abuse and neglect and developing a treatment plan.
2) Document prepared by a probation officer or social worker for the juvenile or family court hearing officer's consideration at the time of disposition of a case. This report addresses the minor's history and environment. Social histories often contain material which would clearly be inadmissible in most judicial proceedings, either because of hearsay or lack of verification or reliability. The informal use of such reports has often been attacked as in violation of due process rights of minors and parents.

SOCIAL REPORT (See SOCIAL HISTORY)

SOCIAL ISOLATION
The limited interaction and contact of many abusive and/or neglectful parents with relatives, neighbors, friends, or community resources. Social isolation can perpetuate a basic lack of trust which hinders both identification and treatment of child abuse and neglect.

SOCIAL SECURITY ACT
Established in 1935 as a national social insurance program, this federal legislation includes several sections particularly applicable to child and family welfare:

Title IV-Parts A, B, C, D (Aid to Families with Dependent Children, Child Welfare Services, Work Incentive Program, Child Support and Establishment of Paternity)
Part A, now included under Title XX as services for children, was designed to encourage families to care for dependent children in their own or relatives' homes by providing services to families below a specified income level. As a condition of receiving federal funding for this program, states must provide family planning services. Part B authorizes support to states for child welfare services developed in coordination with the AFDC program to supplement or substitute for parental care and supervision. These services include day care, foster care, and other preventive or protective programs promoting child and family welfare. Part C offers job training and placement for AFDC parents in an effort to assist them in becoming self-supporting. Part D enforces the support obligations owed by absent parents to their children by locating absent parents, establishing paternity, and obtaining child support.

Title V-Maternal and Child Health and Applied Children's Services
Provides a broad range of health care services for mothers and children from low-income families in order to reduce maternal and infant mortality and to prevent illness.

Title XIX-Grants to States for Medical Assistance Programs (Medicaid or Title 19)
Designed to help families with dependent children and other low-income persons by providing financial assistance for necessary medical services. This act is additionally designed to provide rehabilitation and other psychotherapy services to help families and individuals retain or regain independence and self-sufficiency.

Title XX-Grants to States for Services
Provides grants to states for developing programs and services designed to achieve the following goals for families and/or children: economic self-support; self-sufficiency; prevention of abuse and neglect; preserving; rehabilitating, reuniting families; referring for institutional care when other services are not appropriate.

Mandated child protective service agency programs are primarily funded through Title IV-B and Title XX of the Social Security Act.

SOCIETAL CHILD ABUSE AND NEGLECT
Failure of society to provide social policies and/or funding to support the well-being of all families and children or to provide sufficient resources to prevent and treat child

abuse and neglect, particularly for minority populations such as migrant workers and Native Americans.

SPECIAL CHILD
A child who is abused or neglected or at risk of abuse or neglect because he/she has a special problem with which the parent(s) have difficulty coping or because the child has some psychologically negative meaning for the parent. Also referred to as "target child." If this child is abused, the cause may be referred to as "victim" precipitated abuse."

SPIRAL FRACTURE (See FRACTURE)

SPOUSE ABUSE
Non-accidental physical or psychological injury inflicted on either husband or wife by his/her marital partner. Some experts conjecture that husbands as well as wives are frequently abused, particularly psychologically, but the subject of husband abuse has not gained public or professional recognition to the extent that battered wives has. Domestic violence is the term used when referring to abuse between adult mates who may not be married. (See also BATTERED WOMEN)

STAFF BURNOUT
Apathy and frustration felt by protective service workers who are overworked, undertrained, and lacking agency or supervisory support. This is a common problem, and workers who do not leave protective services (see STAFF FLIGHT) or who do not have supervisory support often lose sensitivity to client needs. (Also referred to as Worker Burnout)

STAFF FLIGHT
Continous change of child protective services staff due to staff burnout (see STAFF BURNOUT). This creates the need to provide frequent training for new workers. Informed estimates place the overall national turnover rate of protective service workers at 85% annually.

STAFF SATISFACTION
Structuring a supportive and encouraging environment for protective service workers with regular periods when no new cases are assigned, thereby decreasing staff burnout and staff flight. Supervisors and administrators need to develop programs including the following elements: manageable caseloads, in-service training, participation in and responsibility for agency decision-making.

STANDARD OF PROOF (See EVIDENTIARY STANDARDS)

STANDARDS
Guides developed to ensure comprehensiveness and adequacy of programs or services. Issued by relevant agencies, such as the National Center on Child Abuse and Neglect for state and local level programs and the Child Welfare League of America for member agencies, standards have various levels of authority.

STATE AUTHORITY
State authority refers to the state department of social services (state department) and a state child protection coordinating committee (state committee). As designated in state law, these structures are to accept responsibility for child abuse and neglect prevention, identification, and treatment efforts. The standards on state authority, as specified in the National Center on Child Abuse and Neglect *Revision to Federal Standards on the Prevention and Treatment of Child Abuse and Neglect (Draft),* include:

Administration and Organization

1 The state department should establish child abuse and neglect policies that are consistent with the state law and conducive to state-wide delivery of uniform and coordinated services.

2 The state department should establish a distinct child protection division (state division) to facilitate the implementation of departmental policies.

3 The state department should designate child protective services units

(local units) within each regional and/or local social services agency.
4. The state committee, as required by state law, should be representative of those persons and agencies concerned with child abuse and neglect prevention, identification, and treatment.

Primary Prevention

5. The state division and the state committee should work together towards primary prevention of child abuse and neglect through formalized needs assessment and planning processes.

Secondary and Tertiary Prevention

6. The state division and the state committee should jointly develop a comprehensive and coordinated plan for delivery of services to high-risk children and families.
7. The state division should ensure that those persons who have reason to suspect child abuse or neglect can make a report at any time, twenty-four hours a day, seven days a week.
8. The state division should transmit reports to appropriate authority for assessment of the degree of risk to the child.
9. The state division should operate a central registry that facilitates state and local planning.
10. The state division's operation of the central registry should ensure that children and families' rights to prompt and effective services are protected.

Resource Enhancement

11. The state division should develop and provide public and professional education.
12. The state division should ensure that training is provided to all divisional, regional, and local staff.
13. The state division should conduct and/or sponsor research, demonstration, and evaluation projects.

(See also LOCAL AUTHORITY)

STATUS OFFENSE
An act which is considered criminal only because it is committed by a person of a particular status, such as a minor. If an adult did the same thing, it would not be an offense. For example, a minor staying out after curfew.

STIPULATION
A statement, either oral or written, between lawyers on both sides of a particular court case which establishes certain facts about the case that are agreed upon by both sides. The facts delineated usually involve such issues as the addresses of the persons involved in the case, their relationships to one another, etc.

STRESS FACTORS
Environmental and/or psychological pressures over a prolonged period which are associated with child abuse and neglect or which, without being prolonged, may be the precipitant event. While a certain amount of stress can be useful in motivating people to change, it is generally agreed that there is an overload of stress in our present society, perhaps because people feel decreasingly in control of the forces affecting their lives. Prevention of child abuse and neglect requires both reducing stress in society and helping people cope with it. Environmental stress which may influence child abuse and neglect includes, but is not limited to, unemployment, poverty, poor and overcrowded housing, competition for success, and "keeping up with the Joneses." Psychological stress besides that caused by environmental factors which may influence child abuse and neglect could include such problems as marital discord, in-law problems, unwanted pregnancy, role confusion resulting from the Women's Movement, and unresolved psychodynamic conflicts from childhood.

SUBDURAL HEMATOMA
A common symptom of abused children, consisting of a collection of blood beneath the outermost membrane covering the brain and spinal cord. The hematoma may be caused by a blow to the head or from shaking a baby or small child. (See also WHIP-

LASH-SHAKEN INFANT SYNDROME)

SUBPOENA
A document issued by a court clerk, usually delivered by a process server or police officer to the person subpoenaed, requiring that person to appear at a certain court at a certain day and time to give testimony in a specified case. Failure to obey a subpoena is punishable as contempt of court.

SUBPOENA DUCES TECUM
A subpoena requiring the person subpoenaed to bring specified records to court.

SUDDEN INFANT DEATH SYNDROME (SIDS)
A condition which can be confused with child abuse, SIDS affects infants from two weeks to two years old, but usually occurs in a child less than six months of age. In SIDS, a child who has been healthy except for a minor respiratory infection is found dead, often with bloody frothy material in his/her mouth. The cause of SIDS is not fully understood. The confusion with child abuse results from the bloody sputum and occasional facial bruises that accompany the syndrome. However, SIDS parents rarely display the guarded or defensive behavior that many abusive parents do.

SUMMONS
A document issued by a court clerk, usually delivered by a process server or police officer to the person summoned, notifying that person of the filing of a lawsuit against him/her and notifying that person of the deadline for answering the suit. A summons does not require the attendance at court of any person.

SUPERVISION
1) Provision of age-appropriate protection and guidance for a child by a parent or caretaker. This is a parental responsibility, but in some cases of child abuse and neglect or for other reasons, the state may have to assume responsibility for supervision. (See also CHILD IN NEED OF SUPERVISION)
2) Process in social work practice whereby workers review cases with supervisors to assure case progress, to sharpen the workers' knowledge and skill, and to assure maintenance of agency policies and procedures. Unlike many practitioners in law and medicine, social workers do not generally practice independently or make totally independent judgments. In general, social work supervisors hold Master's degrees, but in some local public agencies these supervisors may be just out of graduate school and have little experience. Since good supervision is a critical factor in reducing the problem of staff burnout and staff flight, it is important for child protective service agencies to provide training and continuing education opportunities for supervisors.

SUPPORTIVE SERVICES
Supportive services are a wide range of human services which provide assistance to families or individuals so that they are more nearly able to fulfill their potential for positive growth and behavior. The concept implies that individuals have basic strengths which need to be recognized, encouraged, and aided. Thus, a wide range of financial, educational, vocational, child care, counseling, recreational, and other services might be seen as supportive if they do indeed emphasize the strengths of people and de-emphasize their occasional needs for help in overcoming destructive and debilitating factors which may affect their lives.

SURROGATE PARENT
A person other than a biological parent who, living within or outside the target home, provides nurturance. This person may be self-selected or assigned to fulfill parental functions. A surrogate parent may nurture children or abusive or neglectful parents who were themselves abused as children and therefore are in need of a nurturing parental model. (See also PARENT AIDE)

SUSPECTED CHILD ABUSE AND NEGLECT
Reason to believe that child abuse or neglect has or is occurring in a given family. Anyone can in good faith report this to the local mandated agency, which will investigate and protect the child as necessary. However, all states have statutes which provide that members of certain professions must report and that failure to do so is punishable by fine or imprisonment. For specific criteria for suspecting child abuse or neglect, see INDICATORS OF CHILD ABUSE AND NEGLECT and FAMILIES-AT-RISK.

SUTURE
1) A type of immovable joint in which the connecting surfaces of the bones are closely united, as in the skull.
2) The stitches made by a physician that close a wound.

SYPHILIS (See VENEREAL DISEASE)

TARGET CHILD (See SPECIAL CHILD)

TEMPORAL
Referring to the side of the head.

TEMPORARY CUSTODY (See CUSTODY)

TEMPORARY PLACEMENT
Voluntary or involuntary short term removal of a child from his/her own home, primarily when a child's safety or well-being is threatened or endangered, or when a family crisis can be averted by such action. Temporary placement may be in a relative's home, receiving home or shelter, foster home, or institution. Temporary placement should be considered only if service to the child and family within the home, such as use of a homemaker or day care, is determined to be insufficient to protect or provide for the child or if it is unavailable. If the home situation does not improve while the child is in temporary placement, long term placement may be warranted. However, authorities agree that too many temporary placements unnecessarily become permanent placements. (See also CUSTODY)

TERMINATION OF PARENTAL RIGHTS (TPR)
A legal proceeding freeing a child from his/her parents' claims so that the child can be adopted by others without the parents' written consent. The legal bases for termination differ from state to state, but most statutes include abandonment as a ground for TPR. (See also ABANDONMENT)

TESTIMONY
A declaration or statement made to establish a fact, especially one made under oath in court.

THREATENED HARM
Substantial risk of harm to a child, including physical or mental injury, sexual assault, neglect of physical and/or educational needs, inadequate supervision, or abandonment.

TITLE IV (See SOCIAL SECURITY ACT)

TITLE V (See SOCIAL SECURITY ACT)

TITLE XIX (TITLE 19, MEDICAID) (See SOCIAL SECURITY ACT)

TITLE XX (See SOCIAL SECURITY ACT)

TORUS FRACTURE (See FRACTURE)

TRABECULA
A general term for a supporting or anchoring strand of tissue.

TRAUMA
An internal or external injury or wound brought about by an outside force. Usually trauma means injury by violence, but it may also apply to the wound caused by any surgical procedure. Trauma may be caused accidentally or, as in a ease of physical abuse, non-acciden-tally. Trauma is also a term applied to psychological discomfort or symptoms resulting from an emotional shock or painful experience.

TRAUMA X
Designation used by some hospitals for a child abuse and neglect program.

TREATMENT FOSTER CARE
Foster care for children with diagnosed emotional and/or behavioral problems in which foster parents with special training and experience become part of a treatment team working with a particular child. Treatment foster care may be indicated for abused or severely neglected children.

TREATMENT OF CHILD ABUSE AND NEGLECT
1) Helping parents or caretakers stop child abuse and neglect and assisting them and their children to function adequately as a family unit. 2) Providing temporary placement and services as necessary for abused or neglected children until their parents can assume their parental responsibilities without threat to the children's welfare. 3) Terminating parental rights and placing the children in an adoptive home if the parents abandon the children or absolutely cannot be helped. Experts believe that 80% to 85% of abusive and neglectful parents can be helped to function without threat to their children's welfare and, more often than not, without temporary placement of the children if sufficient supportive services are available.

Treatment for child abuse and neglect should include treatment for the abused and neglected children as well as for the parents.

Treatment for child abuse and neglect includes both crisis intervention and long term treatment. The mandated agency may provide services directly or by purchase of service from other agencies. Since a multiplicity of services is often necessary, a case management approach to treatment is usually most effective (see CASE MANAGEMENT). Because mandated agencies necessarily focus on investigation of suspected cases and crisis intervention, long term treatment is best assured through use of a community team (see COMMUNITY TEAM).

Both crisis intervention and long term treatment will usually require a mix of supportive and therapeutic services. Supportive services could include homemakers, day care, foster grandparents, parent education, health care, family planning, recreational activities, housing assistance, transportation, legal services, employment training and placement, financial counseling and assistance. Therapeutic services could include psychotherapy, casework, lay therapy from parent aides, group therapy, family or couple therapy, and self-help such as Parents Anonymous.

TURGOR
Condition of being swollen and congested. This can refer to normal or other fullness.

TWENTY-FOUR HOUR EMERGENCY SERVICES
Local services available at all times to receive reports and make immediate investigations of suspected cases of child abuse and severe neglect and to perform crisis intervention if necessary. The mode of providing twenty-four hour emergency services varies in different localities. However, often mandated agency protective service workers are on call for specific evening and weekend assignments. Often the after-hours number rings the police or sheriffs department which then contacts the assigned worker. (See also COMPREHENSIVE EMERGENCY SERVICES)

UNFOUNDED REPORT
Any report of suspected child abuse or neglect made to the mandated agency for which it is determined that there is no probable cause to believe that abuse or neglect has occurred. Mandated agencies may or may not remove unfounded reports from their records after a period of time. (See also EXPUNGEMENT)

VASCULAR
Of the blood vessels.

VENEREAL DISEASE
Any disease transmitted by sexual contact. The two most common forms of venereal disease are gonorrhea and syphilis. Presence of a venereal disease in a child may indicate that the mother was infected with the disease during the pregnancy, or it may be evidence of sexual abuse.

VERBAL ABUSE (See CHILD ABUSE AND NEGLECT)

VERIFICATION OF CHILD ABUSE AND NEGLECT
Substantiation of child abuse or neglect following investigation of suspected cases by mandated agency workers and/or assessment by a diagnostic team. Also referred to as a founded report.

VICTIM-PRECIPITATED ABUSE (See SPECIAL CHILD)

VISITING FRIEND (See PARENT AIDE)

VITAL SIGNS
Signs manifesting life, such as respiratory rate, heartbeat, pulse,.blood pressure, and eye responses.

VOIR DIRE
1   Procedure during which lawyers question prospective jurors to determine their biases, if any.
2   Procedure in which lawyers question expert witnesses regarding their qualifications before the experts are permitted to give opinion testimony.

VOLUNTARY PLACEMENT
Act of a parent in which custody of his/her child is relinquished without a formal court proceeding. Sometimes called voluntary relinquishment.

VOLUNTEER ROLES
1) Extension and enrichment of direct services to families by unpaid, screened, trained, and supervised persons who generally lack professional training. Common roles are parent aides, child care workers, outreach workers, or staff for helplines. 2) Development and advocacy of child abuse and neglect programs by unpaid persons through participation on community councils. agency boards, or community committees. Scarce resources in relation to the magnitude of the problem of child abuse and neglect demands that volunteers be used increasingly.

WANTON
Extremely reckless or malicious. Often used in court proceedings in conjunction with "willful" to establish certain kinds of unlawful behavior only vaguely distinguished from careless but lawful conduct.

WARRANT
Document issued by a judge, authorizing the arrest or detention of a person or the search of a place and seizure of specified items in that place. Although a judge need not hold a hearing before issuing a warrant and although the party to be arrested or whose property will be seized need not be notified, the judge must still be given "reasonable cause to believe" that a crime has occurred and that the warrant is necessary in the apprehension and conviction of the criminal.

WHIPLASH-SHAKEN INFANT SYNDROME
Injury to an infant or child that results from that child having been shaken, usually as a misguided means of discipline. The most common symptoms, which can be inflicted by seemingly harmless shakings, are bleeding and/or detached retinas and other bleeding inside the head. Repeated instances of shaking and resultant injuries may eventually cause mental and developmental disabilities. (See also SUBDURAL HEMATOMA)

WILLFUL
Done with understanding of the act and the intention that the act and its natural consequences should occur. Some conduct

becomes unlawful or negligent only when it is done willfully.

WITNESS
1. A person who has seen or heard something.
2. A person who is called upon to testify in a court hearing.

WORKER BURNOUT (See Staff Burnout)

WORK-UP
Study of a patient, often in a hospital, in order to provide information for diagnosis. A full work-up includes past medical and family histories, present condition and symptoms, laboratory, and, possibly, X-ray studies.

WORLD OF ABNORMAL REARING (WAR)
A generational cycle of development in which abused or neglected children tend to grow up to be abusive or neglectful parents unless intervention occurs to break the cycle. The diagram which follows outlines the WAR cycle. (Heifer)

X-RAYS
Photographs made by means of X-rays. X-rays are one of the most important tools available to physicians in the diagnosis of physical child abuse or battering. With X-rays, or radiologic examinations, physicians can observe not only the current bone injuries of a child, but also any past injuries that may exist in various stages of healing. This historical information contributes significantly to the assessment of a suspected case of child abuse. Radiologic examination is also essential to distinguish organic diseases that may cause bone breakage from physical child abuse.

Acronyms

AAP	American Academy of Pediatrics	**PET**	Parent Effectiveness Training
ACSW	Academy of Certified Social Workers	**PINS**	Person in Need of Supervision
ACYF	Administration for Children, Youth and Families (formerly Office of Child Development), U.S. Department of Health, Education and Welfare	**CPS**	Child Protective Services
		CWLA	Child Welfare League of America
		DART	Detection, Admission, Reporting, and Treatment (multidisciplinary team)
		DD	Developmental Disability
ADC	Aid to Dependent Children (Title IV-A of the Social Security Act) (also referred to as AFDC)	**DHEW**	U.S. Department of Health, Education and Welfare (also referred to as HEW)
AF	Alleged Father	**DPW**	Department of Public Welfare
AFDC	Aid to Families with Dependent Children (Title IV-A of the Social Security Act) (also referred to as ADC)	**DSS**	Department of Social Services
		EPSDT	Early and Periodic Screening, Diagnosis, and Treatment
		ER	Emergency Room
AHA	American Humane Association	**FTT**	Failure to Thrive
AMA	Against Medical Advice; American Medical Association	**GAL**	*Guardian ad l item*
		HEW	U.S. Department of Health, Education and Welfare (also referred to as DHEW)
APA	American Psychiatric Association; American Psychological Association	**IP**	Identified Patient
		LD	Learning Disability
APWA	American Public Welfare Association	**MINS**	Minor in Need of Supervision
CALM	Child Abuse Listening Mediation	**NASW**	National Association of Social Workers
CAN	Child Abuse and Neglect	**NCCA**	National Center for Child Advocacy
CAP	Community Action Program	**NCCAN**	National Center on Child Abuse and Neglect
CDAHA	Children's Division of the American Humane Association	**NIH**	National Institutes of Health
CDF	Children's Defense Fund	**NIMH**	National Institute of Mental Health
CES	Comprehensive Emergency Services	**OCD**	Office of Child Development (now Adminstration for Children, Youth and Families). U.S. Department of Health, Education and Welfare
CHIPS	Child in Need of Protection and Supervision		
CLL	Childhood Level of Living Scale		
CNS	Central Nervous System	**OHD**	Office of Human Development (now Office of Human Development Services), U.S. Department of Health, Education and Welfare
OHDS	Office of Human Development Services (formerly Office of Human Development), U.S. Department of Health, Education and Welfare	**PL 93-247**	Child Abuse Prevention and Treatment Act
		SCAN	Suspected Child Abuse and Neglect
PA	Parents Anonymous		

SIDS	Sudden Infant Death Syndrome	**VD**	Venereal Disease
STD	Sexually Transmissible Disease	**WAR**	World of Abnormal Rearing
TPR	Termination of Parental Rights	**WIN**	Work Incentive Program
UM	Unmarried Mother		

www.ingramcontent.com/pod-product-compliance
Lightning Source LLC
Chambersburg PA
CBHW082037300426
44117CB00015B/2519